All the Fishes come Home to Roost

All the Fishes come Home to Roost

an American Misfit in India

Rachel Manija Brown

Cover photographs © Gary Powell / Photonica and Samba Photo / Photonica
Quote on pages 24–25 from *Gravity's Rainbow* by Thomas Pynchon, used with permission of Penguin Publishers.
New Yorker cartoon quoted on page 339 © 2005 New Yorker Magazine Alex Gregory. Use by permission of The Cartoon Bank. All rights reserved.

Printed in the United States of America
Rodale Inc. makes every effort to use acid-free ♾, recycled paper ♻.
Book design by Tara Long

Library of Congress Cataloging-in-Publication Data

Brown, Rachel Manija.
All the fishes come home to roost : an American misfit in India / Rachel Manija Brown.
p. cm.
ISBN-13 978–1–59486–139–0 hardcover
ISBN-10 1–59486–139–0 hardcover
1. Brown, Rachel Manija—Childhood and youth. 2. Americans—India—Biography. 3. Eccentrics and eccentricities—India. 4. Ashrams—India. 5. India—Biography. 6. California—Biography. I. Title.
CT1508.B76A3 2005
915.404′52—dc22 2005014275

Distributed to the trade by Holtzbrinck Publishers
2 4 6 8 10 9 7 5 3 1 hardcover

We inspire and enable people to improve their lives and the world around them

For more of our products visit **rodalestore.com** or call 800-848-4735

If you're opening this book for the first time,
it isn't dedicated to anyone yet.

But if you've already finished reading it and you've turned back to the beginning, feeling a little less lonely, a little less strange, or a little more cheered than you did when you began, then you will know: I wrote it for you.

Contents

Acknowledgments

Thanks to my parents and stepmother for providing the raw material and for being supportive rather than litigious. Also, thanks to Dad for providing the laptop I wrote it on, and to Dad and Kebi for the celebratory lunch.

Thanks to Nancy Wall, Emma Bull, and Will Shetterly for teaching me most of what I know about writing.

Thanks to the memoir's first readers, critiquers, and cheerleaders: Bill Bratton, Lissa Knudsen, Aram Krikorian, Ian McDowell, and Karen Williams.

Thanks to the writers of Dueling Modems for sharing your collective experience and wisdom with me. No one could have had a better set of mentors.

Thanks to Brian DeFiore for believing in me and my book, selling my book, giving me brilliant editing suggestions, and generally being DeFiore, Superagent.

Thanks to Leigh Haber for making the whole thing possible.

And special thanks to Starbucks for providing a congenial writing environment.

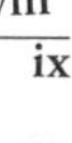

"If you have skeletons in the closet,
you may as well make them dance."

—George Bernard Shaw

All the Fishes come Home to Roost

I

An Officer and a Gnome

The Indian sun struck fiery glints from the train tracks, the wind sent dust devils whirling down the street, my father glowered, and my mother prayed. I plunked down on a suitcase and began reading *The Blue Sword*.

It was my eleventh birthday, and we were on a relaxing vacation.

"What was it that guidebook of yours promised?" asked Dad. "'Charming hotels?' 'Delightful old-fashioned hotels?'"

Mom's eyes shut and her head bowed in prayer. Her lips parted and closed in tiny silent movements, like a goldfish.

Dad yanked a copy of *Lonely Planet* from Mom's bag, opened it to a dog-eared page, then brandished it like a prosecutor displaying a blood-stained knife.

"'Quaint Raj-era hotels,'" declaimed Dad. "Do you see anything 'quaint' around here? Anything 'Raj-era?'" He ostentatiously peered around the desolate landscape. "What about anything 'hotel-like?'"

"Please don't be sarcastic, Joey," said Mom, without opening her eyes or moving her hands from the prayer position.

"I tell you what, Da-nonna. I'll stop being sarcastic if you stop praying."

Mom's parents had wanted a son named Daniel. When they got Mom instead, they vengefully named her Dan-Anna. Unsurprisingly, Mom hated her name. But she didn't like any other enough to change it. So she compromised by pronouncing it Da-nonna.

"Beloved Baba," implored Mom, turning her face to the sky and squinting against the glare. "If it's your will, please send us a way up the mountain. Pray with me, Mani," she urged, prodding me with a sharp elbow.

"God must have more important things to do than call us a taxi," I muttered.

"Mani!" exclaimed Mom, jabbing me again. "Don't say such things. Beloved Baba cares for each and every one of us, and he will always look out for us, no matter what."

Dad said, "So where's Baba's taxi?"

We all glanced around, just in case. No taxi.

If only I'd stayed in Los Angeles, I thought, we'd be in a place where shops were decorated for Halloween with witches and pumpkins. When we'd lived in America, I'd loved having my birthday fall on October 29th. I could pretend the holiday preparations were just for me. But Halloween wasn't celebrated in India, and I was apparently here to stay.

I blamed my parents for this state of affairs. Also Baba.

Baba was an Indian guru whom my parents believed was God. Outside of India, he is probably best known for having been Pete Townshend's guru and thus inspiring a number of songs by The Who, including "Baba O'Riley." He's also moderately famous for keeping a vow of silence for forty-four years and for coining the insipid motto "Don't worry, be happy."

Like The Who, Baba's heyday had been in the sixties, which was when my parents had discovered him. Mom and Dad had given up tie-dye and pot with the change of the decade, but they hadn't abandoned their guru. In 1980, when I was seven, we moved from LA to Baba's ashram in Ahmednagar in order to worship him full time.

Ahmednagar is an obscure backwater town in the west-central state of Maharashtra, India. Its residents usually explained where it was by saying, "Get on a train in Bombay, and go east for nine hours."

The Ahmednagar ashram, or spiritual commune, was located in what I had previously thought of as the most desolate place in India. But this expanse of brown-baked weeds about a hundred miles west of Ahmednagar was giving it some serious competition.

Ahmednagar was even hotter in October than LA in August, so my parents had decided we should take a vacation in the hill-station called Matheran. Hill-stations are resort towns built atop hills that rise above the heat of the plains.

The procedure was to catch a train to the base of the hill, transfer to another train that climbed the hill to the outskirts of town, then take a tonga, or horse-drawn carriage, to one of Matheran's quaint Raj-era hotels. But when we arrived at the train station beside the hill, which was situated in the middle of fifty miles worth of barren plains and the occasional crow, we discovered that the train to Matheran only ran on Tuesdays. It was Wednesday afternoon, the daily train from Ahmednagar had already left, and the nearest hotel was in Matheran.

"Is there a taxi?" Dad had asked the train station's only inhabitant, a bored clerk lounging in an office knee-deep in dusty papers and empty teacups.

"Driver is out of station," the clerk had replied. That was an Indianism that meant that the driver wasn't around, was off-duty, or didn't feel like driving.

"Is there any other way to Matheran?" asked Dad.

The clerk shook/nodded his head. The shake/nod, a side-to-side tilting of the head, is an all-purpose Indian gesture that can mean "Yes," "No," "Maybe," "I don't know," or "I have no idea what you're talking about."

"Where's the stationmaster?" demanded Dad.

The clerk yawned. "He is out of station."

As my parents accused each other of failing to check the train schedule, I immersed myself in a Robin McKinley fantasy novel. The novel's heroine, Harry, was a foreign girl who gets kidnapped by desert nomads and learns to ride bareback and do magic.

Certainly I could identify with the "kidnapped and taken to a foreign desert" part, though I wished I were enjoying my experience as much as Harry was enjoying hers. I also wished three of her magnificent desert steeds would appear, so we could ride them up the mountain.

Mom poked me. "Don't just sit there with your nose in a book. Pray with me."

On second thought, perhaps only one steed.

"Excuse me."

We all jumped. A leathery little man had appeared out of nowhere. His diminutive stature, wizened face, and pointy white beard reminded me of a china figurine I had of a gnome riding a pig.

"I have jeep to Matheran," announced the gnome. "One hundred rupees."

"Oh, thank Baba!" exclaimed Mom. "See, Joey, I told you Baba would provide."

"Where's the jeep?" asked Dad.

The gnome beckoned. We picked up our luggage, which consisted of a suitcase for Dad, a suitcase for Mom, a bulgy cotton bag filled with leaking fruit for Mom, and a tote bag of paperbacks for me, and followed him.

The path went along the train tracks, winding past a lone acacia tree and stopping at an asphalt road that began abruptly in the midst of a thistly field. A jeep was parked in the middle of the street.

"Jeep," explained the gnome.

We piled in alongside an Indian family. Two teenage boys were eating sandwiches, and their parents were sharing a newspaper. They seemed to have been there for some time.

The gnome removed a can of gasoline from under the seat and tipped it into the fuel tank. "I get driver," he said, and then vanished.

After about half an hour he returned, accompanied by a man carrying a metal tube contraption. The gnome opened the hood of the jeep, while his companion positioned the metal thing that resembled a welding arc but couldn't possibly be one, because no one would weld a fueled and working engine, especially when there were people inside the vehicle.

The man fired it up and began to weld the engine. Blinding white sparks fizzed out. I looked at my parents for guidance.

"Baba, Baba, Baba," said Mom.

Dad was silent.

"Um," I said, "That guy's welding the engine, right? Isn't that dangerous? Shouldn't we get out?"

"Baba, Baba, Baba," said Mom.

Dad shrugged.

Just then the man working on the engine turned off the welding arc, slammed down the hood, and walked off.

"Hey, isn't that guy the driver?" I asked the gnome. "Where's he going?"

"Not driver," he replied. "Is engineer. Driver will come."

Again we waited. Fumes began to issue from under the hood of the jeep, and the gnome hurriedly opened it to release the vapors.

Another jeep came rumbling up, one painted in camouflage blotches. An army officer got out and marched over to us. I couldn't help ogling the officer.

In India, the army is not a dumping ground for people who can't function in civilian life, but a quality career path. Officers tended to be polite, helpful, and good-looking. This was not universally the case—the border state of Kashmir, which is the site of a low-grade perpetual war, suffered from anti-civilian violence and looting by Indian soldiers as well as the Pakistani guerillas they fought, but we were far from Kashmir, and all the officers I'd ever met were perfect gentlemen.

This one was slim, dark, and handsome, with a neatly combed moustache and wire-rimmed glasses. I could tell that he was going to get a starring role in my daydreams for months to come.

Over the gnome's protests, the officer peered at the smoking engine. I noticed that he stood as far away as possible and seemed poised to run. His eyebrows shot up, and he scolded the gnome in Hindi. Then he came around to the back of the jeep and addressed the Indian passengers, who seemed to disagree with him. Finally, he turned to my parents.

"I have examined this jeep," said the officer in English. "It is very unsafe. You should not ride in it."

"Is there any other way to Matheran?" asked Dad.

"There is Matheran train."

"That only runs on Tuesdays."

The officer shook/nodded his head. "This jeep is unsafe. The engine is very bad. Better to take train."

Dad said, "Thank you, sir." He sounded sincerely appreciative, if you ignored the fact that he'd clearly never had any intention of taking the officer's advice.

The officer got back into his jeep and drove away.

Mom turned to Dad. "Joey, maybe we shouldn't take this jeep."

"You're the one who wanted to come to India," replied Dad. "Well, this is India."

"But he said the jeep wasn't safe."

"What else can we do? You notice the other family's not getting out."

As Mom and Dad quarreled, a third party arrived. This time, a dwarf.

I don't mean that he resembled a dwarf, as the man I thought of as "the gnome" resembled a gnome: He *was* a dwarf, a pudgy man with stubby arms and legs and an elongated torso, an inch or two shorter than my 4′ 4″ self.

"Is driver," announced the gnome.

We all stared at the dwarf. A slow grin spread across his face, widening and widening until all his teeth were showing. It was a smile of utter vacuity, the sort of blandly demented leer that generally heralds drooling or gibbering or claims to be the Easter Bunny.

"Heh, heh, heh," he chuckled, staring at Mom's breasts.

Mom folded her arms over them.

With the empty smirk still plastered over his face, he clambered into the driver's seat and slid down to reach the gas pedal. That put his head beneath the steering wheel. He then tried sitting on a pillow, which proved that if he was high enough to see over the steering wheel, he would be too high to reach the pedals.

"The driver is a *dwarf*," I informed Dad.

"I noticed," he said.

"Well, how's he going to drive when he can't see over the steering wheel?"

In case this sounds implausible, I note that although my parents' memories of the driver are not identical to mine, to this day they agree on the crucial issue of his height relative to the steering wheel.

Mom recently e-mailed me, "As for the story of the trip to Matheran, you are absolutely correct in that it appeared that the driver was a midget—well, whether officially he was a midget by height or just a very very stuntedly short person is debatable."

Dad's recollection is that the driver was short because he was a twelve-year-old boy.

The dwarf slid down, his feet barely touching the pedals and his head level with the hub of the steering wheel. The gnome hopped into the back of the jeep. We all squeezed over to make room for him. But rather than sitting down, he stayed where he was, clinging to the door frame, his feet on the running board, and his body hanging out the back.

"Neutral!" called the gnome.

The jeep leaped forward. My neck snapped back.

"Neutral, neutral!" shrieked the gnome.

The dwarf turned all the way around, still grinning. "First gear?" he asked.

"Second gear, second gear!"

The dwarf's head disappeared from sight, and the jeep slowly rolled into a fence post.

"Watch the road!" shrieked Mom.

"I am watching," he replied from somewhere beneath the dashboard. "What gear?"

"Reverse!" yelled the gnome. The engine made a horrible grinding noise. "Clutch!"

Mom turned on him. "This driver of yours doesn't know how to drive."

The Indian family, urgently speaking to each other in Hindi, had evidently come to the same conclusion, but seemed no more willing to leave the jeep than we apparently were.

"He knows *automatic*," explained the gnome. "Jeep is manual. Second gear!"

I nudged Dad and whispered, "Why doesn't the other guy drive? He obviously knows how."

Dad gave me a withering look, one clearly polished and refined from years of practice. In response, I cringed.

"*Obviously*, he's teaching the young guy," Dad told me.

"Oh."

The gnome continued to shout instructions, and the jeep shuddered into motion, bouncing up the winding mountain road. As we climbed higher, the ground fell away on the left and rose on the right.

Soon we were weaving and jolting along a narrow road between a vertiginous cliff and a granite hillside. There was no rail, but the drop side was lined with rocks painted white, so drivers could see where the edge was.

The dwarf turned around, leering. "What gear?"

The jeep drifted to the left and knocked a white rock over the cliff. The rock tumbled down, down, down, thousands of feet down, finally disappearing from view.

"Look out!" screamed Mom.

"Watch the road!" shouted Dad.

"Third gear, third gear!" yelled the gnome.

"Lean to the right, the right!" I shrieked, and pushed all sixty of my pounds into the right side of the jeep.

The dwarf turned back around and wrestled the jeep into the middle of the road.

"Baba, Baba, Baba," chanted Mom.

I fatalistically decided that if we were going to die, we were going to die, and somehow began to see humor in our situation. Certainly Harry would have faced death bravely, I thought.

"Along the Cliff of Death rode the ten of us," I declaimed. For the first time, I saw the point of my school's requirement that we memorize epic English poems.

"Be quiet," said Mom. "Baba, Baba, Baba."

"Death to the right of us, death to the left . . ."

"Clutch! Clutch!"

"Baba, Baba!"

"Lean! Lean!"

"Watch the goddamn road!"

"Baba, Baba, Baba . . ."

"A *dwarf* is driving us, safety now is lost to us, along the Cliff of Death rode the . . ."

WHAM!

As the dwarf turned away from the road, apparently to inquire about the gear, the jeep slammed into the cliff side at about twenty miles per hour. I dropped *The Blue Sword.*

"You goddamn moron!" yelled Dad. "Idiot! Idiot! Idiot!"

The Indian family began congratulating each other on their lucky survival.

"Oh, thank Baba we're alive!" said Mom.

We had been packed in so tightly that despite the lack of seat belts, nobody had even fallen out of their seat.

I picked up *The Blue Sword* and clambered out of the jeep. Mom was right behind me.

"You are leaving?" said the gnome. "Paint only is damaged."

"I want my money back," said Dad.

"Is agreement," said the gnome. "Jeep is not damaged."

"The jeep crashed. The driver doesn't know how to drive a stick shift."

"Is agreement. We drive up hill."

"He can't even see over the steering wheel."

"Twenty rupees return."

"We have to walk fifteen kilometers uphill with all our luggage because your driver is a defective midget!"

"Fifty rupees." The gnome held up a wad of bills. "I pay petrol . . . I pay driver . . . I pay engineer . . ."

Dad grabbed the fifty rupees. "Fine."

The Indian family stayed in the jeep. With the dwarf at the helm and the gnome clinging to the back door, the jeep lurched ahead of us and vanished up the hill. We stood and contemplated our suitcases, bundles, and tote bag, and the vast length of the road ahead.

"It's Baba's blessing that we're alive," said Mom, a little doubtfully.

Dad made a snarling noise.

I picked up my tote. Dad balanced the suitcases on his head. He looked like a coolie. I was tempted to snicker, but feared the Wrath of Dad. We began the six-mile trek uphill.

From a loop of the road high above us, a faint voice drifted down. "Second gear!"

2

TOAD MAHAL

My life was completely normal until I turned seven and moved to India. Or so it had seemed to me.

I was born in a redwood forest north of Santa Cruz, California, where Mom taught natural childbirth and Dad was a teacher at a school for the blind. I was three years old and loved three things: books, animals, and books about animals. I was obsessed with Florida swamp rabbits. It was probably a Florida swamp rabbit, though some believe it was a nutria, which had attacked Jimmy Carter, forcing him to fend it off with a canoe paddle and setting a threshold for embarrassing presidential moments not equaled until George H. W. Bush threw up in the Japanese Prime Minister's lap. I had a lop-eared rabbit named Jarabso, and I wanted to study Florida swamp rabbits when I grew up. The origin of

Jarabso's name and my fixation on Florida swamp rabbits remain mysteries to this day.

My troubles began when I entered kindergarten. I had taught myself to read the year before and was delighted to discover that my classroom contained a small library. My teacher was less than delighted with my discovery and cornered my father when he came to pick me up.

"Mr. Brown," said the teacher. "I'm sorry to have to tell you this, but your daughter is not normal."

Dad glanced at me. I was reading in the library corner, with my stomach on a carpet-covered block and my knees and elbows on the floor.

"Yes, she likes to get into funny positions," he said. "We think she'll be a Flying Wallenda when she grows up."

"That's not what I meant," she replied. "Instead of playing normally, she sits there and pretends to read."

"What do you mean 'pretends to read'?" asked Dad. "She does read."

"Children that age can't read."

"Mani can."

I flipped a page, pleased with the chance to read a little more before Dad took me home.

"I'm a teacher, and I'm telling you that your daughter is not reading. She's just sitting there turning pages."

Dad clapped his hands. "Mani!"

"Huh?" I said.

"Come over here," said Dad. "Bring the book."

I trotted up to the desk.

"Read it out loud," instructed Dad.

I opened the book to where I'd left off.

"Mr. Brown," said the teacher. "Really, this is . . ."

"Read," said Dad.

"'Anne put Helen's hand under the faucet and ran cold water over it,'" I read obediently. "'As the water poured over Helen's palm, Anne spelled the word w-a-t—' "

"That's enough," said Dad.

I didn't understand why my teacher looked so angry. Had I done something wrong? I glanced at Dad for reassurance.

He patted my shoulder. "As you can see, my daughter can read. I'm a teacher too, by the way, and I can tell you that Mani reads better than a lot of kids in high school. Any other complaints?"

I got lots of reading time after that, for the teacher never addressed another word to me.

When I was five or six, Mom and Dad sold the house and moved to Hawthorne, a crime-ridden, low-rent area in Los Angeles, and I had to give Jarabso away. Our new neighborhood was not the best. The convenience stores had bars on the windows, and when our neighbors went on vacation, an inventive gang of thieves pulled up a moving van and moved all their furniture. But though I barely noticed the urban blight, I missed having trees to climb and was outraged by the landlord's refusal to allow cats or dogs.

Still, I made up for the shortage of large animals by collecting small ones: Ratsy the rat, a parakeet named Chatter who fired his droppings through the bars of his cage to splatter against walls three feet away, a box tortoise named Starlight, a garter snake that died, goldfish named Peach, Apricot, Tangerine, and Silver, and fifteen toads in a wire construction in the backyard called the Toad Mahal.

Ratsy, whom Dad semi-affectionately referred to as "That Revolting Rodent," was my favorite. He was a hooded rat, with black eyes, a white body, a black head, and a black stripe down his back. I trained him to come when he was called, stand on his hind legs, drink beer from a tiny spoon, and jump through hoops. The hoops were glass bangles that Dad bought in India for ten cents and sold for a dollar, size extra-large. I held them vertically and two feet in the air, so Ratsy had to leap straight up and through the hoop, turn in midair, and descend through it nose first. I did Ratsy the Amazing Performing Rat Shows to demonstrate his tricks for the local kids and also gave tours of the Mani Brown Zoo.

Most of my memories of Hawthorne involve animals, books, and my friends and family. I had to dig deep to uncover any recollections of my parents' spiritual master. Baba was always in the background of my life—I can't remember not knowing about him—but I failed to register his significance.

Our house was full of photographs of Baba as an old man with a hooked nose and a big smile, and as a young man with blazing eyes and wild hair, but they had all the emotional resonance of wallpaper to me. For one thing, he was dead. He'd died in 1969, four years before I was born, so it wasn't like I'd ever meet him.

My parents went to weekly Baba meetings, which consisted of adults sitting in a circle discussing free will and reincarnation and other concepts I didn't understand, but I spent them reading in the corner. Mom often told me that Baba loved me and I should love him, and she made me recite a prayer to him before I went to bed, but I couldn't stir up much interest in a person I'd never met. I supposed he was God, since my parents said he was God, but I was too young to either question or truly believe. Like sex, God/Baba was a somewhat abstract and mildly implausible concept which I shrugged and accepted, figuring I'd understand it when I was older.

The only Baba-related issue I had a solid grasp of was that most people had no idea that he even existed, let alone that he was God. So if anyone at school inquired about my religion, I'd say I was Jewish to avoid the hassle of explaining that God was some Indian guy no one had heard of. I also had no intention of introducing the phrase "Baba-lover" to a bunch of mockery-prone six-year-olds.

But one thing that set me apart couldn't be avoided: my name. My parents had considered naming me Arwen Evenstar after the

elf maiden in *Lord of the Rings* but apparently nixed that name, while sufficiently embarrassing, as too easy to pronounce. So they named me Manija, after one of Baba's female disciples. It's an old-fashioned Persian name meaning precious gem. The Buddhist mantra "*Om mani padme hum*" means "Hail to the jewel (i.e., the Buddha) on the lotus."

My father's father, my Grandpa Artie, was at the hospital when I was born, and a confused nurse asked him how to spell my name. Impressively, he only got one letter wrong. But he was not one to admit fault, and for the rest of his life he pronounced my name according to the spelling he'd dictated for my birth certificate, which was Manijay.

Having my name misspelled on my birth certificate was the first in a lifetime of annoyances caused by a name which few people can spell, pronounce, or take seriously.

(I changed my name to Rachel the summer between high school and college. What a relief that was.)

My parents nicknamed me Mani, pronounced "money." If I introduced myself as "Money," kids would yell, "Gimme some money, Money! Ha, ha, ha!" So I started to pronounce it Mah-ni. This wasn't as funny to them, but it was more confusing. Also kids tended to mishear it: "Manny, Moe, and Jack! Ha, ha, ha!" Revealing my full name, Manija, didn't help. It's pronounced with a hard j, like Jim. But since it looks Spanish, teachers always pronounced it Maniha when they called roll, which prompted my classmates to call me Minnihaha.

Parents, if you do not want your children to write tell-all memoirs when they grow up, do not name them KhrYstYll, Pebble, or Shaka Zulu.

Despite its drawbacks, Hawthorne had the benefit of being near Grandpa Artie's condo. The two of us often had lunch together, then explored the beaches or hiked in the hills. He was grumpy and hot-tempered, but he seemed to know everything there was to know about nature and could explain it to me simply and without condescension. I adored him.

At the time, I didn't realize that Grandpa Artie was not your run-of-the-mill American grandfather.

"The American Communists were very misunderstood," Grandpa Artie would observe, passing me a bowl of Manhattan clam chowder. "You want oyster crackers with that, Manijay?"

"Yes, please."

Dad's mom, my Grandma Janet, had died two years before, when I was four. The only memory I had of her was of a visit to the zoo. She'd leaned against a wire enclosure, and a tapir had eaten the sleeve of her blouse. I remembered her laughing at the absurdity of the incident even as a sodden rag of expensive silk vanished into the tapir's rubbery snout, but nothing else.

I sat swinging my legs on Grandpa's kitchen countertop and arranged the crackers in a circle atop the soup.

"Don't play with them unless you're going to eat them," warned Grandpa Artie.

"I'm going to eat them." I rearranged them into a heart. "Go on about the Communists, Grandpa."

"I was a union organizer in those days," he said, pouring me a glass of milk. "Unions make sure working men—and women—are treated right and get a fair wage. But I also worked for the Civil Rights Congress. That was the part of the Communist Party that fought for equal rights for black people. Did you know that when your daddy was a boy, black people and white people couldn't drink from the same water fountains?"

"How did they know whose was whose?"

"They had signs that said "White" and "Colored."

It sounded so bizarre that I giggled.

"It's not funny," Grandpa Artie admonished. "It may sound silly, but when you have separate drinking fountains, you also have separate schools. Separate everything. We had to fight to make it so black kids and white kids could go to school together. Can you imagine that, Manijay?"

"I guess so." I tried to picture my school with only white kids in it. No more getting shoved by Troy the bully . . . but also no more eating lunch with Isa or Elizabeth. I didn't think I'd like it.

"You're old enough to understand this," Grandpa said. "There's nothing more important than justice. If people aren't treated equally, that's wrong. If they can't live a decent life, that's wrong. If anyone ever tells you it's okay for women to earn less money than men, or for people to live on the streets, or for children to work in factories . . . they're wrong."

"There was a Baba meeting last week," I said hesitantly. "They were saying . . . " I looked up to the ceiling to recall the exact quote. "They said, 'Life is an illusion. Earthly justice is an illusion. The goal of life is to love Baba until you achieve union with Him.' An illusion is something that's not real, right? So if justice isn't real . . . and life isn't real . . ."

The skin around Grandpa's eyes and mouth crinkled like tissue paper. I couldn't tell if he thought what I'd said was funny or sad.

"See here, Manijay," he said. "Your parents believe in God and all that bull—that stuff. I don't believe any of it. I believe that this life is all you get, and when you die, you're gone."

The doorbell rang. It was Mom coming to pick me up.

"You keep an open mind," he said. "One day, you'll be old enough to decide for yourself what you believe in."

Grandpa Artie lifted me off the counter. I started to run toward the door.

"Dammit, Manijay!" he yelled. "Come back here."

I returned to the kitchen.

"You always leave your empty glasses on the counter. Put them in the sink when you're done."

"Sorry, Grandpa."

He went to open the door. I stood on tiptoes to take my glass off the counter, then on tiptoes again to reach the sink. I was too short to see into it, so I reached across as far as I could, then dropped the glass in.

A horrendous cacophony of crashing, crunching, grinding, and smashing noises filled the condo.

I screamed. From the doorway, Mom screamed louder: "MEHER BABA! MEHER BABA!"

"Jesus H. Roosevelt Christ!" yelled Grandpa. "What the hell did you do?"

Everyone ran into the kitchen. Grandpa peered into the sink, then hit a switch on the wall. The horrendous din ceased. "Dammit, Manijay! You dropped the glass into the garbage disposal."

"I put it in the sink, just like you said," I protested. His face turned red, then purple, then he began to make strange spluttering noises, like a drain. Mom wrung her hands. I started laughing.

"GODDAMMIT!" exploded Grandpa Artie. "DON'T LAUGH AT ME!" He was so enraged that he began leaping up and down in place.

"Keep jumping, Grandpa," I begged him. "You look like the Tasmanian Devil."

"Don't laugh, Mani," said Mom. "Artie, please calm down. Meher Baba, Meher Baba."

"GODDAMMIT . . . DAMN BABA . . . MY NEW GARBAGE DISPOSAL . . ." spluttered Grandpa, leaping higher and higher, like an ice skater on TV.

Mom grabbed me by the hand and dragged me from the kitchen.

"No, Mom," I protested. "I want to see him jump."

She whisked me into his bedroom and locked the door. Grandpa followed us. "Goddammit, Dan-Anna, don't hide in my bedroom. Are you out of your mind?"

Mom got down on her knees. "Meher Baba, Meher Baba," she prayed.

"Don't be ridiculous!" yelled Grandpa. "Are you *praying* in there?"

"Baba! Baba, Baba, Baba, Baba, Baba," replied Mom.

I lay down on the bed, happily observing the mayhem. I hadn't seen anything that entertaining since Dad's hand had gotten stuck in a pickle jar.

Months later, Grandpa Artie waved a newspaper clipping at us. "There's an article here on garbage disposals," he said. "It says if you want to keep the blades sharp, every now and then you should feed it an old glass you don't want any more. How 'bout that? Ha, ha, ha, ha, ha!"

It was not long afterward that my parents sat me down on the couch and said they had something to tell me. Even at that early stage of my life, I knew that those words never ever portended good things.

"We're moving to India," said Mom. "We're going to live in Beloved Baba's town with Beloved Baba's mandali."

"Who?"

"The mandali, sweetie. You know who they are. They're Baba's disciples."

I turned to Dad. "*India?*"

"Uh-huh," he said.

Mom and Dad had visited India twice before I'd been born, and the second time, they'd stayed on the ashram for six months. They'd taken me there on their third trip, but I'd been so young at the time that I didn't remember it. But Mom had shown me photographs and told me they were planning to move there some day . . . when they could afford it . . . when the time was right . . . But I wasn't good at remembering vague talk about the future. Or else I hadn't wanted to think about it. I'd seen India from the classroom globe. It was on the other side of the world.

I stared out the window, trying not to cry. Then I turned to Dad. "Forever?"

But Dad had vanished from the room.

"We'll see," said Mom. "Oh, Mani, this is such a wonderful opportunity for you. It'll be such an incredible learning experience. You'll be surrounded by the most loving and spiritual people on Earth."

"Can I take Ratsy?"

"No, sweetie. But we'll find him a good home."

I would never see Ratsy again or any of my pets. Or Becky from Brownies, or Angela from school, or Rochelle from next door. Like Jarabso, gone forever.

"I'll never see my friends again."

"Don't cry, sweetheart," said Mom. "It's for the best. You're not happy here. You don't fit in at school."

"I do fit in," I sobbed. "Mrs. Young said I was one of the best students she'd ever had."

When I'd started second grade a few months back, the school had determined that I could read at a college level, and now I got to leave my regular classroom for an hour every day to get special lessons from Mrs. Young.

"Yes, but honey, American schools don't know how to deal with kids as bright as you are. Remember how your teacher didn't believe that you knew how to read?"

"That was years ago."

"I know this is hard for you now. But you'll be so happy there. You'll be the only child in the world who'll get to grow up in Baba's own home. It's Baba's will."

I didn't care about Baba or his home or his will. But I knew there was nothing I could do. There was already an envelope in Dad's dresser drawer containing three one-way tickets to India.

3

Johnny Rebeck's Machine

I bounced up and down on the plastic airport seats. "Do they have ice cream in India?"

"I think so," said Dad, not looking up from the book he was reading, *Gravity's Rainbow*. It was so immense that he needed both hands to hold it. "Listen to this, Mani, you'll like it." He began to read aloud. "'Upstairs in the men's room at the Roseland Ballroom he swoons kneeling over a toilet bowl, vomiting beer, hamburgers, homefries, chef's salad with French dressing, half a bottle of Moxie . . .'"

I started laughing.

"Please, Joey," said Mom. "You know airplanes make me sick."

"We're not on the plane yet," said Dad. "' . . . after-dinner mints, a Clark bar, a pound of salted peanuts . . .'"

Mom's upper lip quivered, threatening tears.

"'And the cherry from some Radcliffe girl's old-fashioned.' Pretty good, huh?"

"Uh-huh," I said. "Can we get hamburgers?"

Mom said, "If you're hungry, I've got peanut butter and jelly sandwiches in my bag."

I eyed her bag disdainfully. Other kids' moms had purses. My Mom had big bulgy bags made of Indian cotton. No matter what was in them, they always looked squishy.

"Do they have peanut butter in India?" I asked.

"I don't think so," said Mom.

"What about jelly?"

"Yes, they have jelly. They have wonderful, delicious jelly," said Mom, warming to the subject. "You know the jelly in America is full of horrible, unhealthy chemicals—well, the jelly I buy isn't, it's organic, but the jelly in supermarkets is. But in India, all the jelly is organic."

I scowled. I liked the unhealthy supermarket food I ate at my friends' houses better than Mom's healthy organic food. But if the whole country was organic, my friends in India would have the same kind of food Mom did.

"In fact," continued Mom, "when I first went to India—that was before you were born, sweetheart—I visited the Compound, where we're going to live. Firoze was having lunch. You know how Baba is like Jesus—I mean, Baba *is* Jesus, he's Jesus reincarnated. And you know how Jesus had twelve disciples? Well, Baba had disciples too, and Firoze is like Saint Peter. He was Baba's chief male disciple."

I began surreptitiously reading over Dad's shoulder. The page he was on was full of words I didn't know and was even more boring than Baba and his saints.

"You'll love Firoze so much," said Mom. "When I first met him,

I was just some nobody who was interrupting his lunch, but he looked at me with his wonderful loving eyes, and he gave me a chapati spread with mango jam. It was such a beautiful gift."

Mom was so moved by this memory that tears began to drip down her cheeks. She made no attempt to hide them or even wipe them away. The people in the seats across from us began to stare. Dad lifted *Gravity's Rainbow* higher, hiding his face.

"What about pizza?" I asked hopefully. "Do they have pizza in India?"

I bounced up and down on the airplane seat. The plane had been on the ground for ages. I'd read the in-flight magazine, memorized the emergency instructions, and laughed at the barf bag. Now I was bored.

The plane made a small lurch, and Mom emitted a loud shriek. "BABA!"

The plane began a slow and majestic turn around the runway. I flattened my nose against the window.

"Baba, Baba, Baba, Baba," chanted Mom, clutching the armrests as if the gravity might go away at any moment.

"Relax," said Dad kindly.

"Baba, Baba, Baba, Baba," said Mom.

"Is everything all right?" asked a stewardess.

"My wife's afraid of flying," explained Dad.

"I want to die with Baba's name on my lips," explained Mom. "Oh Baba, Baba, Baba, Baba, Baba."

The stewardess backed away slowly.

The plane taxied down the runway. I leaned forward, testing myself against the acceleration that tried to shove me back against the seat.

Dad leaned back, engrossed in *Gravity's Rainbow*.

Mom's fingers dug into the armrests. "Baba, Baba, Baba, Baba, Baba, Baba," she chanted, her volume increasing with each Baba.

The plane leaped into the air.

"Wheeee!" I squealed.

"BABA!" shrieked Mom. "BABA, BABA, BABA!"

"Relax, dammit!" ordered Dad.

"We're flying, we're flying," I cried out. "Oh, look at the tiny little cars."

The plane wheeled out over the ocean, then up over a billowing expanse of white wispy softness. I wanted to get out of the plane and roll in the clouds.

Mom's chanting became background noise. Dad went to the bathroom and didn't come back. When I got up to go myself, I found him leaning on the wall near the toilets, talking to a man with a scraggly beard and a backpack.

"You were Commies?" asked the backpacker. "Far out."

"Oh, yeah," said Dad. "I was born right before it came out about the atrocities that were going on in Russia. After that, my parents quit the party. But I'm not named Joe after Joseph and Mary; I'm named after Stalin."

"You must have had a strange childhood."

"It had its moments. The FBI used to come to our neighborhood to spy on my Dad when my brothers and I were kids. But we always knew who they were, because they were the only people in the neighborhood who wore hats. One day, I was walking home from school, and I saw a man wearing a suit, which nobody who lived there would ever do, sitting in a parked car and reading an upside-down newspaper."

Dad saw me and winked. He knew that he was getting to my favorite part of the story. "So I walked up to him, and I said, 'Hey, mister, did you know your newspaper's upside down?' Then I laughed and ran away."

The backpacker and I laughed too. Then I went into the bathroom. When I came out, two more passengers were standing by the emergency window, listening to Dad, entranced.

"We spent our summer vacations at Nature Friends," said Dad.

"It was an anarchist-communist commune in the woods of New Jersey. We picked wild blueberries and hiked in the hills. One year, the adults had the idea of having the kids hold Olympic games. They divided us into teams and said we could each pick a country we'd represent. And all the kids—all of them, immediately—said, 'We wanna be Russia! No, we're Russia! No, we are!' It almost caused a riot."

Dad paused for laughter and to take a drink of bourbon from a plastic cup. An Indian lady in a sari, who had emerged from the toilet, stopped to listen.

Dad added, "Baba's ashram, which we're moving to, is out in the country and run by volunteers, just like Nature Friends. It's karma."

"This Baba you go to see," said the Japanese businessman. "He is guru, yes?"

"You could call him that," said Dad. "But we believe that Meher Baba is God in human form. Or was; he dropped the body in 1969, so we never got to meet him."

That was the most common way of referring to Baba's death, with "shed the mortal coil" coming in a close second. I imagined sound effects every time I heard those phrases, a thud for "dropped the body" and a slither for "mortal coil," which I conceived of alternately as a curled-up snake and a Slinky.

"But his mandali are still alive," said Dad. "It's from the word mandala. It means his inner circle."

The college girl smoothed her blonde bangs. "How'd you get into this Baba?"

I knew this was a good story too.

Dad swished a sip of bourbon around his mouth. "I met my wife, Danonna, at Berkeley. We were on the debate team, and I was going to be a lawyer. I'd have made a good one. But unfortunately, it was the sixties, and we both got heavily into drugs. We ended up dropping out of college—getting a degree didn't seem important at the time."

Dad glanced at me. I nodded, indicating that I would never get into drugs and drop out of school, and that I thoroughly understood the importance of a degree.

Reassured, he continued. "Da-nonna and I were seeing a counselor at Berkeley, Dr. Bergmann. He had a corkboard on his office wall with a collage of business cards, want ads, psychedelic art, that sort of thing. One of them was a photo of Baba with a quote by him.

"I found out later that hundreds of students got into Baba because of Dr. Bergmann's bulletin board. But Da-nonna and I can't remember what the quote was any more, and neither can any of them. And nobody has ever seen that particular quote or photo again."

Like a magic shop in a fairy tale, I thought. It sold them something that changed their lives, then disappeared.

"Da-nonna took one look at that photo, and she started crying. Well, my wife cries pretty easily. But I looked at it too, and for some reason, my mind was just blown by it. 'Whoa!' I said. 'Who *is* that?' Dr. Bergmann told me that it was Meher Baba, an Indian spiritual leader, and that there was a Baba club that met on campus.

"We went to the Baba club and watched a documentary on him. He'd grown up as an ordinary boy, then he became spiritually awakened as a teenager. When he was thirty-one he began keeping silence, and he never spoke again. He communicated with gestures and an alphabet board. There's a moment in the documentary when Baba looks straight into the camera—at least, Da-nonna says he looked straight at her, and she knew that Baba was God, and she had to devote her life to him.

"I don't remember him looking at me. Actually, we've seen that film hundreds of times since then, and he never looks into the camera. He must've done it just for my wife. But I went to Baba meetings, and I read the books he wrote, and I realized that Baba had the only explanation for the meaning and purpose of the universe that made any sense. So we both became Baba-lovers."

"So what's the meaning of life?" asked the backpacker.

Dad took another drink. "According to Baba, what we perceive as reality is actually an illusion. It's nothing but a dream in the mind of God. Our goal in life is to transcend the illusion of life, our selves, and the world, and so become one with the real reality, which is God."

The college girl yawned. The Indian lady pulled a loose thread from her sari. The Japanese businessman looked at his watch.

"A funny thing happened after we got into Baba," said Dad. "Danonna and I took some LSD one night. Now, Baba had said that before he died, he would break his silence."

"Oh, so he did speak?" asked the college girl.

"No, he didn't," said Dad.

"But . . ."

"It was a test," explained Dad. "He made some predictions that didn't come true, so the people who were only after fortune-telling would get disillusioned and leave, and the ones who stayed would be the ones who truly loved him. At least, that's what most Baba-lovers think. Personally, I think he said some things just to keep people off balance. Sort of a divine joke.

"Anyway, he'd said—gestured, that is—that a great spiritual awakening would occur when he broke his silence. He'd also predicted that three-quarters of the world would be destroyed, and a lot of Baba-lovers thought that it would all happen at once.

"So after the acid had taken hold, Da-nonna and I both knew, without speaking, that Baba would break his silence that very night. Then there was this incredibly loud siren, and people started screaming, and we realized that was it. Baba had broken his silence.

'It's the end of the world,' said Da-nonna.

'Yeah,' I said. 'But on the bright side, tomorrow we won't have to go to work.' "

"But what really happened?" asked the backpacker.

"A fire," said Dad. "And a fire engine. The only thing that was three-quarters destroyed was the pizza place across the road."

We landed ("BABA Baba Baba!"), and I was hauled through the grubby vastness of the Bombay airport. Once we retrieved our luggage, I was hustled briefly through the sauna-like night air, then whisked into a taxi for the all-night drive to Ahmednagar. Dad gazed out the window as the taxi hurtled past the airport, dodged a boy on a bicycle, and missed an oncoming truck by inches.

"Baba, Baba, Baba," began Mom, her eyes glazing over with terror. It seemed that she was also afraid of taxis. A light rain spattered the windows, and the taxi flew over the oil-slicked streets like a hovercraft. It hit a bump and for a brief and delicious moment was actually airborne. Mom shrieked. I fell asleep.

It was late morning when I awoke. I had fuzzy memories of the taxi stopping at all-night roadside stalls for tea and snacks and trips to the bathroom, but most of the nine-hour car ride was a sleepy blur.

Our car was parked at an all-purpose station jammed with taxis, buses, oxcarts, motorcycles, bicycles, donkeys, motor scooters, trucks painted in psychedelic swirls, two-wheeled carriages drawn by wretched bony horses, and rickshaws. The latter are three-wheeled motorcycles with a driver in front and up to three passengers in a seat in the back, with open sides and a black and yellow canvas roof. A line of them began in the lot and overflowed into the street.

"We're here!" Mom exclaimed. "Look, Mani, this is Ahmednagar. We're in Baba's home."

I looked, but I looked at her first. She was transfigured, as radiant beneath her crumpled traveling clothes as a peasant woman catching a glimpse of the Virgin of Lourdes. Dad seemed grumpy and put out, as if we'd just pulled out of the driveway for a camping trip and he already missed hot water and his morning paper.

The air was hot, but it was a tolerable dry heat, like a Los Angeles summer. I smelled sewage, garbage, and gasoline. Gritty dust floated in the air and lodged in my nose and throat. Cats, cows, goats, and huge black water buffaloes with horns twisted like driftwood wandered loose and mingled with traffic. Some of the cows had bells around their necks and their neatly upturned horns painted sky-blue or crimson.

A crow swooped to the side of the road, then flew off with a disemboweled mouse in its beak. It flapped heavily across a sky as blue and bright and intense as the first squeeze from a tube of paint, free of clouds but filled with wheeling fork-tailed hawks.

Stinking gray slime oozed along the gutters. There were no sidewalks, only narrow dirt paths on both sides of the single road. Both street and parking lot were covered with trash and bright red splatters. A rickshaw driver spat into the street, creating another crimson splotch.

Dad caught my pop-eyed look. "It's not blood," he explained. "It's paan—betel nut wrapped in a leaf. You know how your tongue turns red when you suck a cherry Popsicle?"

I nodded, hoping they had Popsicles in India.

It was all so different from anything I'd ever encountered that I had no idea how I felt about it. Ahmednagar was overwhelming and beyond analysis, like a new primary color.

My parents crammed themselves, our luggage, and me into a rickshaw. "Baba's ashram," said Dad to the driver, and we took off in a cloud of fumes and dust.

Mom also appeared to be frightened of rickshaws.

The driver wove along the main road. It had more and more varied traffic than any surface street in Los Angeles, some of it traveling at high speeds. There were no signal lights, signs, or even lines painted on the potholed asphalt. "Drive on the left" and "the larger vehicle has the right of way" appeared to be the only rules, and both of those seemed somewhat theoretical.

There were always at least three more people aboard any given vehicle than it was designed to contain. Tottering bicycles carried families of five, oxcarts were stacked with children three layers deep, and entire villages seemed wedged into open-bed trucks. One truck had six men clinging to the *roof*.

The buildings lining the road consisted of concrete cubes, rectangles, and the occasional triangle stuck together randomly, like a 3-year-old's Lego sculptures.

"Baba, Baba, Baba, Baba,Baba, Baba," chanted Mom, pausing only to choke on dust or exhaust.

The rickshaw zigzagged through a herd of water buffaloes, missed a billy goat by inches, then slammed on the brakes for a massive traffic jam. We idled behind a truck painted with swirls of pink and green radiating from a potbellied man with a halo circling his elephant's head. A mysterious message was emblazoned beneath the holy monster: "HORN OK PLEASE."

"What's that?" I wrinkled my nose at the stench emanating from a furry mound that blockaded the footpath and spilled over into part of the street.

"Oh, Baba, how awful!" exclaimed Mom. "Mani, don't look!"

I craned my neck to get a better view. It was obviously a dead animal, but I couldn't figure out what kind. The mound was about three feet tall and five around, and had too many different colors of fur, not to mention too many rigid paws, to be any familiar creature.

Then I realized that it wasn't a single animal, but many. Once I knew that, the nature of the pile was obvious. It was an immense mound of bloated dead dogs.

I later discovered that this was not a one-time occurrence, but Ahmednagar's eccentric nod to public sanitation. Three or four

times a year, dead dog collectors scoured the city and left their findings on that street corner. And there they stayed, a great mound of decomposing puppies, until the last dead dog had joined the heap. Then they were loaded into a truck and taken away. The entire process took about five days. It was not used for rats, cats, goats, sheep, cows, buffaloes, horses, or birds. All those animals were left to rot where they lay. Pick-up service was reserved for dogs.

But I had no inkling of this upon our arrival and thought that a doggie epidemic was sweeping the town. I had hoped to get a puppy at long last, but it seemed that all the dogs in town were dead.

"And all the neighbors' cats and dogs will never more be seen," sang Dad cheerfully in his not-bad-for-an-amateur tenor. "They all have gone for sausages, in Johnny Rebeck's machine."

The truck lumbered away, and the rickshaw driver whipped into a U-turn. He pulled up at a collection of gray concrete buildings at an intersection with a battered sign reading "ALL WEHICLES STOP." Hot pink bougainvillea spilled over a tree by the gate, blazing like frozen fireworks.

The canine corpses were directly across the street and quite smellable.

"Welcome to Baba ashram," said the driver.

4

The Kaliyuga Age

"Stop staring at those disgusting dead dogs," hissed Mom, pulling me through the gates.

We were in the Compound, one of the three branches of Meher Baba's ashram. The others were Meherabad (Meher's Blossoming) and Meherazad (Meher's Freedom), located on opposite ends of Ahmednagar, where the town ended and the countryside began. The Compound was an afterthought, which was why it didn't have a Baba-related name.

It was a walled-off circle of adobe buildings with a courtyard in the middle. As we cut through the center, I dawdled at a huge gnarled tree beside a dry fountain. Its corrugated bark was studded with jewels of crystallized sap. I pulled one off and poked at the sticky spot where the bead had formed. India might be smelly, but it was full of interesting things.

"Come on, Mani," said Mom.

"It's amber!" I exclaimed. "Sometimes amber has fossil insects inside. Maybe some of these have bugs in them."

"You'll have plenty of time to check out the tree later," said Dad. "You'll have years; this is where we're going to live."

We walked into the main office. A chorus of "*Jai Baba!*" arose. That meant "Glory to Baba" and was an all-purpose greeting, exclamation, and goodbye. The more formal version, which was shouted in unison after prayers and when mandali were leaving or arriving, was "*Avatar Meher Baba Ki Jai!*"

I spent the next few hours being introduced to a selection of middle-aged Western residents and elderly Indian mandali. (Any non-Indians were called Westerners, but all of them seemed to be American.) A number of Indian servants popped in and out, sweeping, dusting, and passing out tea and cookies, but they were not introduced.

In the entire ashram, there were about thirty residents, twenty mandali, and fifty servants, hired help, and itinerant hangers-on, and I met half of them in my first hour there.

All the mandali pinched my cheeks, and some of them pinched my chin as well. It was like being introduced to some annoying ancient relative at Thanksgiving, except that there were twenty of them, and they were not going to go away when the holidays were over.

We were enthusiastically welcomed by all those people I didn't know whose names I hadn't caught. They were all sure that Baba's will had brought us there. *Jai Baba!* Tears of joy slid down Mom's cheeks, and a small smile curved Dad's lips.

A pink-cheeked female mandali, Zireen, beckoned to Mom. "You must dress your child properly for India. She may not wear pants or shorts. Girls must wear skirts or dresses."

"You're wearing pants," I pointed out. I hated skirts and dresses.

"Mani!" exclaimed Mom. "Don't ever contradict a mandali."

Zireen smiled. "When you're older, you may wear the *salwar kamiz*."

She indicated her own outfit of dark pink cotton pants and a long split tunic, with a light pink gauzy scarf around her neck. "But now you're too young."

She tugged at a lock of my hair. I ducked. "Her hair is loose. It must be braided. And she has no hat. She must wear a hat when she goes in the sun. If you allow her to play in the sun with her head uncovered, she will get sunstroke. That is very serious. She could die."

She took the scarf from around her neck and tied it over my hair. "Here, wear this until your mother buys you a hat." It was like an accessory from a fairy princess costume, and somewhat made up for the prospect of having to wear skirts all the time.

Zireen steered me to a mirror. "See how pretty you look." My face was tiny and pale, swallowed up in cloth.

The mirror was the only thing on the wall that wasn't Baba-related. Baba's image beamed from paintings and photos on the walls, from pins on the mandali's shirts and lockets around their necks, from paperweights, from pictures on desks, from the covers of every book on every table, from the letterhead of the stationery, and from the dashboard of every car.

One of the mandali, Firoze, a stocky old man who radiated trustworthiness, noticed me eyeing a painting that portrayed Baba in a white robe on a white horse, flying through a psychedelic colorscape.

"You like that picture?" asked Firoze.

"Sure," I said. "Did he really have a white horse?"

"It's symbolic." Firoze adjusted his black-rimmed glasses. They gave him a studious, Clark Kent appearance. "The picture shows Baba in his incarnation as Kalki, the rider of the white stallion. Baba has had many incarnations: Jesus, Buddha, Mohammed, Rama, Krishna, Zoroaster . . ."

I noticed what all Baba's incarnations had in common, apart from being God. "Can't God ever be a woman?"

"No."

"Why not?"

"That's not a woman's role. But," he added consolingly, "only a woman can be the mother of God."

Who wants to be God's Mom? I thought. Hovering at the edges of my mind, just a glimmering rather than a fully-formed idea, was another thought: *That's not fair.*

Of the mandali, I liked Firoze, who was at least attempting to make me feel included, and Zireen, whose lecture had been delivered kindly.

I took an immediate dislike to Coconut, who asked bewildering questions and wouldn't take "Huh?" for an answer. There was no need to explain his nickname: He was brown, hairy, and spherical. Just when I thought he was getting bored, he produced the most peculiar inquiry yet.

"Are you my mummy?" he demanded.

"What?" *I'd like to mummify you*, I thought.

"Are you my little mummy?"

Mom intervened. Sort of. "Mani, mummy is how they say mommy here."

"Come with me," said Coconut. "I will tell you why it is that you are my mummy."

I shot a "Help!" look at Mom.

"Go with him, Mani," she muttered through clenched teeth. "He's one of the mandali."

He's a sixty-year-old man named Coconut who thinks a seven-year-old girl he just met is his mother, I tried to telepathically convey to my mummy—mommy—Mom. *He's a nut.*

But I followed him into his office. He crouched down. His shirt stretched taut across his belly, and his breath smelled like spice and licorice. "Say, 'because this is the Kaliyuga age, and anything can happen then.'"

"What?"

"Repeat after me: 'because this is the Kaliyuga age, and anything can happen then.'"

"Because this is the Kaliyuga age, and anything can happen then," I parroted, wondering what I was saying and if it was dirty.

Coconut laughed heartily. I was experiencing many things for the first time that day, and here was another one: someone who really did shake like a bowl full of jelly when he laughed. Then he pinched my cheek, hard.

"Ow!"

He laughed again. "Now, why are you my mummy?"

"I already said it." Now I was convinced that it was dirty.

"Once more, so I know you know it."

Sulkily, I recited, "because this is the Kaliyuga age, and anything can happen then."

"Very good! You have an excellent memory."

I couldn't stand it anymore. "What does it mean?"

Coconut winked. "It is a great mystery."

He escorted me back into the main office. "Your daughter is very wise," he told Mom and Dad. "Listen: Why are you my mummy?"

Feeling like a performing seal, I said, sing-song so everyone would know I was only quoting, "Because *this* is the *Ka*li*yu*ga age, and *anything* can *ha*ppen then."

Everyone laughed. I appealed to Firoze, who seemed to be the sanest person there. "What's the Kaliyuga age?"

"It's the time we live in now," he said. "Yuga means age. Kaliyuga means the age of Kali: a very bad time. It is the last age before the end of the world."

"Oh." It still didn't make any sense. But at least it wasn't dirty.

"Can I have a glass of water?" I asked. My tea had grown a repulsive skin on top while I'd been off getting coached by Coconut.

Firoze walked me to the water pots. They were unfired black clay, the size of beach balls, hanging on ropes from the ceiling of

the porch outside. The water within permeated the clay, so they were moist and cool to touch and smelled pleasantly of deep dark caverns.

"You may drink this water," said Firoze. "But you must never drink water from the taps or at a restaurant. You must never drink soda or juice with ice—ice is also water. It is not safe."

"Okay."

He took a tumbler from a rack and scooped water into it from a ladle. "And you must not touch your lips to the cup. Everyone drinks from the same cups. Drink like this." He tipped his head back, opened his mouth, and poured a stream of water through his lips from two inches away.

I took the glass and tried the same trick. A flood filled my nostrils, and the rest drenched my shirt. But it was a fun way to drink, like a circus trick, so I took the ladle and tried again. I filled my mouth on the second try, and only a tablespoonful or so overflowed.

Water from American taps was tasteless, except for overtones of "flat" or "chemical." This water had a scent like earth after rain and a flavor like the smell of granite. The only time I'd ever tasted anything like it had been when I'd drunk from a creek in the woods while on a camping trip. But that water had been too cold to have more than a hint of flavor.

I had finally found something that Ahmednagar did better than Los Angeles.

American residents flowed in and out of the Compound. All of them were white, which I noticed because my neighborhood in Hawthorne had been mostly black.

A loud-voiced, fleshy-faced man bounced in. His collar was unbuttoned to display a tuft of chest hair which he'd carefully curled out over the V-neck. "Yo, Bro, gimme some dough!"

When no one showed signs of comprehension, he elaborated,

"Money, honey, the moola for your room and board. The Goldberg is collecting."

Dad laughed. "Sure thing. How's the show, bro?"

Soon Dad and the man who referred to himself as The Goldberg were cracking jokes like best buddies. At first I thought that The Goldberg had grown up in a black neighborhood, but he didn't sound like any actual black person I'd ever heard. Then I realized that he was imitating black people in the movies.

If you talked like that in Hawthorne, I thought, *someone would go upside your head with a tire iron.*

I wouldn't have taken notice of the man who walked with his shoulders hunched and his neck pulled in, as if he expected someone to slap him in the face at any moment, except that he was introduced as Shinork—pronounced Shnork—Aberjanian. Considering the pain my own funny name had caused me, I refrained from throwing myself to the floor and howling.

Dad was engrossed in debate with The Goldberg. "That's interesting," said Dad. "I've always interpreted that passage to mean that Creation was a causeless whim in the mind of God."

"A causeless whim in the mind of God," repeated The Goldberg. "Yeah! I love you, bro." He announced to the room at large, which was not paying attention, "Hey, can my bro turn a phrase, or what?"

But there were no children, except for the servant kids who worked alongside their parents, and as no one acknowledged them in any way, I got the idea that I was not going to be playing with them.

"Aren't there any kids?" I finally asked.

"You'll meet some at school," said Mom. "But you're the only resident child. This is a great opportunity for you, Mani. No other child in the world has a chance to grow up this close to Baba. You're the only one."

"But there's other American kids in town?"

Dad said to The Goldberg, "Einstein said energy can neither be created nor destroyed, so that means . . ."

"Consciousness remains after death," replied The Goldberg. "Yes! Gimme five!" They slapped hands.

"Sometimes pilgrims bring children," Shinork volunteered. "You can play with them while they're here."

Firoze put me out of my misery. "You're the only foreign child in the town. Was that what you were asking?"

I nodded.

"But you'll never be lonely," said Shinork. "Baba will always be with you."

An invisible intangible silent presence was not what I'd had in mind.

"Is there a library in town?" I asked without much hope.

"There's a library right here," replied Shinork unexpectedly. "Want to see it?"

"Yeah!"

I followed Shinork to a room the size of an American kitchen. Beat-up paperbacks packed tottering metal bookcases and moldy built-in shelves. Dust puffed out in clouds when I experimentally pulled out *Steppenwolf*, hairy spiders spun elaborate webs in the corners, and termites gnawed through the section on alternative healing.

"There's not many kids' books," said Shinork apologetically. "Everything here was donated by pilgrims, so it's just whatever people brought to read and didn't feel like taking back with them."

I could see how that worked. My parents had owned a number of the same books: *The Tao of Physics*, *The Magus*, *Siddhartha*, *Cat's Cradle*, and *Zen and the Art of Motorcycle Maintenance*.

Then I saw a shelf labeled "Children." I pounced. Shinork was utterly forgotten as I scooped up *The Peacock Garden*, *Wild Animals I Have Known*, and *The Adventures of Sudhir and Shailie*.

"Arrrr!"

I spun around, clutching the books to my chest.

A tall Indian with matted hair and a tangled beard towered over me, snarling. His clothes were stained and crusty, and his cheeks and neck were a raw red mass of boils and sores. Moldy bread crumbs speckled his beard.

I squeaked in alarm and backed up against the wall.

"You . . . " he ground out in a voice like rusty machinery. "You . . . GET OUT!"

But he was blocking the doorway. I darted away from the ogre and toward Shinork, who was at the back wall, looking embarrassed.

"Ratanji, this is Mani Brown," said Shinork. "Mani's the daughter of the new residents."

"Arrrr," snarled Ratanji.

"Mani, this is Ratanji, the librarian."

"What?" I exclaimed involuntarily.

"You . . . " said Ratanji. "You . . . *child* . . . keep out!"

"This is a library, Ratanji," said Shinork. "She's allowed to come in and read."

With a final, lingering growl, Ratanji stalked out.

"*He's* the *librarian*?" I said.

"He's Coconut's third cousin," explained Shinork. "He was very close to Baba."

"How am I supposed to check out books when the librarian hates kids?"

"He doesn't hate kids," said Shinork, a little doubtfully. "He's only . . . detached from worldly affairs. I tell you what. Just take the books you want to read, and put them back when you're done."

Semi-randomly, I snatched up *The Black Stallion and the Girl*, *A Dog Like No Other*, *Bob, Son of Battle*, *National Velvet*, and *Danny Dunn, Invisible Boy* and stacked them atop the three I already had. If I had to get past Ratanji every time I came here, I might as well take as many as I could carry.

Shinork showed my parents and me to our new home, a single room with three narrow beds, a flagstone floor, and whitewashed walls.

The bathroom, which was only for bathing and had no toilet, was separated from the house by a long dark hall. When I washed my hands, I discovered that there was no hot water, and it was impossible to get more than a listless film of bubbles from the cracked cake of yellow soap. The minerals that flavored Ahmednagar's water made it so hard that cleaning anything required relentless scrubbing. Washerwomen swung wet laundry over their heads, then slammed it down on a rock slab with a crack like a gunshot. The clothes got very clean but wore out quickly.

There was a kitchen where the servants cooked our meals and a communal dining room. Both were decorated with paintings of Baba's beaming face, of a haloed Baba stepping forth from a misty cityscape, of Baba riding, Baba walking, Baba holding out his hands in blessing.

As we were shown the grounds, I was introduced to a few of the higher-ranking servants: the head gardener, the chief cook, the number one driver. But the residents and mandali did not socialize with servants and knew little or nothing of their lives . . . though they must have known plenty about ours. They had been born servants, and their children would grow up to be servants. As I was often reminded, they were not like us.

The ashram's charities encompassed health care and elementary education for the lower classes, but social justice was not part of the program.

The shared toilets, which could be smelled from yards away, were bean-shaped porcelain holes in a cement floor. I went into one of the stalls and squatted over the hole, then used a small pot, or lota, to scoop up water from a bucket and (cringing) used my left hand to wash myself clean. There was no toilet paper.

Mom had gone over this procedure with me at the airport. She had insisted that Indian toilets were more sanitary than Western ones, which were dirty because you sat your butt down where other people's butts had been, and because toilet paper smeared the filth around rather than removing it. "Not the way I do it," I'd said indignantly.

I dragged my underwear over my dripping nether parts. My panties clung and chafed as if I had wet myself. As I walked out of the stall, moving awkwardly so I wouldn't get an embarrassing damp spot on my pants, I heard a scuffling noise. The next door over was ajar. I opened it.

An enormous black rat and I stared at each other. It was bigger than a guinea pig and bigger than a cat, and it bared gray needle teeth at me. I took a step back. It dove down the toilet, stuck momentarily in the hole, then wriggled through and vanished.

I had hoped to get another pet rat in India, but I didn't think they made hoops big enough for that one.

5

Another Arti

"Wake up, munchkin," said Mom.

I blinked up at her, baffled by the yards of cotton mesh that framed her face. Then I remembered that our beds had to be draped like tents to keep out mosquitoes.

"It's still night," I protested.

"It's morning," corrected Mom. "Arti starts at dawn."

I couldn't remember what arti was, other than my grandfather's name, but I rolled out of bed anyway. The stone floor was cold under my feet, and Mom had to remind me to shake out my shoes before I put them on. A scorpion might have crawled inside during the night.

Mom flew about, almost skipping, humming happily to herself. "Have some tea. I had the servants put ginger in it." She handed me a cup. "We're going to visit Meherabad," she sang to the tune of "We're Off to See the Wizard." "Baba used to live there. Isn't that exciting?"

Dad sat on his bed, looking disheveled and grumpy. I sipped the spicy tea. Riding out before dawn to go who knows where seemed appealingly adventurous.

The three of us emerged into the dark before dawn. Mom had made me wear a dress, so my legs were freezing. We piled into the waiting rickshaw.

"*Meherabad jaiye*," said Mom to the driver, her Hindi phrase book open in her hand.

"Yes, madam," he replied. Pebbles sprayed out from under the three wheels as he stomped on the gas.

"Baba!" exclaimed Mom. "Slower."

"Yes, madam," said the driver, speeding up. We raced through the town. There were no street lights, and the buildings were dim shapes in the darkness. The road was empty except for the occasional donkey or water buffalo.

Dad leaned back and closed his eyes. "Baba, Baba, Baba, Baba, Baba," recited Mom. "Mani! Keep your head inside."

We passed through the town in minutes and through the desiccated plains beyond. The light brightened to gray. Then the rickshaw squealed into a left turn and deposited us in front of a cemetery. The gravestones featured Indian names with nicknames listed in quotation marks, such as "Nervous," "Padre," and "Barsoap."

"Baba liked to give the mandali nicknames," said Dad. "Barsoap got his because he saw something that he thought was a piece of cheese and started eating it, but it turned out to be a bar of soap."

I snickered appreciatively.

"They were very fortunate people," said Mom. "They devoted their entire lives to Baba."

Eyeing the grave of "Asthma," I wondered if I was in a very strange place full of very strange people, or if my life was actually quite ordinary, and I was the one who was odd. Mom and Dad certainly didn't seem to think Ahmednagar was at all unusual.

We walked past the cemetery and up a hill, along a dirt path lined with trees and whitewashed rocks. When I strayed off the path, the weeds crunched under my feet. Except for the leaves of the trees, the landscape was a uniform yellow-brown. The path was coated with dust as fine and dry as talcum powder. At the top of the hill was a pavilion attached to a domed stone building.

"That's the Tomb," whispered Mom, her voice suffused with awe. "It's where Baba's physical form is buried."

I was more interested in the three brown-and-white mutts playing in front of it. I whistled to them, but they put their tails between their legs and slunk away.

About thirty people, both Indians and Westerners, stood chit-chatting in bare feet on the stone floor of the pavilion. A long line of shoes formed a border outside.

A sour-faced female mandali, Urmila, poked me in the ribs, then turned to Mom and said, "Too skinny. You must feed her better." Having been mutually insulted, Mom and I were momentarily united in irritation.

A wild-haired man crouched beside me. "Hello." He had an odd accent. "I am Eyvind Lindstrom. Would you like me to imitate the famous bird of Sweden, the Swedish Orr?"

"Er . . . sure," I said.

Eyvind threw back his head. A noise like a panicked choking victim emanated from his throat. Everyone stared.

"The Swedish Orr," he explained.

I was delighted. "Do it again."

"Shush!" snapped Urmila.

Everyone stood up, put their hands in the praying position, and began reciting prayers in unison. The first was one which I later learned had been written by Baba, to Baba:

"You are without color, without expression, without form, and without attributes . . .

You are in the firmament and in the depths, you are manifest and unmanifest; on all planes, and beyond all planes.

You are in the three worlds, and also beyond the three worlds. You are imperceptible and independent . . ."

And so forth. I was a smart kid with an exceptionally good vocabulary, if I do say so myself, but although I knew that prayer by heart before my first month had passed, I had no clue what it meant. Though I'd gathered the impression that God was a sort of invisible gas.

As the prayers were recited, and the hymns were sung, the sky brightened into dawn. Swarms of mosquitoes attacked my bare legs. I fidgeted and tried not to slap them too loudly. My feet hurt, my legs were cold and achy and itchy, and I felt no kinship with the swaying, enraptured worshippers. I opened my eyes and watched their faces. None of them seemed bored or tired. Apparently, I was the odd girl out.

Suddenly, everyone shouted, "*Avatar Meher Baba Ki Jai!*"

I hastily shut my eyes. Mom nudged me. "You can open your eyes now," she whispered. "When you feel like it, you can take darshan. Just watch what other people do." Then she closed her eyes and returned to communing with Baba.

The procedure seemed to be to step over the threshold of the inner sanctum and bow at it, bow down with your head on a marble

slab and kiss it, bow down with your head on the floor and kiss that, get up, back out slowly and reverently, bow at the threshold, then take something from Urmila with your right hand cupped over your left, and put it in your mouth. Only then could you sit down.

I really wanted to sit down. But I was afraid that if I went in immediately, everyone would know that it was only because I wanted to rest my feet. But once Dad went, I figured I'd waited long enough to fool them.

I went inside. The interior was painted with blobby figures of worshippers bowing to an altar with a blobby figure of Baba. The white marble slab was piled high with flowers and was cold on my forehead and lips. I felt vaguely guilty that I didn't feel anything when I kissed it other than awkward and out of place. I backed out and headed toward Dad, forgetting about Urmila.

The woman grabbed me with a bony claw. "Take your prasad," she said, forming my hands into the correct position. "It's blessed by Baba."

It was a thumbnail-size candy, shaped and flavored like an orange segment, dusty with powdered sugar—the highlight of my visit to the Tomb.

A minute or so after I sat down, I felt a pinch at my waist, under my dress. I slapped at it. The mosquitoes were driving me crazy. It bit harder, and I felt it large and hard and wriggling under my palm.

I shrieked, leaped up, and tried to rip my dress off. Mom rushed over and yanked my dress up, exposing my panties and an inch-long black ant with its mandibles sunk into my flesh.

I screamed even louder. Mom pulled at the ant. To my horror, half the body came off, leaving the head and part of the thorax attached. My scream then could have shattered stone. A crowd of looky-loos clustered around.

"Stop this noise," scolded Urmila. "It's only an ant."

"Hold still," said Mom. "I have to get the mandibles."

Mandibles! "AIIIIIIIIIIIIIIIIIEEEEEEEEEEEEEEE!"

Out of the corner of my eye, I saw Dad retreat into the interior of the Tomb.

"There you go," said Mom, dropping the last ant part on the ground.

I yanked my dress down. My side hurt, I'd had a monster bug on me, and everyone had seen my underpants. I crammed my feet into my shoes and fled.

I fetched up in another graveyard behind the Tomb, this one for Baba's pets. He'd had cats, dogs, birds, even deer and foxes. My mood brightened. If God had pets, I could have pets.

A green lizard as long as my forearm was sunning itself atop the tomb of Bhooty the mastiff. It had spines along its neck and back, a dewlap, and black beady eyes. I crept up behind it and grabbed it behind the head, so it couldn't bite. It struggled, but my grip was firm. I proudly returned to the Tomb with my captive.

"Look what I fou—"

"*Chee! Chee!*" exclaimed Urmila. "Put that down."

I promptly thrust it at her.

"Da-nonna," called out Urmila, backing away. "Make your child take that lizard away. They are dirty and poisonous."

"Iguanas aren't poisonous," I said. "The only poisonous lizards are the Gila monster and the Mexican beaded lizard."

"Do what Urmila says," said Mom. "Let it go."

"I want to keep it as a pet."

"Mani," said Dad, manifesting at my elbow. "Put that reptile back where you found it."

Sulkily, I returned to the graveyard and released it.

"Don't worry, you can catch more later," came a man's voice. "They're all over the place."

I turned around. A stocky American with red-blonde hair and bright blue eyes stuck out his hand. "Harry Carroll. Pleased to meet you."

"I'm Mani." I shook his hand. He didn't hate lizards, and he hadn't said anything bizarre within the first ten seconds of introducing himself, so it was possible that he might be a normal person. I hoped so.

"See? There's another one." Harry pointed to another lizard on a high tree branch. His shirt rode up, exposing hard muscle and a foot-long white slash.

"How'd you get that scar?" I asked. It wasn't disfiguring, so I didn't think he'd mind.

"Knife fight," he said, as if it was no big deal. "I'll tell you about it some time."

I revised my opinion. Harry was not normal. Harry was *cool.*

"Mani!" Mom called. "Arti's over." I trailed behind my parents, Harry, and the rest of the Baba-lovers as they walked back down the hill. Grandpa Artie would have enjoyed the walk: There was wildlife everywhere. I was squatting to examine a slim curled snake I'd found under a rock when I heard a voice.

"What are you looking at?" It was a plump woman in a white sari. She'd been introduced as Saraswati and was one of the few American residents who had taken an Indian name. She was also the only female resident who wore a sari. All the other Western women wore the comfortable salwar kamiz.

"Nothing." I quickly replaced the rock.

"You mustn't do that," said Saraswati. "There could be scorpions under them. There could even be snakes."

"Really?"

"There's a lot of poisonous snakes here. So if you ever see a snake, tell a grown-up immediately."

"What do the poisonous ones look like?"

"It doesn't matter. Just call a grown-up if you see any snake, and they'll kill it for you."

"But most snakes are harmless." I quoted Grandpa Artie. "They won't bother you if you don't bother them."

Saraswati clapped her hands, squashing a bloated mosquito. "Baba said people should kill snakes whenever they see them." She wiped the blood off her palms. "Snakes can't be reincarnated into higher forms until they're killed by a human. So you're actually doing them a favor."

"Oh." I resolved to never ever reveal the location of a snake to a Baba-lover.

When I reached the base of the hill, I wandered off by myself. I walked past the graveyard and found a row of joined houses with a wide shared porch.

An old man in a white robe was shuffling around on the path in front of the verandah, bent over double like a candy cane, his face a foot from the ground and his long fingers fumbling about in the dirt.

"Did you lose something?" I asked.

He ignored me and kept searching. Maybe he didn't speak English. Or maybe he was a bit deaf.

"Excuse me," I said, louder. "Are you looking for something?"

The fingers froze in the dust. The man didn't stand up or straighten his back, but his neck twisted, and his head slowly turned toward me. His face was slack, and his eyes were empty. His mouth worked and twitched as he stared at me from over his shoulder. His fingers began to writhe.

Instinctively frightened, I took a step back.

The madman opened his mouth and let out a hoarse, wordless roar. Still bent double, he scuttled toward me.

I bolted in the opposite direction. Before I'd gone five steps, I smacked into Harry Carroll.

"There's a crazy man," I babbled, ducking behind him for safety. "He's all twisted up, and he yelled at me."

"He's not crazy," explained Harry. "He's a mast."

"He must?" I repeated blankly. "Must what?"

The crazy man had gone back to poking through the dust. Every now and then, he picked up an invisible object and hid it in the folds of his robe.

"His name is Malik the Mast," said Harry. "M-A-S-T. Masts are so close to Baba that they act a little funny. They're drunk on God. But they're not crazy. Baba said, 'Mind working is man. Mind working too fast is mad. Mind slow is mast. Mind stopped is God.' See, there's his sign."

Harry pointed to a signboard on the verandah. It read, "WOMEN ARE NOT TO APPROACH MALIK THE MAST."

"Is he dangerous?" I asked.

"No, no," said Harry. "He's very loving."

"He's picking up stuff that isn't there."

"He calls the invisible stuff deesh," said Harry. "He has a collection of it under his cot."

"He talks?"

"Sure, he talks. He talks about Baba. Only he calls him Dada."

I got a horrible suspicion. "Are you making this up?"

"Nope. Ask anyone." Harry beckoned to a nearby pilgrim man. "Hey, tell little Mani your Malik story."

The man smiled radiantly. "Oh, it was incredible. Malik was saying Baba's name, the way he does: Dada, Dada . . . "

I giggled. Malik let out a weird bleat, then went back to collecting deesh.

The pilgrim continued, "And he held something out to me: a gift. It was . . . "

"Deesh!" I suggested.

"Uh, no. It was a wad of toilet paper. Stinky used toilet paper. Before I could decide what to do with it, he stuffed it in my pocket."

"Ewww," I said.

"Yeah, that's what I thought. But it was a present from Malik, and Malik's a saint, so I couldn't just throw it out. But when I got undressed that night, you know what I found? Malik's . . . er . . . droppings had turned into chocolate! It was a miracle prasad from Malik and Baba."

"Did you eat the chocolate?"

"Of course."

I wrinkled my nose. "I wouldn't have."

The pilgrim looked hurt. "It was perfectly good chocolate."

In Los Angeles, Mom would grab my hand and run across the street if she saw a smelly old man talking to himself. But here in Ahmednagar they gave crazy people jobs and places to live and said they were close to Baba. It was confusing.

But I was sure of one thing: Poop that turned into chocolate was still poop, and that pilgrim was crazier than Malik to have eaten it. Come to think of it, Urmila had said the holy candy at the Tomb had been blessed by Baba. I hoped Baba hadn't created it out of something gross.

6

The Face in the Tree

The next morning my parents and I visited Meherazad. That was where most of the mandali lived and where most of the spiritual activities other than arti took place. As soon as I arrived, I had to go through yet another round of introductions to elderly, cheek-pinching mandali.

Dari, a mandali man with a shock of bristly white hair, hugged me tight, then suddenly thrust me away. Staring deeply into my eyes, he said, "Nice of you. Good of you. Cat says meow."

"Er . . . nice to meet you too." I had stopped expecting that what people said here would make any sense at all. I'd never liked *Alice in Wonderland*—it filled me with an inexplicable sense of anxiety—but it was becoming more relevant by the second.

A firm hand came down on my shoulder. It was

Coconut. I tried to wriggle away, but he held tight. "See this child," he said, beckoning a group of pilgrims to watch the show. "She is my little mummy. How is it that she is so young, and I am so old, and yet she is my mummy? Tell them how it is that you are my mummy."

"I don't know," I said. Mom was gazing worshipfully at Coconut, so there was no help to be found there. Dad had gone off somewhere with The Goldberg.

"She is shy." He pinched my cheek.

"Ow!"

"Why are you my little mummy?" he repeated, yanking on my cheek like a brush through tangled hair.

I gave in. "Because this is the Kaliyuga Age, and anything can happen then."

Coconut's belly jiggled against my side as he laughed heartily. The pilgrims all laughed at me too. It wasn't fair. They should be laughing at Coconut, not me.

You're nothing but a pack of cards, I thought.

Coconut released me, and I started to dash away. But before I could get up much speed, a voluptuous blonde woman swooped down on me. "How adorable!" she exclaimed. "Oh, what a sweet little child. Look at her! She's so *tiny*!" Smothering me in her ample bosom, she said, "You are so cute! I just know that we're going to be *bestest* friends."

If I'd had as much nerve as she did, I'd have bitten her.

"I'm Darlene," she said to Mom and me. "Shall I show you two around?"

"I've visited the ashram before," said Mom. "So has Mani, but she was too young to remember."

"Then I'll just walk with you," said Darlene.

She proceeded to take us on a tour of yet another set of sacred places: Baba's Hall, Baba's Bus, Baba's Caravan, and Baba's Rose Garden. The latter was dotted with little water tanks with floating

frogs that dove for the bottom when I tried to touch them. There were butterflies everywhere, huge ones with lacy black and white wings and pulsating hot pink bodies, tiny banana-colored ones, and medium-size ones patterned black and bright blue.

"You were an actress?" Darlene asked Mom. "I was too. I must have been in hundreds of plays. What were you in?"

"Plays, like you," said Mom. "And I guest-starred on *Mission: Impossible* and *Lassie*."

One of Mom's best routines was her version of the latter role, in which she played a coed who was contemplating jumping off the Golden Gate Bridge.

Suicidal Hippie Chick: "Nobody loves me. Maybe it's time to end it all. What do you think, Lassie?"

Lassie: "Woof!"

Suicidal Hippie Chick: "What's that, Lassie? *YOU* love me?"

Lassie: "Woof!"

Suicidal Hippie Chick: "Oh, thank you, Lassie! Now I have a reason to live!"

That was how Mom used to dramatize the role for my amusement; I never saw the episode. When Dad overheard her re-enacting it, he would insist, to my delight and Mom's annoyance, that "Woof!" was collie-speak for "Jump!"

Darlene said, "I was also a model."

"So was I," said Mom. "Did you feel self-conscious, seeing your face in magazines? I did."

"Mmmph," said Darlene.

"Isn't it wonderful how Baba works?" said Mom. "We have so much in common, and he brought us both to him."

Though I didn't notice it without a reminder, Mom was beautiful, a free love maiden turned earth mother with ink-black hair down to her hips and enormous brown eyes that glowed amber in the sun. But her looks had not been an asset to her career. Casting directors thought she was too ethnic to play white-bread all-American roles but not ethnic enough to play brash Jewish stereotypes, and she had been too genuine a hippie to be palatable to filmmakers trying to market a movement they didn't understand to audiences who wanted either sanitized or demonized versions of it.

She quit acting the day she went to audition for a B-movie and was handed a synopsis reading, "A group of hippies form a commune in the woods. At first, all is peace and love, but then their true natures emerge, and they revert to cannibalism."

A black bee bigger than Dad's thumb dive-bombed my head. I ducked.

Darlene pointed. "That's Baba's Tree. About twenty years ago, his face appeared on the trunk."

"I don't see it," I said. "Where's it supposed to be?"

"Right there." Darlene indicated an unexceptional swirl of bark.

"That's a face?"

"Oh, look at his loving eyes," said Mom. "There, Mani."

"Where?" I asked.

"It's hard to see now," admitted Darlene. "The bark's grown a lot since it first appeared. Let me show you a photo from when it was new."

She took us to Baba's Room, which contained a photo of the tree. "See?" said Darlene. "It's Baba wearing a crown."

I saw two lopsided eyes, a grinning clown's mouth, and electroshock hair. Or possibly a spiky crown.

"Isn't it amazing?" asked Darlene. "A Baba-lover who's an engi-

neer wrote a monograph for the Baba newsletter analyzing the probability of that having occurred by chance. He found that it was impossible. That face scientifically proves the existence of God."

"Oh, he's so beautiful," said Mom. "You can see it now, right, Mani?"

"I see a face, all right," I said.

We walked to Baba's Porch for the final round of Meet the Mandali. The Porch was the realm of Baba's chief female disciple, Paribanu.

She was a delicately pretty Indian woman in her sixties, enthroned in an armchair beneath the inevitable Baba painting and surrounded by pilgrims. The female pilgrims hugged and kissed her, but men only bowed from a distance.

"Baba forbade Paribanu to ever touch any man but him," explained Mom. "Every incarnation of God has a consort, and she was his."

I recalled the word 'consort' from the *Arabian Nights*. "They were married?"

"No, no." Mom sounded shocked. "Never say that." Her voice dropped to a whisper. "You know that married people have sex to make babies."

I nodded.

"Baba and Paribanu never did that. She was like his *spiritual* wife. Do you understand?"

I didn't, but I nodded again.

Satisfied that I wasn't going to repeat the word "married," which was apparently dirty when applied to Paribanu or Baba, Mom introduced me to the consort.

I was sick of saints. They all squashed me and pinched me and said things that made no sense. Since Paribanu was the biggest saint of all, she'd probably make less sense and pinch harder than any of the rest.

"*Jai Baba*," I said unenthusiastically.

"*Jai Baba*," replied Paribanu. She leaned in, and I caught a pleasant scent of baby powder. I braced myself for a mauling, but she only kissed me lightly on the cheek.

“Do you have a favorite Baba story?” inquired Paribanu. “I’ll tell any story you’d like to hear.”

From the looks on everyone’s faces, I could see that this was a huge and unusual honor.

Remembering the pet cemetery, I asked, “Did he ever have a pet rabbit?”

A bearded pilgrim laughed loudly. Paribanu gave him a reproving glance. “As a matter of fact, he did. When it was a baby, one day it was hopping around in the yard when suddenly a crow swooped down, grabbed it by the ears, and carried it away. I started chasing the crow, but it flew into the forest, and—“

Quick as a swooping crow, a pilgrim woman leaped on to the porch. “Oh, Paribanu!” she exclaimed. “I’m so blessed to meet you. Thank Beloved Baba for giving me this chance to come here—I’m so happy—You are the purest woman in the world, and I am so blessed—Oh, thank you, Baba!”

Then, as abruptly as she had arrived, the woman jumped off the porch and fled down the garden path, her arms and clothes flapping behind her.

Paribanu watched her go, an expression of bemusement on her wrinkled face. “What a stupid girl,” she remarked thoughtfully. “Dumb, dumb, dumb.”

I decided that I liked Paribanu.

“We found the hare under a tree,” she went on. “It wasn’t hurt except for sore ears. So we took it to Baba, and he cuddled it. Such a lucky hare, to have come from a crow’s beak to the loving hands of the Avatar of the Age.”

Then she told a story about how Baba had thrown a plate across the dining room table because he had demanded total, unquestioning, to-the-letter obedience, and a mandali had given him a white plate instead of the blue one he’d asked for. Paribanu said that Baba’s willingness to discipline his mandali proved how

much he loved them. A chorus of assent rose from the surrounding pilgrims.

I thought of dinners in LA. Dad often refused to speak to Mom, and Mom frequently burst into tears and ran out of the room. But at least no one threw dishes.

"I remember when Baba spoke on obedience," chimed in Nona Gosling, an elderly American pilgrim who had met Baba. Though she was not a mandali, her pilgrim-plus status was apparent from the way everyone fell silent when she spoke.

"We were all sitting in a circle around his beautiful feet," said Nona.

That was the fifth reference I'd heard that week to "Baba's beautiful feet," "Baba's exquisite hands," even "Baba's lotus feet." Did anyone ever rhapsodize about "Baba's delightful toenail clippings?" I snickered to myself.

"Baba asked us if we were ready to give him true obedience," continued Nona. "Of course, we all said we were. He asked if we'd give up our money, our jobs, even our lives for him. We all said we would.

"Then one by one, Baba asked us if we would be willing to kill our relatives or loved ones if he ordered us to.

"One by one, everyone said yes, they would. Then he came to me, and he signed out on his alphabet board, 'Would you kill your children for me?'

"My son was just five years old then, and though I knew I ought to be willing to do anything that Baba ordered, I just couldn't. I started crying, and I said, 'No, Baba, I wouldn't.'

"Baba smiled at me with the most wonderful compassion, and he signed, 'Don't worry. God will never ask you to do anything you're not able to do.'"

Nona's audience sighed happily, as if the credits had started to roll at the end of a good movie.

"That was when I realized the full depth of Baba's loving kindness,"

Nona said. "Of course, I should have said yes, Baba, I would do anything for you. But he had compassion for my weakness. He . . ."

I had been listening with growing horror, and at that moment, I burst into tears. Then I jumped up and ran.

I darted around the building and fetched up at the side of a well. There was a turtle at the bottom. I sat on the edge and watched it fumble at the stone walls with its front flippers.

I was still crying when Mom found me. She sat down beside me. "Sweetie, you don't think I'd ever hurt you, do you?"

I shook my head.

"Then what's the matter?"

I *didn't* think Mom was going to kill me, so why was I crying? "I don't know," I sniffled.

"Baba was testing them," said Mom. "He'd never really ask anyone to kill another person. Come on now, let's go wash your face."

As I splashed cool water over my eyes, I realized what had bothered me about the story.

Grandpa Artie always said you should never do something just because someone else tells you to. Not even if it's the president of the United States.

But Baba hadn't told Nona that he'd never really ask anyone to kill anyone. He hadn't said that she had been right to say she'd disobey. All he'd said was that he wouldn't ask *her*, because she wouldn't be able to obey him, and he didn't want to put her on the spot.

Baba had been testing his followers, all right, but for obedience to him and nothing more. The one who would rather have saved her children than obey his orders had been the one who'd failed.

7

Grunting Scales

"Arrr."

The growl came through the window over my bed. It was a small snarl, almost a polite one. My window overlooked a walkway, so I assumed it was some resident or servant clearing the evening dust from his throat.

"Arrrr."

That was no cough, but a true growl. And it sounded close. I huddled nervously under the covers, wondering if my parents could hear it too.

"Arrrr."

Mom's bed was only two feet from mine, so she had definitely heard that, unless she was asleep already.

"Arrrrrrrrr!"

That one was so loud that Dad must have heard it from across the room. Why weren't they doing anything?

"Mom? Dad?" I called out.

"What is, pumpkin?" asked Mom sleepily.

"There's someone outside, growling at me."

"Arrrrrrghhh! Raaaaarrrhhh!"

Dad blearily crawled from his mosquito netted bed and parted the curtains. The mad librarian, Ratanji, was visible in silhouette several feet away, a tall stooped figure with matted hair and tangled beard.

"It's just Ratanji." Dad closed the curtains and returned to his bed. "Go back to sleep."

"ARRRRRGGHHH! WHAAAAAARRR!"

"But he's howling outside my window," I protested.

"So?" said Dad. "He's outside. He can't hurt you."

"HAAAARRRGGGHHH!"

"Mom!" I wailed.

"Just ignore him, sweetie-pie. He's Coconut's cousin, you know. And they say he was very close to Baba."

"But . . ." I fell silent. If my parents didn't think there was anything weird or wrong about a crazy man howling outside my window, repeating *but he's howling outside my window* seemed unlikely to convince them.

"Arrrr."

A low note.

"Arrrrr."

A little higher.

"Arrrrrr."

Higher still. In fact, it was a *mi*: "Mi, a name to call myself." I had seen *The Sound of Music* several times on TV and knew "Do, a Deer" by heart.

Ratanji had abandoned simple growling in favor of singing scales. Well, grunting scales.

"Arrrrrrr."

Fa.

"Arrrrrrrr."

So.

"Arrrrrrrrr!"

Ratanji was straining for the high note, and he was only on *La*. This did not bode well.

"Arrrrrrrrrr!"

Ti.

"Arrrrrr—"

His voice cracked.

"YAAAAAAAAGGGH!!!! RAAAAAARRR!!!!

HAAAAAAAARGGGGH!!!!"

BOOM-BOPPA BOOM-BOPPA BOOM-BOPPA-BOOM!

A massively amplified drum machine's disco beat smacked down Ratanji's bellows like a cement truck crushing a pickle.

"Baba!" yelped Mom. "Joey, what's that?"

Finally, something that got her attention.

"I know," I said. "It's the movie theater. Shinork said it was loud."

WHOMP! WHOMP! WHOMP!

"Christ," moaned Dad. "They've got outdoor speakers."

"Shinork said it's the only movie theater in town," I said, eager to show off my knowledge. "He said all their movies are four-hour musicals. In Hindi."

BOOM BOOM DA-BOOM!

"Four hours?!" squeaked Mom.

"DISCO DA-NONNA! DISCO DA-NONNA! UH-HUH, UH-HUH, UH-HUH!"

"It's singing your name." I was amazed.

Dad began to sing along. I joined him. "Disco Da-nonna!" we caroled. "Uh-huh, uh-huh, uh-huh."

"Stop that, Joey. Stop that, Mani," said Mom. "I don't like this song. It sounds dirty."

It was true that the singer had a low and oily voice and sounded as if he was licking his lips on each "uh-huh."

"DISCO DA-NONNA!" came the blast from the speakers. "DISCO DA-NONNA! UH-HUH, UH-HUH, UH-HUH!"

"ARRRRRGGGH!" added Ratanji. "YAAAAARRRRGH! BWAAAHAAAAHAAAA!"

I pulled the pillow over my head. Ratanji couldn't possibly last for more than another half-hour, but if Shinork was right, the movie had three hours, fifty-nine minutes, and thirty seconds to go.

8

First Day at Holy Wounds

The world might be an illusion, but I still had to attend one of its schools.

Ahmednagar had two: one private and one public. The latter was taught in Maharashtra's state language, Marathi. Being public, it was free, and the consensus at the ashram was that it couldn't be any good if the children of servants and villagers were taught there. More tactfully, Mom said I'd have more in common with the middle-class town kids who attended the private school. Since I was justifiably afraid of going to a school that was taught in a language I didn't know, I lobbied for the English-speaking school.

And so, despite being Jewish by birth and a Baba-lover by parental decree, I was sent to Holy Wounds of Jesus Christ the Savior Convent School.

My parents escorted me to Holy Wounds for the first day of school, early in the morning, so I could get oriented before the other students arrived. We took a rickshaw from the Compound, but that was for their convenience. Ordinarily, I would walk there and back.

The rickshaw pulled up before a spiked iron gate capped with an immense painting of an anatomically correct veiny heart, wrapped in thorns and bleeding realistically.

I was alarmed by the fetishistic depiction of the thorns stabbing into the tender flesh and the excessive amount of dripping blood. It was going to be depressing to walk under that every day. And what if it was meant as a representation of how it felt to attend the school?

I kicked dust at the unwelcoming gates. It rose in a cloud, then settled on my patent leather shoes. They were part of the Holy Wounds school uniform, which Mom had thoughtfully purchased in advance so I wouldn't stand out on my first day. The rest of it consisted of white bobby socks, a brown pleated skirt, a long-sleeved white shirt, and a choking scarlet tie. Per Holy Wounds regulations, Mom had made up my hair in two braids, then doubled them over and tied them together, so they looked like hound dog ears.

My final adornment was an out-of-uniform green cotton hat which flopped over my head like a wilted cabbage leaf. My parents had petitioned the principal to let me wear it.

Each element alone was ugly, even the shirt; as an ensemble, it achieved a ghastliness striking even to a confirmed tomboy like me. I especially resented the tie, as I had thought that one advantage of being a girl was that I would never have to wear one. Nervous and spiteful, I stuck the end of it in my mouth and ripped off a scarlet thread.

We passed under the mutilated heart and into the main building. The principal, Sister Rose, met us in her office. She was an old In-

dian in a full black habit and wimple. A silver cross pendant hung between her breasts, or between the probable location of her breasts; her figure was completely muffled in yards of fabric. Her thin cheeks had an unhealthy yellow tone.

"This is our daughter, Mani," said Dad.

He pronounced it "Money." It occurred to me that one benefit of living in India was that that no one would tease me about my name.

"Such a sweet child!" exclaimed Sister Rose, and pinched my cheek. I caught a waft of heavy perfume and the dusty musk of old age. I thought of decaying flowers, brown and slimy, and mentally dubbed her Sister Rotten Rose.

I wouldn't tease other unfortunates about their funny names, but I had no qualms about inventing nicknames for my own private amusement. God did it too.

A nun so ancient that she looked like the Egyptian type of mummy tottered from the office and tremblingly fumbled at my chin. "I am Sister Perpetua," she whispered.

Sister Purple. I was on a roll.

A young nun, also in full habit, waltzed up. She had plump cheeks and bright black eyes. "Ah, the foreign girl!" She pinched my other cheek with her long glossy nails.

"Ow," I said warningly.

"Oh, that didn't hurt. Did it now?" She pinched harder.

"Yes."

She laughed merrily. "I'm Sister Barbara."

Black and white, with claws. *Sister Badger.*

My parents took off, leaving me alone with the nuns. They looked at me and smiled. There was no escape.

Sister Badger escorted me to the playground, a bleak gravel lot adorned with two concrete benches and a single dispirited tree. It wasn't yet eight in the morning, but it was already uncomfortably warm. Holy Wounds smelled like dust and hot metal and children's sweat. It smelled like heat itself, if heat could have a smell. As the sun grew brighter, the lot filled up with uniformed schoolchildren in neat lines.

I was the only foreigner in the entire school.

I was also the only student who wore a hat.

Sister Badger introduced me to my teacher, Mrs. Joshi. She was not a nun, but a slender, sharp-featured woman who barely topped five feet, wrapped in a tidy green sari. I was so relieved that I didn't nickname her.

I lined up with the rest of the students in her class. This, explained Mrs. Joshi, was assembly and how each school day began.

I waited for someone to nudge me, point at me, or ask me where I was from, but nobody made a sound. They stood rigidly at attention, their faces turned up toward a balcony. I was nervous. But they seemed scared.

Sister Rotten Rose appeared on the balcony. The students shouted in sing-song unison, "Good mor-ning, Sis-ter Ro-ose!"

"Good morning, students," she said. "Good morning, teachers. We will now sing the national anthem."

The students sang a cappella and in perfect unison:

"Jana gana mana adhi nayaka jaya hai!

Bharat bhagya vidhata . . . "

I hadn't yet learned any Hindi other than "yes," "no," "hello," "thank you," "bring hot water," and "dog," so I mentally translated the lyrics into Paranoia:

"Down with America

Death to all foreigners

Especially the tiny little American

With the stupid floppy hat."

At the end of the song, they shouted, "*Bharat Mata Ki Jai!*" ("Glory to Mother India!")

The national anthem was followed by a series of hymns. Sister Rotten Rose had assured us that most of the students were Hindu, that most of the non-Hindus were Muslims or Sikhs, and that no attempts were made to convert anyone. I hadn't paid much attention, as evangelism wasn't on the list of things I was worried about. But here were those Muslims, Hindus, and Sikhs, plus one ancestrally Jewish but officially Baba-loving foreigner, inescapably singing praise to Jesus.

"Oh, taste and see

That the Lord is good

For he tastes like honey in the rock."

How could you taste God? By sticking out your tongue and licking his cheek? And how could there be honey in a rock?

"Assembly dismissed!" said Sister Rotten Rose.

I had no idea why the students had all acted like they were about to face a firing squad, unless they had a massive case of collective stage fright, but they visibly relaxed once they were dismissed.

"Thank-you Sis-ter Ro-ose!" chanted the students, sounding genuinely thankful. For what?

We marched in single file into a classroom. It had a blackboard at the front of the room, a pencil sharpener at the back, and tattered posters on the walls. Except for the writing on the posters, it was reassuringly familiar.

Everyone sat down. Mrs. Joshi motioned me to an empty desk. Then she went outside and almost immediately came back inside.

The students leaped to their feet. "Good mor-ning tea-cher!" they chorused.

"Good morning, students," said Mrs. Joshi. She sat down at her table.

The instant her butt met the chair, five of the students leaped up and began dashing about, cleaning erasers, wiping the windows, and neatening the posters.

The students who weren't doing chores were staring at me. The students who were rushing around were also staring, as best they could without colliding with the scarred wooden desks. But I was a new girl who had joined in the middle of the year. They would have stared no matter where I was from.

I stared right back. For the first time in my life, I was not the smallest person in the class, but only one of the smallest. Three of the girls were about my height, and one, a wisp of a thing in a pixie cut, looked substantially lighter.

The boy clapping erasers caught my attention. Unlike the rest of the black-haired, brown-eyed, brown-skinned class, he had auburn hair, green eyes, and freckles; Indian, but not from around here. His eyes were big and set far apart, giving him a look of permanent surprise. I wasn't sure if he was handsome, or just eye-catchingly different, and as soon as I thought that, I was embarrassed and turned away.

The girl next to me had uncombed hair and a rumpled uniform. She was the only person in the room who wasn't watching me. She stared out the window, the whites of her eyes showing above and below the iris, like a mouse in a glue trap. Her right ear was filled with pus and blood, crystallized amber and scarlet like stained glass. Patches along her chin and neck were glazed like cake frosting, from where her ear had dripped.

She absently scratched her chin. Bits of amber crumbled away and pattered to the desk. Then she put down her hand. She had never taken her gaze from the window.

I couldn't figure out how she could resist picking her ear clean. I'd never be able to leave it alone, no matter how strictly I was forbidden to touch it.

Then I realized that no one had told her that it would never heal if she picked at it. If she had a doctor, or even parents who cared, she would have shown some signs of being taken care of. Her ear never would have gotten that bad. Someone would have at least made her wash her face.

The boy in front of me also had oozing infections. Both his dirt-gray elbows had hillocks of inflamed flesh at the joint, red volcanoes with pus-filled craters. He caught me staring and jabbed the needle tip of his protractor in my direction.

I guessed I wasn't in Kansas anymore.

A bell rang. The students who were out of their seats bolted back to them and plopped down.

"We have a new student," announced Mrs. Joshi. "She comes from America, and her name is Mani."

The students burst into muffled snickers. A few of them chanted a whispered phrase that I couldn't catch. Ignoring them, Mrs. Joshi said, "Please open your Marathi readers to page thirteen."

I opened my reader to a Marathi poem illustrated with a motherly looking cat in an apron.

As I didn't read or speak Marathi, it took me a while to figure out what was going on. But, as Mrs. Joshi had the students read aloud, and occasionally explained points in English, I realized that we were reading a nursery rhyme called "Mani Mao," which was baby talk for "Mrs. Cat."

Mani Mao, Mani Mao,

Unga tujay kittay mao.

This is not a literal translation, but it captures the spirit of the rhyme:

Puddy-Tat, Puddy-Tat,

Aren't you a pretty cat.

"*Mani Mao!*" whispered a girl and tittered.

"*Mani Mao, Mani Mao*!" chanted the boy with infected elbows, pointing and snickering.

"*Mani Mao*!" chorused the students, barely audible so Mrs. Joshi wouldn't hear. "*Mani Mao! Mani Mao*!"

It was my first day in school, and I had just been introduced as "Our new student, Humpty-Dumpty."

9

The Sidewalk of Meaninglessness

As if Hindi and Marathi weren't hard enough, I had to relearn English as well. Erasers were now rubbers, soccer was football, and you thrashed people instead of beating them up. It had been forty years since India had been a British colony, but it still conformed to *London Times* standards. The nuns at Holy Wounds scolded me for misspelling "color" and "honor," mispronouncing "schedule," and using the word "bloody" (in reference to a skinned knee.) Though my parents tried to be sympathetic, they had to stop laughing first.

To add to the confusion, the Hindi teacher was named Mr. Engineer, the engineering teacher was Mr. Kar, and the geography teacher, who was South Indian, was Mrs. Ganapathyvenkatasubramanyam.

Though I quickly learned to copy words in the

Devanagiri alphabet, I hit a snag when Mr. Engineer had me read them aloud. I might read English at a college level, but my Hindi and Marathi skills were stuck at kindergarten.

When Dad decided to learn Hindi, I hung around to see if he'd have better luck. His search for a tutor began with asking Firoze for a recommendation. Firoze referred him to Abdul the driver, who referred him to Sarosh the gardener, who referred him to Thaki the cook.

Thaki was a wide-built matriarch whose years of dough-kneading had given her biceps like a West Hollywood gym rat. Everyone said she was an excellent cook, but it was hard to tell. She and her army of assistants fed us rice and dal and chapatis at least four nights a week, and it's hard to do much with rice and dal and chapatis. (Dal is lentil curry, chapatis are wheat tortillas, and rice is rice.) I liked brown dal better than yellow dal, but Thaki preferred yellow by a ratio of 3:1.

She varied this regimen with forays into gluey okra, which Indians call lady-fingers but look more like alien fingers, a delicious curry made with whole hard-boiled eggs, which appeared infrequently because I was the only person who liked it, and a yellow-green buttermilk curry that looked and smelled like toxic waste. If it had appeared in a movie, the hero would have fallen into it and become Dioxin Man. I longed for the days when the scariest thing on my plate was creamed corn.

But I respected Thaki. Her father was an alcoholic bum who sometimes staggered into the Compound to hit her up for money. One night he hung around loudly demanding more after she'd already paid him off for the month. She punched him in the jaw and knocked him out cold. As he was drunk and elderly, it wasn't exactly a fair fight. But he was a head taller, and it took nerve to punch out one's own Dad.

Nobody messed with Thaki.

When asked about acquiring a Hindi tutor, Thaki recommended Mr. Kripalani. He was a retired deliveryman who had participated in Mahatma Gandhi's Quit India movement and had met Jawaharlal Nehru, another leader of the fight for Indian independence and India's first Prime Minister. That was the sum total of Mr. Kripalani's credentials. But whatever a freedom fighter wanted, a freedom fighter got. And Mr. Kripalani wanted a low-stress part-time job.

Shinork, who also wanted to learn Hindi, chipped in to hire Mr. Kripalani. The tutor was a shrunken man in a Nehru jacket and a Nehru cap, which nobody else wore anymore but were presumably there to remind people that he was a freedom fighter.

"Goo mowwing," said Mr. Kripalani. "I aw Wawweff Kwipawwani."

Mr. Kripalani had no teeth.

Shinork gave Dad a panicked look. Dad suppressed a chuckle. I smiled evilly, for I knew what further horrors lay in wait.

As I had anticipated, they came to grief on the second letter. "Ka," said Mr. Kripalani.

"Ka," repeated Dad and Shinork.

"Naw ka," said Mr. Kripalani. "That," he pointed to the first letter, "iff ka. Thiff, " he pointed to the second letter, "iff ka."

"Ka," repeated Dad and Shinork.

"No, no," said Mr. Kripalani. "Not ka. *That* iff ka. *Thiff* iff *ka*."

"Ka," said Dad and Shinork, looking slightly desperate.

Mr. Kripalani shook his head pityingly. "No, no. Now wiffen cawefuwwy. Ka."

"Ka," said Dad. Shinork had fallen into a wretched silence.

"Vewwy goow," said Mr. Kripalani. "Onshe mowe. Ka."

"Ka," repeated Dad.

"No, no," said Mr. Kripalani. "*Ka*."

Meanwhile, I sat in the corner and flipped through their textbook. It had been written during the British Raj and included phrases like "six mutinous sepoys will be hanged at dawn," "cholera has broken out in the cantonment," and "please pull the punkah." Finally Mr. Kripalani gave up on ka and moved on to the equally troublesome ga.

"Ka" is not the only sound represented by two letters with different pronunciations that sound identical to Americans. That category also includes "ga," "la," "tha," "ja," "ta," "sha," "na," "ra," "da," and "cha." Spelling in Hindi is phonetic, but if you can't hear the differences in sounds, it's possible to write words in which every single letter is the wrong one. I did that repeatedly over the years, to the fury of my teachers, who were convinced that I did it on purpose.

"Pewhaph we shouw twy a sentence," suggested Mr. Kripalani.

I discreetly fled the room. Dad later informed me that the sentence, which Mr. Kripalani wrote out phonetically after Dad and Shinork failed to hear it after seven repetitions was "*Ek gaon mai ek kisan hai.*" "In one village is one farmer."

Three lessons later, Dad and Shinork were still on "*Ek gaon mai ek kisan hai.*" They were also still on ka. Six lessons later, when Gums Kripalani, as Dad nicknamed him, had given up on ka and had started on ta, my supremely conflict-averse father was trying to figure out how to discreetly get rid of him. This proved to be difficult.

Tactful inquiries established that if he fired a freedom fighter, he'd offend the Compound's entire thirty-servant staff and Thaki in particular. If Thaki got mad, the food didn't get cooked. Dad and Shinork were forced to soldier on with Gums.

The toothless freedom fighter was still on ta when The Goldberg began taking Dad to visit the city bus station. Dad had been made The Goldberg's assistant, and The Goldberg's ashram job was to organize transportation. They worked about two hours a day, as there wasn't much transportation to be organized. But The Goldberg liked to drop in at the bus station to chat with its manager, Mr. Gear. Business in India was conducted over tea and snacks, which meant free food. And as few of the residents were even remotely busy, they spent much of their time looking for ways to kill it.

After a few visits, Dad noticed that when he addressed the stationmaster, Mr. Gear looked pained, and his clerks, twelve men who hung around his office but were never observed to do any work, giggled. But Dad didn't get a chance to ask why until one day when Mr. Gear wasn't there.

I had tagged along, as attracted as Dad by the prospect of snacks and entertainment. I also enjoyed rifling through the stationmaster's bundles of papers marked for recycling in search of calendars adorned with full-color pictures of gods and goddesses. I had heard that there were thirty thousand gods in the Hindu pantheon, and I wanted to collect a complete set.

"Where's Mr. Gear?" asked Dad.

The clerks snickered softly. The chief clerk, Ravi, volunteered, "He is out of station."

"But is he coming soon, babe?" asked The Goldberg.

Ravi shook/nodded. "He is just now coming."

Ravi snapped his fingers, and a clerk scampered out for tea and biscuits. I blew the dust from a picture of Kali with blood dripping from her fangs, dancing atop the corpse of her husband, Shiva, and admired her necklace of skulls and belt of children's hands. That one was definitely going in the collection. As all Gods were Baba, and Baba was all Gods, even the gruesome ones, Mom could not object.

"Hey, Ravi," said Dad. "How come everyone laughs when I say 'Mr. Gear'? Am I saying it wrong?"

The clerks looked at each other and tittered.

"It is like this," said Ravi. "'Gear' means his name. But you are saying 'Gear.' 'Gear' means goat."

"How do you say his name?"

"'Gear.'"

"'Gear,'" repeated Dad.

"No, no," said Ravi. "That is the goat. 'Gear.'"

"'Gear,'" said Dad.

"'Gear,'" I tried.

Ravi looked upon us pityingly. "I am thinking you cannot be saying this in American."

Dad and The Goldberg continued drinking tea while I selected the warrior goddess Durga gorily slaying a demon, a baby Krishna stealing butter, an adult Krishna driving a war chariot, and an adult Krishna playing the flute for an audience of scantily clad cowherdesses.

I was fond of the God Krishna. The child Krishna was mischievous and loved butter, which I could identify with; the warrior Krishna was skillful, wise, and brave, which I admired; and the lover Krishna was . . . well, I couldn't have explained then exactly what it was that I liked about that aspect. Later on, when I could have explained, I would have rather dropped dead than do so.

"When did you say Mr. Gea . . . When's the stationmaster coming?" asked Dad.

"He is just now coming," reassured the clerks.

Half an hour later, Dad and The Goldberg were becoming impatient.

"Where does Mr. . . . —Where's your main man live?" asked The Goldberg. "We'll stop by his house."

The clerks shook their heads. "He is not there."

"He's not here, babe. He must be there."

"He is not there."

"How do you know?"

"He is in Sholapur," explained Ravi.

"What?" exclaimed Dad. Sholapur was a six-hour drive from Ahmednagar.

"Then he's not coming in today, bro," said The Goldberg. "Not if he's in Sholapur."

"Not today," agreed Ravi. "You come back tomorrow."

Years later, I realized what had been going on. In India, it's considered rude to say no directly or bluntly turn down a request. Instead, people politely put you off until you figured out that whatever you were asking for wasn't available. But since no one was aware of the nature of the culture clash, the Indians thought the ashram residents were clods, and the residents thought the Indians were insane.

Dad and The Goldberg and I headed back to the Compound in a fog of bewilderment. As we drove past the concrete headquarters of Wable (pronounced "Wobbly") Construction Company, Dad said, "Why didn't they say he was in Sholapur to begin with?"

"It's like that." The Goldberg pointed to the sidewalk.

It was the only sidewalk in Ahmednagar. It was quite a nice one, smooth and white and equipped with an elegant brass railing. The only thing wrong with it was that it began halfway down one block and came to an abrupt end a third of the way down the next block.

"Bro, that's been there for years," said The Goldberg. "Why does the only sidewalk in Ahmednagar start nowhere and go nowhere? Nobody knows."

"I know," I said. "It's because . . ."

"But you know what it means, bro?" continued The Goldberg. "It's a sign that nothing in this world of illusion makes any sense. It's like Gear the man and Gear the goat who's coming any moment even though he's in Sholapur. It's the Sidewalk of Meaninglessness, babe. It's a concrete manifestation of the Divine Madness of this Crazy Century."

Dad and The Goldberg slapped hands. I sulked in the backseat. I'd asked Abdul the driver about that sidewalk a week ago. He said that the city had hired someone's cousin-brother (male cousin) to do the job, and the man had done part of it, then pocketed the rest of the money and fled with it, as cousin-brothers were wont to do. Sidewalk of Meaninglessness, my foot.

10

The Grand Illusion

By now you must be wondering about the person without whom this book would not exist: Baba. So was I. Though he hadn't interested me when he'd just been a picture on the wall of our Los Angeles apartment, now that he was many pictures on every wall, the focus of my parents' existence, and the reason why I was suddenly living in Ahmednagar, I became quite curious about him. With Mom's enthusiastic approval, I began reading my way through her extensive Baba library. Here's what I learned:

Baba was born in 1894 in Pune, a town a few hours' drive from Ahmednagar. His parents were middle-class Parsis. Parsis are the descendants of refugees who fled religious persecution in Iran. Their numbers and status roughly correspond to that of Jews in America: a small but successful minority with a scholarly tradition and a number of famous representatives in arts and entertainment, business, and politics.

They follow the ancient religion of Zoroastrianism, which predates Judaism. Fire is their sacred symbol, and Earth is also considered holy. Corpses, which are polluted, can therefore neither be burned nor buried. Observant Parsis lay out their naked dead in topless Towers of Silence. Vultures swoop down to eat the flesh, and the stripped and dried bones are deposited in a central well. In the coastal city of Bombay, which contains many Parsis and high-rises, every now and then a clumsy vulture drops a scrap from a Tower of Silence, like a child's finger, on some unlucky family's balcony.

Baba's parents named him Merwan Irani. He was a bright and handsome boy, but otherwise seemed ordinary. When he turned nineteen, he befriended Babajan (no relation), a Muslim holy woman who lived under a tree. She had an enormous frizz of white hair and was reputed to be over a hundred years old. One day she kissed him on the forehead. He went into a catatonic state in which he barely ate or slept, but sat staring into space for days at a time.

His family took him to a series of doctors and psychiatrists, but none could cure him. After a year he became more functional but was no longer the promising boy he'd been. In his own mother's words, he seemed to have become an imbecile. He wandered around India until he met up with another holy person, this one male and Hindu.

The holy man pitched a rock at the dazed boy's forehead. Merwan promptly declared that he had become enlightened. His catatonia, he explained, had been the result of awakening to his overwhelming true identity as God incarnate, and being hit over the head brought him back into phase with the physical world. From then on, he was known as Meher Baba, or Compassionate Father.

A rock is preserved in Baba's old house in Pune. It has the heft of a brick and a sizable bloodstain in the center. But it's not the same rock. For some time after the first blow, Baba banged his head against the floor until his forehead bled and all his teeth were knocked loose—in order, he explained, to keep in tune with the illusory physical world and not be overwhelmed by his God-consciousness.

His family was dubious at first. His teenage brother Jal began boasting that he too had special powers. When Baba heard of this, he asked Jal if he could withstand fire. When Jal replied that he could, Baba placed two burning coals on his brother's hand. The boy stood the pain for five minutes. When Baba finally took them off, the skin on his palm came with them. But Jal later decided that this had only seemed cruel and had in fact been a good spiritual lesson. Baba's entire immediate family eventually came to believe that he was indeed God in human form.

Baba amassed a following of hundreds of thousands worldwide over the next fifty years, including Pete Townshend of The Who. I never met Townshend—never even got a concert ticket—but I heard his hymn to Baba, "O Parvardigar," several thousand times.

One of Baba's teachings was that there are always five enlightened Perfect Masters, and that the woman who kissed him and the man who threw a rock at him had been two of them. Five was something of a mystical number for Baba.

So was six. His emblem is a circle formed by the symbols of six major religions. Beneath the circle is the slogan "Mastery in servitude." This is not a reference to bondage and domination, but means that one must serve God before serving humanity and that becoming the slave of God will wipe out the self, enabling the egoless soul to merge with God. Dad wore his wedding band on his left hand and a ring with that emblem on the same finger of his right.

Seven was another mystical number. Baba said there were seven planes of existence. His banner, which flew from the ashram tower and resembled the Gay Pride rainbow flag, had seven stripes. Three was significant too, for the division of consciousness into gross, mental, and spiritual states. Baba claimed that each incarnation of

God had twelve chief male disciples and an "appendage" of two chief female disciples. (Baba's appendage consisted of Paribanu and Zireen.)

Baba had a lot to say about numbers.

Despite all this, Baba-loving is not officially a religion. Baba denied that it was one, and so do his followers. If pressed, they call it a "way of life" or a "spiritual path," or some other term so vague that one might take it for a twelve-step program, a health regime, or a martial art.

This is probably appropriate for a community that does not evangelize, has no procedures for conversion or excommunication, and whose scriptures veer so wildly between the extremely general and the extremely complex that Baba-lovers often have widely varying ideas of what Baba-loving is all about. That last may account for much of Baba's appeal. A great many personal philosophies can find support somewhere in the mass of Baba's writing.

Do you despise religion? No problem: Baba-loving isn't one. Are you a devout Christian? You can be a Christian *and* a Baba-lover. Do you want unconditional love? Baba offers it. Are you a nihilist? Baba said life is an illusion, and God is beyond good and evil. Are you frightened and oppressed by the daily necessity of choice and personal responsibility? Move to Ahmednagar and turn it all over to Baba and the mandali, resting secure in the knowledge that if you follow their orders, you will always be right.

But following orders only exchanges one set of choices for another. Mom often spoke of such dilemmas: If Firoze told her to type six letters while he napped, not to wake him up, and not to leave the room, but his typewriter got hopelessly jammed, should she wake him up, leave the room to get help, or wait for him to wake up on his own?

The humiliation of failing to follow a simple order and being scolded for disobedience, said Mom, was sent by Baba to destroy her ego and remake her as a better, more selfless person. No one said serving God was easy. Firoze had once faced similar quandaries himself, for Baba had often given the mandali complicated orders in which it was impossible to obey one part without disobeying another.

In Baba's early years, he was prone to handing them weird commands to test their obedience or improve their spirituality, like ordering two of them to ignore each other's existence, cutting off all contact between his disciples and the outside world, and making them devote the time between six and six-thirty to killing mosquitoes. But he mellowed as he grew older, and none of the mandali issued bizarre orders after his death.

Though Baba died in 1969, four years before I was born, he was such a looming presence at the ashram that one could almost forget that he had, as his followers said, dropped the body.

At the ashram, Baba's name was on everyone's lips at all times. It was used as punctuation, as a greeting, as an exclamation, as a goodbye, and as a prayer. Mom in particular used "Baba" much as some people use "fuck," as an all-purpose conjunction. "Oh, Baba, what a nice sunny day." "Baba, a cockroach in the dal!" "Oh, Baba, the train's late again." She even followed burps and sneezes with a trailing sigh of "Oh, Baba, Baba, Baba, Baba, Baba, Baba, Baba."

When I saw *The Brady Bunch* episode in which Jan exclaims, "Marcia, Marcia, Marcia!" I knew exactly how she felt.

But of all Baba's attributes, the most notable was his silence. Baba wrote that in his incarnations as Buddha, Jesus, Mohammed, etc, he spoke many words, and they were all misinterpreted. So this time, he was not going to speak.

He proceeded to give innumerable talks via sign language and an alphabet board, and to dictate a book.

Should one be inclined to dismiss Baba as yet another charismatic con man, I must note that he did not amass wealth or stockpile weapons or use his followers for sex or, apparently, ever have sex with anyone. And a lifetime of self-imposed silence bespeaks sincerity. I don't believe that he was God, but I believe that he believed it.

Few of his disciples seemed drawn by his philosophy. Dad, who relished discussions of the abstract and abstruse, was an exception.

But most of them were in love with the man, his presence, his image, his words. Mom saw his face in flickering black and white, and had a revelation that made her devote her entire life to him.

From the outside, Baba-loving is one more weird Indian cult with an inexplicable following among otherwise intelligent people. From the inside, it's the logical explanation of the meaning and purpose of the universe, and a source of everlasting peace and love.

So perhaps it doesn't sound weird to you, the reader who never heard of it before. Perhaps it's ringing out as the message you've sought for your entire life, the one true path that you must follow.

Maybe you're booking a ticket to Ahmednagar right now.

We all have mental magnets for obsession, waiting to encounter an idea or person or practice of the opposite charge. Some of our magnets are more powerful than others, but we all have them. But they're not all made for the same obsessions. Mom's magnet was an exceptionally strong one, and it attracted her to Baba. There's never been an official census, but about a hundred thousand people worldwide seem to have Baba-magnets.

I can't understand why except by analogy. When I was a child, I was obsessed with animals. Now I'm obsessed with martial arts. Grandpa Artie was obsessed with creating a just society. Some people are obsessed with Star Trek, ferrets, or a person they're stalking. I can understand the fascination, even if I can't understand its object.

I don't know why Baba's followers picked him over the other thirty flavors of God, any more than I know why three-year-old me became fixated on Florida swamp rabbits rather than ponies or parakeets or Komodo dragons. It is, as Coconut was fond of saying, a great mystery.

And I can make guesses about trauma, rebellion, or loyalty to Grandpa Artie, but I'll never know for sure why I lack the God magnet. Like a block of wood that was carved and painted, I looked like I should be attracted. I sped toward the Baba-magnet with everyone else, but I only followed their lead. I never felt the pull.

II

Stone and Sand at Holy Wounds

I slid my finger along the lines of my history textbook, now and then frowning studiously. I hadn't needed to use my finger since I was three, but I wanted to look like I was paying attention. Especially since I had no idea what chapter we were on.

"*Swaraj mera janma siddha adhikar hai,*" explained Mrs. Joshi, slashing the air with her ruler to emphasize her point. The students nodded wisely.

I examined a drawing of a warrior queen riding an elephant. She had an arrow sticking out of her eye and was stabbing herself in the heart with a dagger. The caption read, "Rani Durgavati takes her own life to avoid capture by the enemy." I could identify.

Though the textbooks were in English, the classes were usually taught in Hindi. And since the other students already knew far more English than I did Hindi, I wasn't forced to learn their language to communicate. In March I'd been the best student at Hawthorne Elementary, but by June I was failing at Holy Wounds. If they hadn't practiced social promotion, I would never have gotten out of second grade.

The result was that I could read Hindi but not comprehend much of what I was reading, catch the gist of simple conversations but only speak in pidgin, and didn't know my times tables. And as the textbooks were antiquated and often ludicrously over-simplified, for years I was under the impression that Japan has so many earthquakes that all its buildings are made out of folded paper.

On the bright side, to this day I can remember the names of India's three largest producers of milk. They're the Arrey Dairy, the Worley Dairy, and the Kurla Milk Scheme.

"Mani Mao," whispered Gopal, the boy with the infected elbows, jabbing a sharpened pencil at my eyes.

I jerked my head back. Mrs. Joshi was writing in English on the blackboard, so she'd missed the whole thing. The board now displayed the enlightening statement, "1856: Lokmanya Tilak."

I glared at Gopal and held my own pencil ready. "Mani Mao, Mani Mao," he muttered spitefully, then looked around for more unwary prey.

Gopal's evil eye fell upon Shamim, who was scribbling frantically in his notebook. Shamim was the worst student in class except for me, but I was cut some slack for being a foreigner. Shamim was a Muslim in a predominantly Hindu school. As a refugee from Kashmir's houseboats, fields of hyacinths, and cross-border terrorism, he stood out visually more than I did, being redheaded and tall and with startling pale eyes. But he spoke Hindi and he was Indian, which meant he was considered unusual but not a freak like me.

Gopal slithered from his desk and lay full-length in the aisle. He stretched out his arms, one with an open hand and one with a loosely closed fist. Everyone but Mrs. Joshi and Shamim watched him with, if my own feelings were universally shared, a mixture of curiosity, horror, and relief that someone else was going to be the victim.

Gopal yanked on one leg of Shamim's desk, flung a bottle of ink at him, and whisked back into his own seat.

Shamim leaped up with a scream. He was dripping with ink, and everything from his desk was scattered on the floor. "Who did that?" he yelled in Hindi.

"You clumsy boy," said Mrs. Joshi in English. "You have spilled ink and spoiled your uniform and interrupted the class. Wipe up the ink, then come here."

"But I didn't do it," babbled Shamim in Hindi.

"Speak English," said Mrs. Joshi.

Shamim's English was worse than my Hindi, but he was no fool. "Gopal. Gopal do!"

"Ah," said Mrs. Joshi. "Are you saying I should punish Gopal instead of you?"

"Gopal," agreed Shamim.

"I see," said Mrs. Joshi. Since she appeared to be letting him off the hook, Shamim busied himself cleaning up the ink. When he was finished, Mrs. Joshi beckoned him to come forward.

"Gopal do," protested Shamim.

"Children, there is nothing worse than a telltale," said Mrs. Joshi, relentlessly waving Shamim toward the front. "You must be brave, and take your punishment. You must never tell tales on your classmates. Did Gopal really spill the ink?"

The class, confused by the trick question, made the ambiguous shake/nod movement. I hadn't gotten the hang of that yet, so I shrugged.

"If the teacher asks you, you're not telling tales," explained Mrs. Joshi. "Did Gopal spill the ink?"

"Yes, tea-cher," chorused the class.

"Gopal . . . " Gopal bounced up front and held out his hands to take his punishment. He never argued or seemed to mind being hit, qualities that Mrs. Joshi clearly found admirable. "Two for being mischievous."

She smacked him across the palms with her ruler, not too hard. She hit me like that too: hard enough to sting but not hard enough to make me dread being struck. Like being spanked, it was more humiliating than painful. But that wasn't how she hit Shamim.

"Shamim . . . " The big boy slunk forward. "Hold out your hands." He hesitated, then slowly offered them. "You shouldn't have to make me tell you. For that, turn them over." Across the knuckles hurt more.

Shamim turned them over. Mrs. Joshi held her ruler high. But before she could bring it down, Shamim jerked his hands away.

"Shamim . . . " said Mrs. Joshi.

He put them out again. The ruler slammed down. CRACK! Shamim screamed and pressed his hands across his chest.

"Again."

Tears ran down the boy's cheeks. He shook his head and snuffled and bawled. I despised him.

"Buck up, Shamim," said Mrs. Joshi. "Be a man. Your parents would be ashamed if they saw you weeping."

He put out his hands, sniffling. CRACK! The ruler shattered. Everyone ducked. A sharp-edged fragment ricocheted off my desk.

"Look what you made me do," said Mrs. Joshi to Shamim. "Go to Mrs. Phulari's room and ask to borrow her ruler."

Shamim fled, clutching his bleeding knuckles. Mrs. Phulari's room was next door, but he still hadn't returned when the recess bell rang. The kids poured out of the class and on to the playground. I reluctantly grabbed my hated floppy hat and followed, keeping a close eye on Gopal.

"*Durukh aur Mati*!" squealed Chandan, a popular girl. "Ha," agreed the other kids. "*Durukh aur Mati*."

"Come," said Rupali kindly. She was the tiny girl with the pixie cut.

They were playing "sand or stone," a game of tag in which the people being chased were safe if they stood on stone and taggable on dirt. Every time someone was tagged, the safe area switched.

The game favored speed and agility over size and strength, and I was in my element. We dashed about, yelling and laughing. Even Darshana, the sulky girl with the infected ear, seemed to be having fun. I knew I was. Until someone grabbed my hat, ripping at my hair and painfully snapping the elastic band at my throat.

"Ow!"

"Mani Mao," taunted Gopal, waving it by the band. "Mani Mao! Mani Mao!"

The kids turned on me in an instant. "Mani Mao!" screamed everyone but Rupali and the absent Shamim. "Mani Mao! Mani Mao!"

I dashed after Gopal. But my short legs were no match for his long ones. After a few minutes of running hatless and hopeless in the sun, I reluctantly returned to the classroom. I wasn't sure how long it took to get sunstroke, but Mom had insisted that I never take my hat off in direct sunlight. I stood sulking in the doorway. Gopal stole my hat every recess. I was sick of it.

Okay, Baba, I prayed experimentally. *Make Gopal give me back my hat.*

"Mani Mao, Mani Mao," called Gopal, dancing closer and swinging the hat by its band. I made a lunge for it, but he darted away. "Mani Mao!"

Mom said everything was Baba's will, but I couldn't see why Baba wanted me to be picked on. Nobody ever mentioned God's aspect as the Divine Bully. But if he didn't want me to be unhappy, why wouldn't he help?

The next time Gopal came close, I refused to take the bait. He threw the hat in the window of the teacher's lounge, then ran away. We weren't supposed to bother the teachers during lunch, but I fig-

ured they wouldn't mind if I retrieved my hat. I knocked on the door.

Sister Badger opened it. "Bad girl," she scolded. "You must never disturb the teachers."

"Gop—er—" Mrs. Joshi was also in the lounge. "Someone threw my hat inside. Can I get it, please?"

Sister Badger flexed her claws. "You should not have disturbed us for such a thing. Hold out your hands."

My head felt hot and swollen with outrage. If Sister Badger hit me, it would explode. Then she'd be sorry. "It wasn't my fault. Someone stole my hat and threw it in here to get me in trouble."

Baba, if you really love me, make her believe me.

"Bad girl," said Sister Badger with satisfaction. "Telling lies. Making trouble for others. You threw it yourself. Our Lord Jesus Christ the Savior hates it when you tell such lies."

I'm not a Christian, I thought. *Why should I care what Jesus thinks? Anyway, I'm not lying, so if Jesus hates anyone, he hates Sister Badger.*

Oblivious to the hatred of Jesus, Sister Badger picked up her weapon. "Hold out your hands."

I took my four blows from the flexible stick Sister Badger favored. My head didn't explode, though I wished hers would. Sister Badger disdainfully gestured to me to retrieve my hat from the floor. I grabbed it and stomped back to class right before the bell rang.

Mrs. Joshi, who also taught English, was in either a magnanimous or forgetful mood for the next class. Though a new ruler lay on her desk, she didn't use it on Shamim.

In the middle of Chandan's sing-song read-aloud of a Victorian poem about gay frolicking children, I surprised everyone in the class, including myself, by bursting into noisy sobs.

Mrs. Joshi walked up to my desk. "What's wrong?"

I was crying so hard that I couldn't answer.

"Come now," she said. "You may tell me. Someone has done something cruel to you. Who was it? Tell me, and I will punish them."

Of all the times and ways she could have been nice to me, why did she have to pick this one? I thought of laying the rap on Gopal, but he was a favorite of hers.

"Darshana," I blurted out.

Darshana gasped.

"I see," said Mrs. Joshi, eyeing the unfortunate and oozing girl with contempt. "What did she say to you?"

Her name had escaped from my mouth without permission from my conscious mind, but my subconscious must have been working overtime. She was low caste, a charity case, and compounded her gruesome affliction with poor personal hygiene and a sullen demeanor. Though she hadn't done anything to me other than chanting "Mani Mao" with everyone else, I didn't like her, Mrs. Joshi didn't like her, nobody liked her. Darshana could clearly be bullied with impunity.

"Uh . . . " Once again, my subconscious took over. "She said Baba was a liar and he wasn't really God."

"I *never*!" exclaimed Darshana, who must have been too shocked to protest earlier. "I never said that. I never said anything to her."

"Don't lie," said Mrs. Joshi. "That was a terrible thing to say. Class, you must never insult someone else's religion. Think how you would feel if someone said such things about yours."

While Mrs. Joshi laid into Darshana with Mrs. Phulari's ruler, I wondered what had possessed me. I had taken my darkest and most forbidden thought, put it into words I didn't dare claim as my own, and used it as a weapon against someone who had never hurt me.

And it had worked. Words had power. I had power. But I realized I should have used it on Gopal, not Darshana.

I was developing an obsessive hatred for Gopal. I was also developing a similar feeling for my hat. I was convinced that it symbolized my foreignness and was the root of my troubles. I couldn't play with the other kids during recess if Gopal had my hat, because

they played in the deadly sunlight. If he hadn't yet taken it, I had to play while clutching at the thing to make sure he didn't. But beside all that, the brim flopped in my eyes, the shapeless crown made my skull look lumpy, and the entire thing was colored a sickly green that brought out the yellow in my complexion and made me look as if I was about to vomit.

I was sure that if I could just play hatless in the sun along with everyone else, they would forget I wasn't Indian. The more I thought about this, the more feasible it seemed. If everyone else could play in the sun without wearing hats, so could I.

The next time the kids played "*Durukh aur Mati*," I casually left my hat on my desk.

My next recollections are of the hazy sort that filter through a high fever, hallucinations superimposed on memories: strange men shining lights in my face, thorns piercing my eyeballs, water dripping somewhere out of reach. The sheets were turning to slime, and I was sinking through them. Then they were rough granite and rubbing my skin off. My body ached, I was hot and cold and nauseated, and my head was being peeled open like an artichoke. Everything I touched felt gelatinous.

When I recovered enough to ask what had happened, I was told that it had been more than a week since I had collapsed from sunstroke, and I was never ever ever to play in the sun without a hat.

"Then make everyone stop picking on me and throwing rocks at me," I wailed, weak and tearful from fever. "I can't wear my hat if Gopal keeps stealing it. Make him stop."

"You have to ignore him," said Mom. "Bullies are just trying to get a rise out of you."

"I DO ignore him!" I screamed. "It doesn't work!"

"Pray to Baba," suggested Mom. "Come on, I'll pray with you. Beloved Baba, please help—"

"I hate it here," I said. "I hate Holy Wounds. I wish I'd get run over by a truck and die."

"Oh, honey," said Mom, tears welling up in her big brown eyes. "You don't mean that."

"That does it," said Dad. "I'm talking to Sister Rose."

That was the first of many trips Mom and Dad took to talk to Sister Rose. None of them had any effect whatsoever. On my first day back Gopal stole my hat during recess and thirty kids cornered me under the stairwell after school, lobbing rocks and shrieking "Mani Mao! Mani Mao! Mani Mao!"

Whenever I tried to hit one of them, ten would shove me back. They didn't want to fight. They wanted to poke sticks at the animal in the cage.

Suddenly, they scattered. I peered past the bolting bodies, expecting to see Mrs. Joshi enforcing my parents' directive.

It was Mom. Worried that I might not be well yet, she had come to pick me up. I deliberately looked at her, then at the fleeing kids, then back to her. I was humiliated that she had seen me cornered and cowering, but now she knew I wasn't exaggerating. Now she would fix things.

I waited through the rickshaw ride home for her to say something. She was silent. I could almost see the incident erasing itself from her mind. Her child was having the same wonderful spiritual experience that she was. Anything that might contradict that could not be true. It was an illusion, like the rest of the world. In the Grand Cosmic Scheme, it had not happened.

Neener neener neener, she had her fingers in her ears.

It was clear that my parents would not or could not help me out. So why bother telling them anything?

But I had an idea. I was fixated on Gopal as my chief tormentor and the ringleader of the rest. If I could take him out of the equation, maybe everyone else would leave me alone. And I had figured out his weak point.

It wasn't only foreigners Gopal had it in for. He was an equal-op-

portunity bully who pinched the girls and punched the boys and got more kids into trouble with the teachers than just the redheaded refugee, Shamim. I couldn't be the only one who'd enjoy taking revenge on Gopal.

One by one, I approached the boys and girls who seemed like potential converts to my side.

"I saw Gopal throw ink on you," I told Shamim. "It isn't fair. He got you in trouble for no reason. We should hit him when the teachers aren't looking."

"Gopal bullies all the girls," I said to fat Gita, talking hurriedly in the last moments before assembly. "The girls should get him back."

"We're too small to beat Gopal," I whispered to delicate-boned Rupali. "But six of us together could thrash him. Gita and Sita and Shamim and Khushwant and I are going to get him today at lunch. Will you help?"

By lunch my posse had attracted a band of stragglers and hangers-on, who were quickly transformed into allies. "Get some rocks," I instructed. They began to pick up the kind that were thrown at me every day, stinging missiles the size of brazil nuts.

"No, big ones." I hefted a stone the size of a lemon. I couldn't close my hand over it. "Like this."

We cornered Gopal in the same stairwell he'd trapped me in. "Come on!" I yelled, pitching my rock. He ducked, then darted to the side. It was a dead end. He tried to back into the wall. Emboldened, the mob closed in.

Mrs. Joshi came charging up, laying about with a walking stick. She'd never come to rescue me. I couldn't even see Gopal through the angry throng at that point. Once Mrs. Joshi had whacked a couple of the kids over the heads and across the back, the rest scattered.

Gopal lay sprawled under the stairwell. Mrs. Joshi pulled him into her lap. His shirt clung to his chest in wet red patches, brilliant against the starched white cotton. Blood flowed from his head and down his neck, soaking into his collar. His eyes were half shut and glazed over.

"What are you standing around for?" yelled Mrs. Joshi. "Khushwant, Shamim, run and tell Sister Rose to get a doctor!"

The boys ran. I crept away with the other kids.

Rupali patted my shoulder comfortingly. "Don't worry. We'll say it was the boys' idea."

"Yeah, maybe," I said, sure that plan wouldn't fly. I appreciated Rupali looking out for me, but I didn't want to blame someone else. I had never imagined anything like that bloody scene. Had *I* provoked that? Could I have killed him? What sort of trouble was I going to get into if I had?

Mrs. Joshi contacted my parents, which was how I found out that Gopal was not dead, though he did have a concussion and needed fourteen stitches in his head. Dad yelled, Mom cried, and Mrs. Joshi struck my palms six times each with a switch. All things considered, I got off pretty easily. Either the blame got shared around and diluted, or my previous complaints about Gopal carried some weight.

After that Gopal went easier on me. But a boy named Suresh promptly took over as my chief tormentor, and the rest of the students (except for Rupali) continued hurling rocks and insults at me on a daily basis. As time went on, the kids at Holy Wounds communicated their hatred of the foreign girl to the kids at the Marathi school, and pretty soon every kid in town knew to throw rocks at me whenever I appeared outside of the Compound gates without an adult escort. So while I squelched one bully, hundreds of others took his place.

But Mom kept saying that it was all part of Baba's plan to make me stronger, and that view fit in with a hymn Sister Rose often made us sing, "Onward Christian Soldiers." I could believe that Ahmednagar was God's boot camp, but I wondered who the enemy was.

12

Alice's Market

Though I couldn't go into the town alone without being pounced on by a mob of kids, I loved going out with an adult bodyguard. When Dad heard that Ahmednagar had a breakfast specialty called jalebis and bhajias, he set aside a Saturday morning for an expedition to the bazaar to find it.

We threaded our way through the slums outside the Compound and into a maze of alleys packed with open stalls—fifty specialty markets in one sliver of town. Cars couldn't fit in, but rickshaws, motorcycles, and scooters zipped through, throwing up sprays of mud and reeking sewage to splatter the dogs and cats, the water buffaloes and goats, the free-roaming holy cows, the pedestrians who didn't dodge fast enough and the bicyclists with slow reflexes, the children on donkeys, and the horses and oxen toiling in harness.

First came the paan-stalls, beloved of men with rotting scarlet teeth. Their quick-fingered proprietors popped betel nuts, spices, lime, tobacco, and, for the ultra-special and most expensive paan, a dab of hashish, into green leaves, and folded them into neat and unhealthy packages. A line of scruffy men squatted on blankets nearby. They seemed to occupy the same ecological niche as shoeshine men, but instead they removed their customers' earwax with disturbingly long and pointy instruments.

The things-to-hang-on-your-walls shops came next. They sold mirrors, frames, and color prints of Gods, Goddesses, demi-gods, and saints. The monkey God, Hanuman, ripped open his chest to display his loyal heart; the boy saint Dyaneshwar and his saintly baby sister Muktabai perched atop a flying wall and made a water buffalo recite holy verses from the Vedas; the Goddess Durga, patron of warriors and martial artists, rode a lion and brandished weapons in all ten of her hands; the wild God Shiva, destroyer of ignorance, danced to uncreate the world.

Each picture was garish but compelling, like an 8 × 10 Las Vegas. The most exotic elements, such as the many limbs and animal steeds, were visual shorthand for a complex symbolism. The extra arms were not to be taken literally but represented more-than-human attributes. The objects held in each hand were rich with meaning, each lotus or dagger or book meant to remind worshippers of a certain myth, a blessing that Goddess could be petitioned to give, or the people that God held in his especial care.

The God Krishna was said to have been dark-skinned. But that was considered ugly and associated with the lower castes. (If you believe the claims in the matrimonial classified ads, single and desperate Indians are as likely to possess the prized "wheatish" complexion as

their American counterparts are to be Very Good-Looking.) So in a discreet nod to his real skin tone, Krishna was colored robin's egg blue.

Elephant-headed, pot-bellied Ganesh was created when the Goddess Parvati, wife of Shiva the Destroyer, got lonely when her husband was away. She wanted a son, but Shiva wasn't there to help. So she exfoliated her body, removing what my Grandma called "shmutz," but which the myths refer to as "scurf," and molded it into a handsome son. Then she went to bathe, after asking Ganesh (for that was he) to make sure that no one disturbed her.

But she forgot to add, "Unless Shiva comes home unexpectedly. You'll know him by his matted hair, indigo throat, and the cobra around his neck. He can come in, but no one else."

Sure enough, Shiva came home and found a strange young man barring the way. They argued, then the hot-tempered Shiva lopped off Ganesh's head. Parvati rushed out, explained the misunderstanding, and demanded that Shiva fix things. He strode out, exclaiming that he was so sorry that he would take the head of the first creature he saw. This turned out to be an elephant.

One of Ganesh's tusks is snapped short, because he had used it as a quill when he transcribed *The Mahabharata* from the sage Valmiki. He is accompanied by a rat, sometimes tiny and crouched at his feet, sometimes large enough to ride. The rat and its changing size represents Ganesh as the Overcomer of Obstacles, creeping under barriers too big to break through. The sweet in his hand signifies abundance.

If you know the stories, a picture is worth *at least* a thousand words.

The flower bazaar came next. Its perfume floated across the alley to anoint the waiting Gods. Fold-out tables were heaped with garlands of marigolds and roses, jasmine and lilies, zinnias and orchids, ready to hang around a picture of a saint or a photo of an ancestor, to drape a tombstone or a bride.

Further on, women sat behind cones of powder in crimson, saffron, orange, purple, hot pink, forest green, and indigo. They scooped the powder into newspaper wrappings for women to dab on their foreheads, streak down their hairlines, decorate their Gods and saints and honored dead, and tap into intricate stenciled patterns on the swept area before their front doors.

Those doorstep sand paintings are called rangoli and are remade each morning, because by nightfall wind and feet have worn them away. The tin stencils, pointillist renderings of flowers and curlicues and geometric designs, were sold in the metal bazaar three streets down. Some women combined stencils to create large and original patterns, but the traditionalists pinched up the powder in the tips of their fingers and drew their evanescent art by hand.

Next came the vegetable bazaar, an immense selection of greenery under a canopy, emitting a sharp and earthy smell of herbs, onions, and the dirt clinging to the roots that had been pulled that morning. An entire aisle was devoted to squashes: green, orange, yellow, spotted, or speckled; cylindrical, round, oval, acorn-shaped; knobby, very knobby, and ultra-knobby. The king of the squashes was doodie, which can grow up to three feet long and resembles a great green phallus. It's mealy and squishy and almost completely tasteless, but Thaki the cook was inexplicably fond of it.

Years after my first visit to the vegetable bazaar, the much-loathed doodie had a brief and shining moment as an aid to cross-cultural humor. Dad and some of the resident men went on vacation near the Nepali border, where they whiled away the snowy hours by exchanging jokes with their Gurkha guide. The guide's favorite joke was the one called "chi-chi." You may know it as "ooga-booga," or perhaps "walla-walla."

Two missionaries are captured by savages. The savage chief declares, "The penalty for trespassing on our lands is death or chi-chi! Decide now."

The first missionary figures that whatever chi-chi is, it can't be worse than death. "I choose chi-chi!"

"Chi-chi!" yell the savages excitedly. They pounce on the missionary and butt-fuck him till he's almost dead.

The second missionary doesn't want to die, but he can't stand the thought of chi-chi. Gathering his courage, he tells the chief, "I choose death!"

"Very well," says the chief. "Death . . . by chi-chi!"

Apparently buggery humor translates well. A few days after Dad regaled the Gurkha with the chi-chi joke, a fat man dropped a coin at the bazaar. As he laboriously stooped to pick it up, the Gurkha grabbed a doodie from a nearby stall, goosed the looming butt, and shouted "Chi-chi!"

The fruit bazaar was outside the vegetable bazaar, with the wares displayed in wicker baskets on the street: big pale sweet limes, tiny green sour limes, huge spiky jackfruit, pebble-skinned custard apples, mottled papayas, and tamarinds with brittle shells and tangy brown flesh the texture of a fruit roll-up. And . . .

"Peaches!" I exclaimed.

Dad inspected the speckled yellow fruit. "No, those are mangoes. Want one?"

"Sure." I had called his attention to the fruit for another reason, but he had missed his cue. "I guess they're not much like *peaches*," I added, stroking one with my forefinger. "These are smooth. *Peaches* are fuzzy."

Dad handed over the money and took the mangoes. "Did I ever tell the story of your uncle Danny and the peach?"

It was my favorite. I wriggled with anticipation. "Tell the peach story."

Dad began cutting up the mangoes with his Swiss Army knife. "Don't put your mouth on the skin; it hasn't been washed," he cautioned. "Okay, the peach story. This happened a few years before you were born. Your mother's parents didn't approve of me, so they'd disowned her for dating me. But—"

"Why didn't they like you?"

"Because I was a hippie. They hated hippies."

I later learned that the main bone of contention had been that Mom and Dad were unmarried but living together.

"Anyway," continued Dad, "after a while they had second thoughts about never seeing their daughter again. So they invited both of us to come and have dinner with them. Now I'm not sure why, but for some reason we brought my little brother, your uncle Danny. He was about fourteen then. I was nineteen and your mother was eighteen.

"Your mother's parents lived way out in the desert. It was a three-hour drive, and we spent the whole trip . . . er . . . smoking marijuana. By the time we arrived Danny was stoned out of his mind. He lurched up to the house like a zombie."

Dad did a mini-lurch, legs stiff and eyes rolled back into his head. The fruit sellers and their customers stopped their transactions to watch him.

"Of course your Mom and I were stoned too, but we were more used to it. Er . . . you know you shouldn't . . . "

"I'm not going to smoke marijuana," I recited. "Smoking is bad for you. Go on."

"Your Mom's parents were incredibly straight. Like, uber-straight. They sat on a plastic-covered couch, glaring at us, as stiff as if they'd had baseball bats rammed up their . . . spines. Danny passed out in a plastic-covered easy chair and sprawled there with his mouth hanging open.

"Oh, and I had this enormous white-boy Afro at the time. And I was wearing a eucalyptus necklace with bud-shaped beads and a button that said, '(Dad mouthed the F-word) Nixon.'

"We sat there in total silence for what seemed like hours. Then Danny, who had adenoids, began to emit these grotesque honking snores."

To the onlookers' delight, Dad did a few grotesque honking noises. I laughed so hard that I made some too.

"'GNAAAAHHH . . . GNAAAAHHH . . . GNAAAAHHH . . .' went Danny.

"Then Grandpa Howard said, 'How about a drink?'" Dad's "Grandpa Howard" voice was absurdly hearty. "'Or something to eat? Young man!' That was directed at Danny, who woke up with a start.

"Danny babbled, 'Wha'? Huh? Whazzat?' His head was switching back and forth, and his eyes were darting around the room. Pot made him paranoid.

"'Young man,' said Grandpa Howard formally, 'Would you like something to eat?'

"Danny said, 'Wha'? Huh? Oh, no, no, no, no—well . . . yes . . . there is . . . something . . . ' Then he paused, licking his lips." Dad as Danny licked his lips elaborately and wriggled them like a tapir.

"You could see the idea slowly filtering through his mind that there *was* something he'd like, that he'd request as soon as he remembered what it was called. We all watched him, totally fascinated." Dad, as Danny, smacked his lips and rotated his shoulders in happy anticipation.

"'Well?' said Grandpa Howard.

"'I . . . would . . . like . . . ' said Danny, drawing out the suspense. We all leaned forward. 'A *peach*.'" Dad drew out the word into four or five syllables.

"'Oh, sure,' said Grandpa Howard. 'I've got a peach. Want me to cut it up for you?'

"'No . . . '

"'Or I could peel it. Shall I peel it?'

"'No . . . no . . . '

"Grandpa Howard fetched an unadorned peach from the kitchen and presented it. And Danny snatched it with both hands and fell on it, plunging his entire face in, sucking, snuffling, rolling his eyes."

Using the mango as a peach stand-in, Dad as Danny devoured it with uncouth noises of slobbering and delight. Not only was I laughing so hard that I was almost on the ground, but so were the fruit vendors.

Extracting himself from the mango, Dad said, "Well, your Mom and I were watching Danny and cracking up when suddenly Grandpa Howard figured out what was going on. He said, 'That boy is high!' Your Mom and I just laughed harder, and then Grandpa Howard threw us all out."

That, as it turned out, was the bowdlerized version. Dad started telling the story unabridged when I was in my teens. This is what really happened after Grandpa Howard figured out the meaning of the peach:

"This is no laughing matter!" shouted Grandpa Howard. "How dare you bring him here! It's not enough that you're *fucking* my daughter, you have to bring your filthy fucking drugs into my home!"

Grandma Sue, her hands folded neatly in her lap, leaned forward and hissed, "Yes! We know about you! We know what you do! You're *fucking* each other!"

Mom was somewhat inured to this behavior, but Dad was poleaxed. He had often heard the F-word from his father, in reference to misbehaving tools or the FBI, but never from a woman of his mother's generation.

"Fuck you both!" yelled Grandpa Howard.

"Fuck you!" shouted Grandma Sue. "Fuckers!"

"SLUUUUURRRRP!" went Danny.

"GET OUT OF MY HOUSE BEFORE I FUCKING KILL YOU!" roared Grandpa Howard.

Mom leaped up, Dad yanked Danny out of the chair, and they fled the scene, dripping perplexity and peach juice.

Though Ahmednagar lacked peaches, its selection of fruit was otherwise superb: watermelons the size of softballs, pomegranates that opened like treasure chests and spilled out rubies, crisp apples

scented like flowers, tart jamun berries, pink-fleshed guavas, spicy brown chikus, and everyone's favorite, Alphonso mangoes, the perfect balance between sweet and tangy, juicy and creamy.

The fruit sellers waved goodbye to Dad as we headed for the jalebi and bhajia stall. It was surrounded by happy customers eating dripping golden pretzels and yellow fritters speckled with green.

Dad marched up to the counter. "*Do jalebi aur bhajia.*"

The jalebi-and-bhajia man blinked at the unfamiliar and foreign face. "*Che rupia saath paise.*"

Dad offered him a ten-rupee note. The jalebi-and-bhajia man tilted his head back and forth in polite but unmistakable refusal.

Confused, Dad held up six fingers. "*Che rupia?*"

"*Haji. Che.*"

Dad tried to hand him the bill again. The jalebi-and-bhajia man tilted his head and said something in Hindi.

"Note is torn," explained a bystander, swallowing a jalebi fragment and indicating a rip at one edge of the rupee. "No one will accept."

Puzzled, Dad replaced the defective bill and tried another one. That one passed inspection. But the change he received consisted of three rupee notes and four hard candies.

It turned out that the value of the metal in coins smaller than fifty paise was greater than their face value, so they were being sold on the black market and melted down for scrap. Twenty-five-, ten-, five-, and one-paise coins were rarer than atheists in Ahmednagar. But instead of rounding up the prices, shopkeepers gave out substitute change. They either scribbled "25 p" on a scrap of paper or handed out candies. So if you paid for a sheet of bindis with a five-rupee note, you got two rupees and a toffee in change.

Paper money was also problematic. No one would accept bills with dog-ears, tears, stains, creases, crumple marks, or an overly furry texture. The residents, who lacked the Indians' practiced eye for flaws were constantly receiving tattered bills as change, which they were then unable to fob off on anyone else.

While Dad and I were still musing over the edible change, which struck me as straight out of Wonderland, the jalebi-and-bhajia man handed us our breakfast.

The jalebis were crispy hollow tubes filled with sugar syrup, and the bhajias were spongy dumplings spiked with lethally hot green chili peppers.

Taken individually, jalebis are sickly sweet and bhajias are thermonuclear missiles; cold, jalebis have the taste and the consistency of sugared cardboard, and bhajias of spiced Styrofoam. But hot and fresh, eaten in alternating bites, they are a symphony of contrasts, hot/sweet, soft/crisp, spiced/bland.

If only the bazaar and Holy Wounds had made such a delicious alternation of states.

Like an immigrant wandering an American supermarket and marveling at frozen foods and packaged meats, I was delighted with the bazaar partly for its difference from what I was used to, and partly for its lavishness and wealth of product. But every kid in Ahmednagar seemed to hate me on principle, the teachers and nuns didn't much like me either, and I was already sick of prayers and pinched cheeks and Baba, Baba, Baba.

Alice's "eat me" cake and "drink me" bottle had been delicious. But she couldn't taste them without growing tall enough to crush herself or small enough to drown in her own tears.

"Down the rabbit hole," I muttered to myself.

"What?" said Dad.

"Nothing," I replied.

13

A Jolly Good Read

An Indian pilgrim named Freyni Dadachanji caught my attention during her brief visit. The heat, dust, and griminess of Ahmednagar, coupled with the water-saving regulation that forbade pilgrims from bathing more than once every three days, made even the most fashion-conscious of them look bedraggled after a few days. But Freyni still embodied casual elegance after a week at the ashram. I was impressed.

I took a seat beside her on the bus to Meherazad and sat surreptitiously admiring her, from the sleek waves of her hair to her modest yet sexy white linen suit to her slim feet in gold-strapped sandals, with a dab of crimson polish on all twelve of her toes.

That couldn't be right.

I counted them twice, starting at different ends

each time. Yes, stylish Freyni Dadachanji had six toes on each foot. The extra toe was smaller than the little one—the second-littlest one—but not deformed in any way. I squinted to see if her hands, partially hidden in her lap, had six fingers.

"Only the toes," she said, holding up her crimson-tipped fingers for display. I jumped. Her voice was as silky and refined as the rest of her, like polished wood.

"Did the other kids tease you in school?"

"No, because I didn't wear sandals. And even when I do, most people don't notice. You're very observant."

Freyni Dadachanji thought I was smart! "Does anyone else in your family have six toes?"

"Oh, yes. It's from my mother's side. She has six toes, my maternal grandmother has six toes, my maternal aunts have six toes, and one of my maternal uncles has six toes *and* six fingers. On each hand."

"Gosh."

She reached for the book in my lap. "May I?"

"Sure."

She turned it over in her tapering fingers. "*King of the Wind*," she read. "Oh, that's the one about the Arabian horse in England. I loved that when I was a little girl."

I wanted to be Freyni Dadachanji when I grew up. Six toes and all.

"Tell me," she said. "Do you like Enid Blyton?"

"Who?"

"Ah." She smiled mysteriously. I was in love.

A package arrived soon after Freyni Dadachanji left town. It contained six books extolling the virtues of the English boarding school: Enid Blyton's *St. Clare's* series.

India's lingering traces of British rule were easy to detect in its bookshops. An antique Anglophilia packed them with P. G. Wode-

house's intricate farces about brilliant butlers and upper-class twits, Georgette Heyer's comedies of manners masquerading as Regency romances, and Enid Blyton's paeans to boarding school.

Blyton was an immensely prolific writer of incredibly English children's books, the type that are unreadable if you're over the age of twelve but irresistible if you're under it. She wrote mysteries, fantasies, adventures, farm stories, and school stories. Hundreds of them.

She had twelve basic characters who recurred with different names in different books:

1. The brave, sensible, competent English child.
2. The obnoxious foreign child (American, French, or Ruritanian), who bucks up and reforms when exposed to sensible English children.
3. The gentle, easily frightened girl.
4. The hot-tempered tomboy.
5. The hot-tempered Gypsy or circus person.
6. The stupid policeman.
7. The flustered French woman.
8. The wise, super-competent English adult.
9. The extremely intelligent animal.
10. The talking animal.
11. The magical person, creature, or household item.
12. The all-purpose villain.

Mrs. Joshi clearly saw herself as Blyton Type Eight Sub-type C: the strict but fair teacher or headmistress. Perhaps she beat her students out of frustration that we were not Blyton's frolicsome, doughty, enthusiastic children but a rag-tag gang of illiterate cringing brats, oozing bodily fluids and clobbering each other.

Blyton's books revel in lavishly described breakfasts, lunches, teas, suppers, picnics, snacks, elevenses, and midnight feasts, replete with treacle pudding, watercress sandwiches, pork pies, steak and kidney pies, jelly rolls, fried bread, buttered scones, hot cocoa, cold ham, homemade jam, peppermint creams, toad in the hole, lobster salad, tinned pineapple, and strawberries with Devonshire cream.

Interspersed with all that eating (perhaps to work it off) are kidnappings and daring escapes, lacrosse and cricket matches, countryside adventures with no grown-ups in sight, practical jokes, mysteries solved, everlasting friendships, adults who understand, and school that's fun.

Her vision of a child's life, not as it is but as it ought to be, shone through her atrocious prose and smug English conviction that Americans are arrogant, stupid, and have funny accents, and dark-skinned foreigners are cowardly, stupid, and have funny accents.

Blyton's books are so idyllic as to be escapist reading for even the happiest of children. Every child in India who could read English seemed to read them: the girls destined for arranged marriages with men three times their age, the children who hid with their parents when the religious riots broke out, the overprotected urban kids who always had an adult or three checking up on them. And me.

14

Assembly at Holy Wounds

I had attended Holy Wounds for several months before I discovered the significance of Sister Rotten Rose's words, "Assembly dismissed!"

After the last hymn one morning, Sister Rotten Rose did not dismiss us. "You have been unruly today," she announced, though I hadn't noticed any extra horseplay. "You are *not* dismissed."

I waited for her to deliver a mass scolding, but instead she turned on her heels and retreated to her office in a swirl of black cotton.

Nobody moved. Obviously we were in for some sort of group punishment. Mrs. Joshi and the other teachers left their places at the head of the lines. I assumed they were going to go round and whack us. Instead they marched to the staff office, leaving the students lined up in the sunny plaza.

I wondered why nobody broke rank or started giggling or whispering, now that the authorities had abandoned us, but then I saw the curtains pulled at the office. They were watching us.

I shifted from foot to foot. Keeping us standing didn't seem like much of a punishment. We stood out here for half an hour every morning anyway.

Then it started to get hot.

The assemblies ended just before the blazing heat of day began. Now it had begun, and we were stuck in it.

Well, we were out in the sun all recess anyway.

It got hotter.

During recess we could get a drink from a tap or canteen. We had the option of ducking into the classrooms or up against the walls for a bit of shade. And we could move around, so the sun wasn't always beating straight down on the tops of our heads.

For the first time, I was happy to wear the stupid floppy hat.

The sun brightened, relentless. The windows were sheets of blazing light. The reflections off everyone's patent leather shoes hurt my eyes.

The heat had increased exponentially since I had first arrived in Ahmednagar. A week before I had snuck a wall thermometer from the Compound office and put it on the sidewalk. It hit 112 degrees, then exploded. But I had done that at midday. It was still morning now.

It got hotter.

Everyone kept standing at attention, so I did too.

My feet ached. My eyes ached. A jackhammer thudded into my head.

I had acquired the habit of scooping ants and termites from their shaded homes, moving them into direct sunlight, and seeing how long it took them to die. On concrete or asphalt they ran in one or two circles, then curled up, quivered, and died. On dirt they ran

around longer before they fell over, but sometimes revived if I immediately put them back in the shade. They never revived if I'd put them on a rock. I told myself I was doing experiments, but I knew perfectly well that I just liked to watch them suffer.

It looked like I wasn't the only one with that hobby.

I wished I had a pith helmet. How could the rest of the kids stand it, with no hats at all? I supposed, being born here, they were accustomed to it.

I heard a thud behind me. I turned around. Shamim had passed out.

"Don't look," muttered Rupali. "Whoever it is, they've only fainted. You'll be punished if you move."

I turned back around. Surely someone would come and pick him up.

Nobody came.

It was like standing inside an oven. The air wavered with heat. Or was something wrong with my eyes? I couldn't keep anything in focus. Black bubbles floated across my field of vision. I couldn't feel the ground under my feet.

A girl from an upper-level class threw up. Then Rupali did. I didn't look.

Oily green liquid oozed past my left shoe and pooled in someone's footprint. I tried not to look at that either.

I tried not to think about throwing up.

I tried not to think about passing out.

I tried to think about something totally unrelated to what was going on, but I was too dizzy to collect my thoughts. The sledgehammer behind my forehead didn't help.

I was going to keep my feet on the ground. I thought about that. On my feet. On my feet. On my feet.

"Assembly dismissed!"

I looked up. Sister Rotten Rose had appeared on the balcony. We marched back to class. Shamim must have picked himself up at some point, because he came stumbling along at the back of the line with dust in his hair.

I was in bed when Mom came home that evening. "Are you all right?" she asked.

"I have a headache," I mumbled. "Sister Rose made us stand in the sun."

"Oh," said Mom, uncomprehending. "Then stay in bed, sweetie. I'll get you an aspirin and a glass of water. You'll feel better in the morning."

15

WITHOUT A SINGLE MARATHI VOWEL

While rummaging through the dank corners of Ratanji's library, I found an encyclopedia entry on my new hometown. It cited the proverb "*Ahmednagar: bin kana bin matra*" and translated it as "Ahmednagar: without a single Marathi vowel." In other words: "Ahmednagar: there's no there there."

I lost no time in quoting it to Coconut.

"You are wondering what this saying means," said Coconut.

"I know what it means," I said. "It means there's nothing interesting here."

"No, no. It is a play on words."

"I know that. It's a play on words that means—"

"It cannot be translated," said Coconut. "It is a joke. But it does not say anything bad about this town. Ahmednagar is the town chosen by Avatar

Meher Baba. It is a very special town. It is the town where my little mummy lives." He made a grab for my cheek. I ducked.

I later mentioned the saying to Paribanu. "Well, dear," she said, "To tell you the truth, none of us mandali were very happy when Baba told us that he had decided to establish his ashram in Ahmednagar. 'Oh, Baba darling,' I said. 'Are you sure you want to live *here*?'

"But he'd made up his mind, so I had to follow his will. Maybe he wanted to teach us to make the best of our circumstances. And Ahmednagar has great spiritual significance, even if it's not obvious to the eye."

"Or ear," I added. "Or nose."

Paribanu chuckled.

Ahmednagar's only distinctions other than the ashram were an army base with more tanks than any other single base in India and the Ahmednagar Fort, which was an active military post with an on-site museum. In the fading days of the British Raj, the freedom fighter Jawaharlal Nehru had been imprisoned in the fort for seven years for agitating for Indian independence.

Every few years, the army base held the Parade of the Tanks. Without fanfare, of trumpets or otherwise, they drove hundreds of tanks down the main road. It took most of the day. The treads left four-inch-deep ruts in the asphalt, which remained unrepaired until they were evened out by the next Parade of the Tanks. Apart from that spectacular display of legalized vandalism, the soldiers were only notable for being more polite, more law-abiding, and having snappier uniforms than the cops.

But apart from the fort and army base, the town was dismal. The unregulated factories dumped so much waste that the river was a canal of gray sludge, the telephones and mail were as unreliable as the electricity, the roads were mostly potholes and dust, and the seasons consisted of Unpleasantly Hot, Unbearably Hot, and for two months every few years, Soaking Wet.

One of the residents, Edward, came from an isolated town in Michigan where the only entertainment was getting drunk and fighting with other drunken locals until someone was knocked unconscious. But the rest of the residents had never before lived anywhere as dull as Ahmednagar. And Edward had high-tailed it to San Francisco as soon as he'd turned eighteen, so even he had gotten used to a more varied existence.

Edward, incidentally, was a registered sex offender. He'd stumbled out of a party one night and realized that he needed a bathroom, stat. But he couldn't remember which beach house he'd come from, so he decided to piss into the surf. A cop shone a flashlight on him, caught him with his pants around his ankles and his dick in his hand, and booked him for masturbating in public.

But if he had moved to Ahmednagar in the hope of escaping further unwanted and embarrassing sexual incidents, he came to the wrong place. One morning at Meherabad he awoke to a cacophony of grunts and brays, looked outside, and spotted a farm boy taking advantage of a horrified donkey.

"*Ahmednagar: Gadha-chod ki desh.*" ("Ahmednagar: Land of the Donkey-Fuckers.")

As one can only spend so many hours per day in prayer, the residents spent much of their copious spare time on a frantic hunt for entertainment. I, on the other hand, found much of mine in watching them.

They divided neatly into two groups: those who seemed ordinary except for living in an ashram, and those who would have stuck out in an asylum for the terminally peculiar. But even the more normal ones developed tics and eccentricities if they stayed long enough. Or perhaps they developed nothing. They often spoke of the spiritual forge upon which they were beaten and melted until their truer, better selves were revealed.

Something was certainly revealed.

They were a tiny insular community in one of the world's least happening towns, and their claustrophobia and desperation for amusement were fever-intense.

There was no TV. There was no radio. Movies were in Hindi without subtitles. There was no camping, fishing, or hunting. There were no computers or VCRs. There were no bars, no beauty parlors, no classes, no gyms. Because of the servants and semi-communal housing, most residents could not cook, garden, keep pets, drive cars, or remodel their homes. The ashram jobs were mostly part-time.

A handful of residents were Indian, but they didn't socialize much with the Western ones. The mandali were of a higher spiritual class and the servants were of a lower social class, and the inequality was a barrier between them and the residents. Pilgrims could be befriended, but they usually only visited for two weeks. And as not all the residents liked each other, any given resident's social circle often contained fewer than ten people.

I was the only resident to befriend non-Baba-loving local Indians. This mystified me, for while the Indians had no particular incentive to hang out with the Westerners, more pals would have helped cut down on the residents' stultification. I figured them for Grade-A religious snobs.

After I left, I learned that the mandali Zireen had forbidden the residents to associate with the locals. She thought it would distract the residents from serving God if they were allowed to kick back with the townies. She also worried that Americans who hung out at the Army base could be accused of spying and that it would make the ashram look bad if residents had affairs with locals.

Her fears were reasonable. America was regarded with suspicion for being an ally of India's enemy Pakistan, and some of the locals were quite attractive. But the main effect of her prohibition was to make the residents go stir-crazy within months of arrival.

As I was too young to have an affair or be a spy, I was allowed to

visit Rupali at her family's apartment in town. But while I could theoretically associate with anyone, there were so few people my own age who wanted to associate with me that I ended up twice as isolated as even the most hermit-like residents.

The only communal singing was at arti. There was no dancing except performances on Baba-related holidays. We produced plays several times per year. There was Ratanji's library, a volleyball court, and backgammon, chess, and cards. There were a few cassette decks and about twelve cassettes. Most of the residents had bicycles, motorcycles, or motor scooters. And once a year a circus with two elephants and the Psychic Dog came to town. That was it.

Other people in similar situations might tip cows, manufacture crystal meth, or tend their collections of human body parts. The residents preferred to gossip, feud, cultivate eccentricities, and pass around strange theories, fad diets, and books of a spiritual or improving nature.

Another popular hobby was pilgrim-watching. This was most easily enjoyed at Baba's Hall, where pilgrims frequently hijacked the scheduled program with inappropriate revelations of troubling desires. Once a man launched into a monologue about his love-hate relationship with blue jeans and his mother.

"She was always . . . " He quivered with emotion. "Bending over. Stooping. *Wiggling.* Showing me her trim . . . tight . . . rounded . . . buttocks. In blue jeans. *Jean . . . Butt!*"

After Jean Butt left Ahmednagar, he wrote a letter to Dad. It conformed to the guidelines of *The Psychotic's Elements of Style*, being long, single-spaced, and typed on both sides of the page. The letter was a tirade against Dad and The Goldberg for unspecified crimes and threatened to "kill them on the volleyball court" the next time Jean Butt visited Ahmednagar. It was unclear whether or not "kill" was meant metaphorically. This puzzled Dad, because not only had he missed the infamous jean butt speech, he had never even spoken to the man. Neither had The Goldberg.

It's a fact, however, that Dad and The Goldberg were the only residents who wore blue jeans.

But some of the residents would undoubtedly have been peculiar even if they'd had less time on their hands. Milt Frimpkis, for instance. He was a hustler, a wheeler-dealer, forever scheming to get into the mandalis' good graces or score an extra rupee. His plots often involved having pilgrims bring him things from America: a prototype air-freshener, six bottles of Tia Maria, or forty pounds of dog chow. Whenever we saw an exhausted pilgrim hauling an oddly shaped bundle into the Compound, we knew that Milt had gotten to them.

But he had one thing that endeared him to me: a large collection of comic books which he let me read. He was not a true collector, or he'd never have let me lay hands on them. Nor was he a true fan, for he never seemed to read them himself. He just had them, in tottering dusty stacks inside a cabinet.

Thanks to him, I got to identify with the tough women and misunderstood mutants of the X-Men, ponder the mystic adventures of Dr. Strange, and boggle over the Legion of Super-Pets, which consisted of a caped flying dog named Krypto, a caped flying horse named Comet, a caped flying monkey named Beppo, and a caped flying cat named Whizzy.

Somehow a Denny's menu had gotten mixed up with the comics. It was a full-color four-page laminated extravaganza, and I pored over it for hours on end. The glossy photos of hamburgers, french fries, and ice cream sundaes transported me into a dream of America.

I took Milt's example and urged pilgrims to send me food—I even went on a campaign to get them to bring me root beer syrup,

so I could make my own—but I lacked his weird persuasive force. He could convince old ladies with walkers to bring him loads of ornamental bricks, but I was lucky to get a few packets of Lipton chicken noodle soup.

Like many of the residents, Milt was a hypochondriac with a particular preoccupation with the state of his bowels. Perhaps he caught it from the mandali, who enjoyed nothing better than a forty-minute conversation on the topic of their latest bowel movement: shape, color, consistency, aroma, difficulty, number of stools, time spent eliminating, time since last movement, and whether it was painful or pleasurable.

This may have been a hangover from the days when Baba's BMs had been a major topic of concern. The published diary of a mandali has multiple entries with topic sentences like "Today Baba passed three well-formed stools." Dad once speculated at length about how many of those well-formed stools had been secretly collected and saved by the mandali, where they were kept, and what they looked and smelled like now, until Mom shushed him.

But Milt took rectum-gazing to new levels. He eventually became so paranoid about the Compound toilets that he purchased a potty chair for his private use.

I couldn't blame him for wanting to avoid the toilets. Foul during the day, they became downright frightening after dark, when you had to venture across an unlit stretch of gravel that was nearly always blockaded by a goos or two.

Goos is the Marathi name for the bandicoot rat. The goos I saw on my first day was a baby. A fully grown goos is a foot long from its snarling mouth to the base of its scabby tail, and the tail is the same length as the body. In appearance and disposition they resemble *The Princess Bride*'s Rodents of Unusual Size, and they make a daunting, hissing gauntlet to run at 3:00 am.

But keeping a potty chair in the communal dining room behind a screen was, we all agreed, going too far.

The formidable old mandali nicknamed Preacher called Milt into his office to lay down the law. "I hear you have a *chair* . . . in the eating room . . . to shit in. This is disgusting. Remove it immediately."

Milt wrung his hands and cringed. It was his favorite mannerism, even after I read *David Copperfield* and started calling him Uriah Heep. "But the toilets are unsanitary. We Westerners are very susceptible to germs."

The old man glared past his bristling brows. "You crouch over the toilets. You do not touch them. What do you think? You think the germs are going to leap up your ass?"

Other residents turned to creative pursuits to ease the boredom. I discovered Shinork's when he pounced on me as I sat on the rim of the Compound's dry fountain, swinging my legs and reading *Ivanhoe*.

"Jai Baba." Shinork held up a sheaf of papers. "It's an epic poem about the devotional path that leads the spiritual seeker through the thickets of illusion to the fated meeting with the God-Man. Here." He thrust it at me.

I sat on my hands. "It's cursive. I can only read print."

"That's all right. I'll read it to you."

I scuffed my heels against the fountain. "No."

"Why not?"

"I don't know anything about poetry. I won't get it."

Shinork knelt at my feet. He was probably trying not to loom over me, but because I was already elevated, it made me look down at him as if he were a supplicant to a queen.

"Come on, Mani," he wheedled. "You may only be eight years old—"

"I'm seven."

"Okay, seven years old, but you're smarter than most adults. You read more, and more sophisticated books, than most adults. I

respect your literary opinion more than anyone else's here. Except maybe your parents and Firoze."

That was the trouble. Shinork didn't just want me to read his poem. He wanted me to critique it and I instinctively knew I would hate it. Then I would have to tell the truth and crush his feelings. I had an obsession with honesty, which didn't stop me from evasions and secretly reading adult books, but prevented me from telling outright lies. I lived in dread of the day someone would ask me outright, "Do you love Baba?" My only recourse was to refuse to read the poems.

Desperately, I said, "I hate poetry. All poetry. It could be the best poetry in the world, and I still wouldn't like it. I'm the wrong person to read your poems."

Shinork's thin lips pursed stubbornly. "Even if you didn't like it, you'd have intelligent reasons for not liking it."

Seven-year-old me and thirty-something-year-old Shinork stared each other down like gunslingers. Maybe it was Shinork's decision to kneel. But we both knew when I'd gained the upper hand.

"No. Make Mom read it. She likes spiritual poetry."

"Fine. I'll do that." He blew the dust from his manuscript and stalked away. I considered dashing around the hedges to warn her that he was coming and armed with iambs, but I'd never make it in time.

One resident rented a house in town apart from all three centers of Babadom. I didn't know her well because of her geographic isolation, but I envied her freedom. Carla had curly red hair and wore the usual female resident get-up of salwar kamiz dolled up with clunky hippie jewelry and a locket or pin with Baba's picture. Though she didn't talk much, she was worth listening to when she did.

"Even when I was a teenager, I always wanted to have a mystical experience," I once heard her say. "But that wasn't part of my family's life cycle. I was the odd one out. My sister wanted to go to college and join a sorority, and I wanted to go into the desert and chew peyote with Carlos Castaneda's teacher, Don Juan Coyote."

There were other reasons to pay attention whenever Carla started talking. Like most of the residents, she was a former hippie. Unlike any of the others, her hippie friends had once burned down a Bank of America during a student demonstration and she used to be a tarot card–reading witch. I'm not sure which accomplishment impressed me more. I used to beg her to read my cards, but she never would. She also denied having been an actual witch.

"I'm an ordained minister," she explained, "I did aura-readings and tarot-card readings, but it wasn't with a coven, it was with a New Age curse."

But most of the residents were concentrated at Meherabad, with a handful at the Compound and only Carla in town. Few Westerners were ever allowed to stay at Meherazad, where most of the mandali had their homes. It was the ambition of every resident to be invited to live at Meherazad. Dad used to tease Mom that Darlene, who had become her bitter rival for the mandali's attention, and the smarmy Saraswati would both move in before Mom would.

The mandali treasured their scraps of privacy, and I suspect that they found interacting with even the shyest residents tiring. To each other, the mandali were old friends or old rivals or old coworkers; to the residents, they were the Holy Chosen Ones. There's nothing like a worshipful gaze to inhibit relaxation. But they did keep a few residents at Meherazad whose usefulness surpassed their lack of mandali-hood.

Brady was a big husky hunk of a man whom the mandali kept at Meherazad to do heavy lifting. In keeping with his all-American looks, he was very straightforward—so much so that he responded to polite queries with unnecessary honesty. Once Firoze asked him where he had stayed on his last visit to America, and Brady ex-

plained that he had rented a room at a brothel so he could bang the whores at his leisure.

But he didn't get in serious trouble until Firoze requested that he stop shitting in the fields.

"There are toilets," said Firoze. "Use them instead."

"I like the fields better," explained Brady.

"Anybody can see you there," said Firoze. "They see a Western man squatting in the fields. It doesn't look good."

"I like the fields," said Brady stubbornly.

Eventually an ultimatum was issued: Stop shitting in the fields or leave Meherazad. Brady left.

I wondered sometimes if the residents were strange because they lived in Ahmednagar, or if their choice to move to an ashram proved that they'd been oddballs before they left. As the only person in the ashram who wasn't there by choice, I would be the test case. If I turned out like the other residents—if I started writing love poems to Baba, if I volunteered information about my morning dump, if I turned eighteen and decided to stay on as a full-time Baba-lover—it would be because that forge everyone kept talking about had melted me down.

INTERLUDE I: 1990

LIKE A VIRGIN

If you've looked at my bio on the book jacket, you know that I no longer live in Ahmednagar. How did I get out, you may be wondering: Did I leave by myself when I came of age, or did my parents get disillusioned with the ashram and take me back with them? And what in the world had my parents been thinking when they moved there in the first place?

I was still struggling with the latter question long after I left the ashram. I was also still pondering the one I raised at the end of the previous chapter: whether we shape our experiences or are shaped by them. Was I who I was because I had grown up on a bizarro ashram in India? Would my personality have been different if my parents had stayed in Los Angeles? What experiences in my parents' past had made them people who would decide to raise their only child on that bizarro ashram? Or was it all of our inborn personalities that had made our lives turn out the way they had?

While remembering the past is often helpful when trying to understand the present, the reverse can also be true: Examining the present sometimes sheds light on the past. When I was a child, I knew virtually nothing of the forces and events that had shaped my parents. Nor did I realize how my experiences in Ahmednagar were molding me into the adult I would become—or how I was molding my experiences in Ahmednagar. In order to illuminate those issues, I wrote four interlude chapters, which are about what happened to me and my parents after I left India.

I won't yet tell the story of how I escaped. But I will say that Dad and I moved back to America when I was twelve, but Mom stayed at the ashram. I rarely replied to her tissue-thin aerogrammes scribbled over with news of the mandali and reminders that she and Baba loved me. Nobody else's mother was in India worshipping a silent dead guy, and I didn't want to be reminded of just how different I was.

I'd discovered on my first day of junior high that being American in America was not a fit-in-free pass. I had a funny accent and a funny name, I didn't know any slang, I flinched when people made sudden moves, and the only Foreigner I'd heard of was me. And I read books. That was the clincher.

While my peers with social skills were out doing drugs and having sex, I spent the next five years crouched in my room writing clunky short stories about aliens and alienation. Then I stomped around the house waving my rejection slips and moaning that I'd *never* be a published author before I turned twenty.

"Why don't you write about Ahmednagar?" suggested Dad. "I've never seen a story about an American girl who grew up on an Indian ashram. I bet you could sell that."

I gave him a withering look. I was big on withering looks when I was seventeen. "I don't even want to *think* about that part of my life, let alone write about it."

But I could only crush it from my mind for ten months out of the year. I was sent back to visit Mom every summer, and the summer between high school graduation and college was no exception.

I boarded the plane without protest. My previous trips hadn't been *that* bad . . . except for the heat . . . and the open sewers . . . and Coconut demanding that I recite the Kaliyuga line . . . and Urmila yelling at me for sitting with my knees apart . . . and Mom giving me an hour-by-hour commentary on the state of her bowels . . . and . . .

The trouble with trying to forget your past is that you can't learn from events that you refuse to remember. As the plane began to taxi and memories of my previous trips flooded back, I realized that if I hadn't blocked them out before, I would never have agreed to the trip.

Mom and a driver picked me up at the Bombay airport and took me to Ahmednagar. Lulled by Mom's metronomic chant of "Baba, Baba, Baba, Baba, Baba, Baba, Baba," I fell asleep.

When we reached Ahmednagar, the car braked for a trio of cows in the road. A gang of raggedy kids playing marbles glanced up at the car. I favored them with a sorrowful smile. Poor things. They'd never go to college, never even own a book, never—

One of the kids peered at me. Her eyes widened in astonished recognition. "Mani Mao!" she shrieked.

The other children leaped up. "Mani Mao! Mani Mao!"

They clustered around the car, pulling faces, making threatening gestures, and banging on my window. As the driver screeched around the cows and children, I looked out the rear window. A little girl was hurling a rock at us.

"God!" I exclaimed. Those kids must have been toddlers when I left. Had their older siblings passed down the Legend of Mani Mao?

"Don't take the Lord's name in vain," said Mom.

We pulled into the Compound, and residents and mandali

swarmed up to hug and squeeze me. I clutched *The Mists of Avalon* to my chest. It was thick enough to provide some protection.

"Jai Baba," said Coconut, seizing my cheek between pincer-like fingers. "You are my little mummy. Tell me why it is that you're my mummy."

"Jai Baba." Urmila prodded my ribs. "Still so skinny. Still with a book. And what is wrong with your face? You must have Dr. Ambika see to that terrible rash."

I was painfully sensitive about the acne that flared against my pale skin and almost burst into tears. I glowered at the driveway as a preventive measure.

"Still sulky," remarked Saraswati jovially. "Smile!"

"Jai Baba," said Darlene. "My goodness, you haven't grown a bit. You're still so short!"

I was also painfully sensitive about having reached my full adult height at 5′0″. I glared at Darlene, Urmila, Saraswati, Coconut, and Mom for good measure. Then I realized that I didn't have to keep silent.

I said, "Darlene, you shouldn't tell people they're short. How would you like it if I said, 'Wow, you're fat?'"

"Mani!" exclaimed Darlene. "How rude."

"Tell us why it is that you are my little mummy," insisted Coconut.

"No," I said. "I won't."

"Mani." Mom put her hand on my shoulder. "Don't talk back to Coconut."

I shook her off and glared at him. "I'm not saying that line anymore."

Coconut beamed at me. "But you are still my little mummy. Why is it that you are my little mummy?"

I stomped off to Mom's room. She followed, scolding all the way: " . . . He's an old man and one of Baba's beloved mandali, and he loves you very much. It wouldn't have killed you to make him happy."

"Yes, it would." I plucked at my shirt, which was sweaty enough to reveal that my bra was a demi-cup. I turned on the overhead fan and lifted my face to it as it began to lazily stir the air.

"Baba!" exclaimed Mom. "Turn off the fan."

"It's an oven in here," I protested.

"Fans are unhealthy. I'll catch a chill."

"I tell you what," I suggested. "I'll take the bed that's under the fan, and you can have the one over there that's nice and hot."

Mom's lips trembled. "If you don't turn off the fan, I'll catch pneumonia and die. And it'll be your fault."

"Oh, come on. It's a hundred and ten in here."

"Fine, then," said Mom, stalking to her bag and removing a pair of bruised bananas. "Leave on the fan. If you want me to *die*."

"You're not going to die because of a fan!" I screamed, slamming down the off switch. "You're insane!"

"Don't you talk to your mother like that!"

I stomped off to the library and lingered in front of it in pleasant anticipation of all the interesting books pilgrims might have donated to it in the year since my last visit.

The door banged open. Ratanji loomed in the doorway.

"Eeek!"

"Arrr!"

We stared at each other with equal horror. His sores had spread from his face to his grimy hands, and his pants were blotched with yellow stains.

"*You* are here," snarled Ratanji. "To *read*. To read my books."

"That's right," I retorted with all the bravado I could muster. "I'm here to read."

"Rarrrrr," said Ratanji. His lips writhed as if manipulated by unseen strings. "Hurrrrr."

I ducked past him, seized a random book, and held it open in front of my face.

"Graaaaaarrrrr."

I turned a page.

"Yarrrrrr. Kurrrrrrr. Haaaaarrrrgh!"

I continued my perusal of *The Secret Life of Plants*. Unsurprisingly for a book plucked from the ashram library's science shelf, it claimed that houseplants are telepathic and can tell if their owners are having sex thousands of miles away, though it did not explain why they'd care. Several minutes and many guttural noises later, I heard the sweet sound of the mad librarian's footsteps in retreat. I put down the plant porn and picked up *Tally-ho, Jeeves!*

"Jai Baba, Mani."

I looked up from the floor, where I had squatted to read the W's. "Hi, Darlene," I said unenthusiastically.

Darlene gave me a sweet-for-Baba smile. "I'm sorry I said you were short. You're right, it was rude. I was just so thrilled to see you."

"Um . . . Okay."

"My goodness, you're grown up." Her gaze lingered on my sticky shirt. "You must be thinking of boys now."

That was another painful and sensitive topic. I did spend many wakeful nights contemplating the young Bob Dylan, the young Mick Jagger, and the young John Lennon. But teenage boys didn't appeal to me. And since girls were supposed to have crushes on real people they knew, that made me an asexual freak. (The boys I knew called me a dyke, but they were just being creeps. I didn't get crushes on girls either.) My upbringing had obviously stunted my sexual growth and doomed me to eternal virginity.

Besides, boys weren't interested in me. My hair dripped oil, I was practically a midget, my family was in a cult, and I liked to read. No wonder no one had asked me to the prom.

I shrugged. Darlene moved in closer, breathing heavily through her mouth. "I hope you're following beloved Baba's will, even though you're in America."

"What?"

"Are you a virgin?"

Life at the ashram must have finally driven Darlene over the edge. And she was looming over me, preventing my escape.

She loomed some more. "Well? Are you? Have you followed Baba's orders? Are you still a virgin like he wants you to be?"

I finally found my voice. "That's none of your business!"

Darlene took a step back. I stood up, depriving her of the loom factor. Perhaps she sensed that I was about to snap, for she scuttled away.

A week later Coconut was still harping on mummies, Mom and I were engaging in daily screaming matches, and Saraswati had harangued me for being a fallen woman when I refused to confirm or deny my state of virginity. I was ready to commit mass murder. Or at least turn on the ceiling fan. So I convinced Mom to go on vacation. We settled on a hill station called Kandala, which was supposed to be quiet, cool, and relaxing.

The air became soft with mist as the train snaked up the green hills. Mom put a third sweater on top of her second one. "Don't the hills remind you of Matheran?" she asked. "We had such fun on that trip."

"Except for the part where we almost got killed in a Jeep crash."

She passed me a thermos of ginger tea. "But the hotel was so nice. I remember how much you liked the monkeys in the garden"

"Yeah, but two days after we arrived, Indira Gandhi was assassinated, and we had to run for our lives."

"We didn't 'run for our lives.' We just felt it was best to leave."

"Mom, we 'felt it was best to leave' because people were saying the assassins had been sponsored by the CIA, and then all the stores put signs in the windows that said 'closed in case of riots.'"

"We left because of you," retorted Mom. "Your father and I would have stayed, but we wanted to make sure you were safe. Everything we did, we did for you."

"Yeah, blame it all on me."

Mom slammed the thermos back into her bag. An orange juice–colored stain spread across the side. "This is supposed to be a fun trip, so we can learn to appreciate each other as mother and daughter. Why do you always have to pick a fight?"

I didn't know myself exactly what it was that made me want to put a pickax through her head every time we talked for more than ten minutes. "Because I'm a teenager."

We got off the train and into a rickshaw. The driver, whom I had been relieved to note was of normal stature, pulled up at a . . . my jaw dropped . . . quaint Raj-era hotel.

Ensconced in a room with a pleasant pasture view, Mom unpacked and arranged her clothes, a framed Baba photo, two Baba books, three bananas, six guavas, two chikus, four pears, and an apple. Then she retreated to the bathroom. I sprawled on a bed and opened Barbara Hambly's *The Time of the Dark*. Before I finished the first paragraph, a tremendous crash sounded from the bathroom.

"Baba!"

I dashed up to the bathroom door. "Are you okay?"

"I think so," came Mom's shaky voice.

"What happened? Can I open the door?" It was one of Mom's peculiarities that she never locked the bathroom door. It had taken several pitched battles before I could even convince her to close it.

"Yes."

I opened the door. Mom, with her pants around her ankles, was sitting on the toilet seat. Which was sitting on the floor. The toilet had ripped out of the wall when she had sat down on it and was in several ceramic pieces scattered across the floor.

Serpent's tooth that I was, I started laughing. "I'm glad I wasn't the one who had to go."

"Oh, Mani." But she was laughing too. "This is why Indian toilets are better. They can't fall off the wall."

The owner of the hotel apologized and gave us another suite, this one with an Indian toilet and a view of woods with a creek running through it.

"The toilet was Baba's blessing in disguise," said Mom. "See, now we've got a better view."

It began to rain, so we called for room service. The chef recommended the tandoori chicken. It was tender and juicy and went well with the buttered naan. Stuffed and cozy, I couldn't even work up much indignation at having to pray to Baba before going to bed.

A scream woke me up. "Baba!"

I sat up. Rain was beating down on the roof, and Mom was sitting up in bed and staring down at the floor in horror. I put on my glasses and looked where she was looking. "Aaagh!"

The floor was rust-red and moving. That was because it was covered in a wall-to-wall carpet of stinging ants.

I had to leap from bed to chair to chair to get to the phone to call the owner. He appeared, once more full of apologies, with two boy assistants, each carrying a broom and a can of insecticide. Though the ants were soon disposed of, clouds of corrosive vapor remained.

"You should go for a walk," suggested the owner. "The smell will be gone when you return."

Mom's coughing fit stopped in mid-hack. "Oh, no. These are toxic fumes. We want another room."

The owner sighed. "Yes, madam. One couple is leaving this afternoon. You may have their room when you return."

Mom and I walked into the woods. The rain stopped, and a

rainbow appeared. "Look," said Mom. "It's a present from Baba, just for us."

I bristled. But since I could never tell her that I didn't believe in him, I had to try to accept her Baba-track mind.

A flash of sheet lightning reduced the tree trunks and a distant building to silhouettes. Thunder exploded in our ears like a sonic boom.

"Baba!"

The sky went black. We opened our umbrellas, but the wind blew the rain horizontally and each drop stung like a thrown pebble. We ran for the building, which proved to be a ruined monastery filled with bats and pigeons.

"Just the place for a picnic," said Mom, squatting on the rotted floorboards. Like a conjurer, she opened her bag and whisked out a thermos of hot mint tea, a tiffin of cold tandoori chicken, two oranges, and a box of sesame chikki.

I worried a scrap of meat from a thigh bone and watched the rain wash the forest clean. "I love watching storms. It's the one thing I miss about India . . . I mean, the one *thing* I miss. As opposed to people."

Mom's eyes filled with tears. "Oh, Mani. I miss you so much. I know I'm not as entertaining as your father—he's always telling all those funny stories—but—"

I moved quickly to avert an emotional scene. "Mom, you tell funny stories too. You should tell them more often."

"Really? You like my stories?"

"Sure I do." It was odd how her stories all took place in the present day or recent past. Almost none of them predated my birth. No wonder Dad had a wider selection. He was mining a larger range. "Why don't you tell me a funny story from when you were a kid?"

Mom's face went still, like a bucket of water freezing over. "I can't think of any."

"Come on, you must have some."

"No. I don't." Her lips parted in a wide, fake smile. "I'm afraid you have a boring old mother—no stories."

Several puzzle pieces of information suddenly fitted together in my mind. I didn't believe in plant *or* human telepathy, but this instant of realization came so fast and clear that it felt like a psychic flash.

You were abused as a child, I thought. *That explains so much.*

I said, "What was your father like?"

"Oh . . . well . . . we don't really get along."

"Why not?"

"Well, munchkin, you know sometimes it's hard for parents and children to communicate. Even you and I don't always understand each other."

"Yeah, but what sort of things did you fight about?"

"He doesn't believe in Baba, so he didn't approve of my moving to India. That's all." She leaned over and hugged me. "Isn't this wonderful? Aren't we having a fun time, just you and me? Baba must have arranged this storm just for us, so we could have this lovely picnic."

The cold in the air was nothing compared with the cold inside me, as if icy water were filling up my hollow body. Mom's father must have done terrible things to her, but she would never tell me and I could never ask. I could never tell her I didn't believe in the God she'd devoted herself to. That would be saying her whole life was a lie. The rainbow, the storm, and the ruined monastery were romantic stage sets for a long-running play whose actors had long since ceased to believe in their lines.

"Look," said Mom. "It's a full moon."

Our new suite had a picture window overlooking a waterfall tumbling into an elfin glen. The rain never stopped, so we ordered in. It

turned out that tandoori chicken and buttered naan were not merely the specialties of the house, but the only items on the menu. We ate our déjà vu dinner without enthusiasm.

I awoke the next morning to a familiar shriek. "Baba!"

"What now?"

Mom stood in the middle of the floor in a billowing white nightgown, with her black hair tumbled about her shoulders. The overage Gothic heroine pointed a trembling finger as she averted her eyes from the terrible sight.

Once I put on my glasses, I had to agree with her assessment. "Eeeewww!"

The picture window was black and pulsed like a live thing. That was because it was blanketed with flies.

"I guess we could switch rooms again," I said. "But we'd probably get the plague of locusts suite."

Mom shook her head. "This was the last available room. So don't say anything to the owner, or he'll spray toxic chemicals everywhere."

"But what about those flies?"

"We can swat them."

"Mom, that's Planet of the Flies out there. Let's get the insecticide and just use a little bit of it."

"If I inhale any of those chemicals my airway will swell up and I'll suffocate and *die*."

"Flies carry diseases. If we leave them there, maybe I'll catch one and die."

Mom clucked. "Don't be silly."

Three days later, the rainstorm was still going strong, and Mom and I, along with the flies and the three-item menu, were still stuck in the same room. Tempers were flaring, and the fruit was running low.

"Don't you talk back to me," called Mom from the bathroom. She had taken to leaving the door ajar. "Unnnh. Oh, Baba, Baba, Baba. This rich food isn't agreeing with me."

“I’m not going to talk to you at all while you’re on the toilet,” I yelled from the bed. “It’s disgusting.”

“You shouldn’t be ashamed of natural bodily functions,” retorted Mom.

“I’m not *ashamed*, I just think it’s gross not to close the door. I can hear everything.”

“So? Everybody shits.” She said the last word with some satisfaction, daring me to call her on her language so she could lecture me on shitting being a natural bodily function. We’d had that argument at least twice before.

“Yeah, well, everybody shouldn’t hear it.”

“That’s what’s wrong with the West. It’s all mind and technology and no connection to nature.”

Plop.

“I’ve got my fingers in my ears!” I screamed. “I’m not listening!”

I did not, in fact, have my fingers in my ears. I was writing in my diary.

India is the right place for her, all right—just not for me. I’m a city girl. As I write this, I’m worrying about whether she’ll want to read it or ask me what I’m writing or read it on the sly or even accidentally.

If you are reading this, please stop. It’s private. You should be ashamed of yourself.

We went back to Ahmednagar the next day, making a smooth transition between clothes drenched with rain and clothes drenched with sweat. I promptly fled for the library but was accosted before I could reach sanctuary.

“Jai Baba,” said Urmila. “I have been meaning to ask, but you always run away from me. Are you pure?”

"What?"

"Have you kept yourself pure for Baba? Have you? Are you . . ." She eyed my chest. "A *virgin?*"

I ran away.

The day I left Ahmednagar, Darlene thrust an envelope into my hand with instructions to read it in private. I opened it after Mom had wept me onto the plane.

Dear Mani,

I'm writing to apologize. I realize now that I acted inappropriately, and you must have thought I was quite insane! I think a lot of us residents have trouble dealing with the fact that you left us as a child, but now you are a young woman. Anyway, I wanted to let you know that the next time you come here, I will not badger you about matters that are really none of my business.

In beloved Baba's love,

Darlene

An apology! I was pleased and amazed. But I wanted one signed by all the perpetrators of all the virginity interrogations I'd endured in the past two months, with an attachment by Coconut regarding the Kaliyuga age and Mom regarding fans, toilets, and my entire childhood.

In lieu of that, I vowed to erase all vestiges of my past. It would be hard. Even my name, Manija Mehera Brown, was copied from two mandali. Like everything from my childhood, it was a millstone around my neck. No one could pronounce it and every time I introduced myself, a long explanation of matters I didn't want to discuss was required. That put me in a hostile and snappish mood, so I made a bad first impression on everyone I met.

I would change my name. I would choose one that *I* liked, one with no connection to the ashram. It would be easily pronounced and spelled. It would not lend itself to stupid nicknames. It would be from the Jewish heritage that my parents had rejected. And it would mean something to me.

I had reread Milt Frimpkis' "X-Men" comics on my trip and had been struck by how much I had in common with one of the characters. She came from an alternate future where mutants were put in concentration camps. Her face had been tattooed, and she had been forced to use her telepathy to track down other mutants. She escaped into the past but never told anyone what she had done. She telepathically made people think her face was normal and she tried to fit in, but she couldn't live with her memories and finally had another mutant erase them for her.

Her name was Rachel Summers.

Rachel. I was Rachel.

Dad drove me home from the airport. I was determined to ask him about Mom. He'd reply, "What are you talking about?" or "What an awful thing to say!" But I'd repeat the question till I got an answer. Dad and Mick Jagger were singing about Ruby Tuesday, who wouldn't say where she came from. I interrupted them.

"Dad!" My voice sounded stagy and unnatural. "Was Mom sexually abused when she was a child?"

Mick Jagger informed us that yesterday didn't matter once it was gone. I disagreed.

Dad said thoughtfully, "I've always wondered."

"You've what? What do you mean? Don't you know? Why didn't you ask?"

"I don't know if you've noticed, Mani, but your mother doesn't remember any of her childhood before the age of twelve."

"Really?" Psychic flash my ass. In fact, I'd been shamefully unobservant.

"Uh-huh." Dad returned to harmonizing.

"One more thing," I was dying to shock my shock-proof Dad. "I'm changing my name. To Rachel!"

"Okay," said Dad.

"And I never want to go to Ahmednagar again. I don't have to keep visiting when I'm in college, do I?"

Dad shrugged. "Not if you don't want to."

I spent the next few miles brooding over my summer, my mother's past, and the impossibility of getting a rise out of Dad. It was like a cosmic scale weighing Mom's hysteria against Dad's imperturbability to maintain a universal balance. Where did I fit in?

Dad and Mick Jagger were singing about thoughts that they couldn't make disappear. She smiled sweetly, but still they worried. Lay off the disappearing, Mick, I thought. Mom had forgotten her entire childhood, and look where that got her. My attempts to forget mine had made me repeat the same mistake every summer. No, there was nothing to be gained by erasing the past. From now on, I would remember every detail of every moment I'd ever spent in India.

I'd just never tell anyone about it.

16

RAJA NAAG

After I'd been living in Ahmednagar for about six months, I was given permission to explore the ashram grounds by myself. Being allowed to roam the countryside solo was the biggest advantage of my parents' laissez-faire approach to child-rearing. But I had to do it stealthily, lest I be waylaid by interfering mandali, residents, and pilgrims.

As the only resident child, everyone connected to the ashram felt that they had a stake in my discipline. After months of scoldings from just about everyone for climbing trees, playing in the dirt, touching lizards, sitting with my knees apart, having untidy hair, looking sullen, and doing anything at all other than sitting in Baba's Hall and listening to the mandali tell stories about Baba, my demeanor began to resemble that of a spy behind enemy lines.

One day at Meherazad I slunk past Baba's Hall, then paused near the open door of Coconut's office to eavesdrop on the lecture he was giving to a bunch of enthralled pilgrims. I was perversely fascinated by how incomprehensible he was and also by his ability to imply capital letters in spoken words.

"It is the Divine Will," Coconut was saying. "But it is not the Divine Wish. We will not know the Divine Wish until Beloved Baba's Universal Manifestation."

Fingers snapped, calling my attention to Baba's Caravan. Dad looked up from the Caravan bunk he'd been napping on. "Where're you going?"

"Exploring."

"By yourself?"

"I'm not going far."

"Why don't you ask the pilgrim kid to go with you?"

"Zen's seventeen. He's not going to want to go lizard-catching with a seven-year-old girl."

"How do you know?"

"I just do." I regarded the gray-eyed Zen with bedazzlement and awe. He was handsome and older and American and male, and I could no more have spoken to him than I could have ridden a gecko to the moon. Also his two-week stay was almost up, and I'd already been burned by getting attached to visiting pilgrim kids whom I'd never see again once they returned to America.

"You're always going to be alone if you never even try to make friends."

I shrugged.

"All right, then. Go and be by yourself." Dad lay back down and closed his eyes.

I proceeded into Baba's Garden. Pilgrims loved the roses and stiff unscented zinnias, but I liked the Gul Mohr trees best. At the beginning of summer their punkah-fan leaves fall and seedpods appear, long and brown as a child's arm. They rattle when you shake them. When they ripen they split in half with a bang and spill out striped oval seeds the texture of aged marble. At the height of summer, after the last seedpods have fallen and before a single leaf appears, the Gul Mohrs bloom overnight and become shady scarlet bonfires. The flowers are as complex as orchids, as intricately detailed as the rest of the tree.

I picked up a seedpod and brandished it like a sword. Whack! I struck a tall weed dead.

"Mani! Don't destroy the flowers."

"It's not a flower." I held up the battered stalks for Saraswati's inspection. "I read in *India Today* that Congress grass is one of the seven most devastating weeds in the world."

"You shouldn't hit things in Baba's Garden. It isn't peaceful." The resident smoothed her sari. "Why don't you sit and listen to Firoze like a good little girl?"

"Dad said I could walk around." I stuck the seedpod into a water tank and scooped out a yellow-and-black toad.

"Really, Mani," said Saraswati. "You know the mandali don't like you to play with frogs."

"It's a toad. See, it has warts." I extended the toad-on-a-stick toward her.

"Baba! You dripped muddy water on my sari."

"Oops," I said unrepentantly, and stared into her pale eyes.

Saraswati blinked first. "Don't think I won't tell your mother."

She hustled away, and I dismissed her from my mind. It wasn't as if my parents had a lot of leverage in terms of punishing me. What were they supposed to do, ban me from watching our nonexistent TV?

The toad's eyes were old gold shot with black. I placed it in a flowerbed. Frogs could live in water tanks, but toads were land animals and would eventually drown. The chubby toad sat still, then began shoving its hindquarters into the earth. With astonishing

speed, it wriggled its way into the ground until nothing but its golden eyes showed. Then it closed its eyes and vanished. For a moment a tiny patch of earth buckled and humped to show its progress, and then even that ceased.

Despite everyone's efforts to thwart me, I was learning more from the land than I did in school. I marked the spot with a pebble, so I could dig down later and see if it was still there.

"Jai Baba, darling. What are you doing?"

I looked up. It was Darlene.

"Nothing."

"My goodness, that seems to be a favorite game for children—nothing!" Darlene let out a merry tinkling laugh.

I gave her my patented stare. I had discovered that if I kept it up long enough and didn't blink, I would disconcert many adults and cause some to panic and flee.

Darlene wasn't one of them. "Well, Mani, I have some very special news for you. Can you guess what it is?"

"No."

"You've been chosen to have tea with Paribanu this afternoon," she breathed into my ear. "And I'll be serving it. Isn't that wonderful?"

"Uh-huh. Is my Mom serving too?"

The stare hadn't worked but the question did. Darlene's lips compressed and her eyes went squinty, transforming her into The Blonde with No Name.

"Yes," she spat out. "Da-nonna was also chosen."

Paribanu's custom of having tea with a select group of women was the cause of more jealousy, conniving, and outright feuds than any other ritual in the Baba community. She had tea twice a week at a table that seated fourteen. Paribanu and other female mandali took four of those seats. The rest were apportioned among the twenty to sixty female pilgrims and residents who were present. In addition to the seats, two female residents were selected to serve the tea. This was the highest honor of all and was viciously contested, especially by Mom and Darlene.

Darlene patted me on the shoulder, fairly hard. "You get invited to tea every single time you're here. I hope you appreciate what a unique blessing that is."

"It's just because I'm the only kid."

"Yes, you are. And that makes you very special. You know, Mani, sometimes I get the impression that you don't appreciate all the gifts from Baba that you're getting."

I considered digging up the toad and dropping it down her blouse. Instead I added an extra dose of malevolence to my stare.

"Well, Mani? Do you understand what an incredible blessing it is to spend time with Paribanu?"

"I like the tea," I said. "It's got mint in it."

Darlene's mouth twitched. Her ears turned red.

"Jai Baba," I said sweetly. "I'm going to catch some lizards. I'll be back in time for tea."

Before she could launch another offensive, I dashed down the path. I ducked around to the side of the women mandali's bedrooms and checked for spying eyes; then I plucked a sprig of datura, a succulent relative of deadly nightshade whose blossoms were rubbery stars of purple and white. I dabbed away the milky sap, stuck it into my left braid, then searched the bougainvillea for a matching flower. The vines twined around trees and swallowed walls like kudzu, brilliant against bark and concrete. Royal purple, magenta, maroon, scarlet, light pink, dark pink, hot pink, orange, peach, white. I settled on one white and one purple blossom for my right braid.

It was impressive how pretty Baba's Garden was, given the unpromising land it existed on. Ahmednagar's native plants were the spindly weeds and poisonous succulents that can survive in soil that

was often as desiccated as the surface of the moon. But as Mom often said, everything has a bright side, and there's more to a landscape than pretty vistas. The land around Meherazad was scrubland, all hills and valleys and the twisting, interlocking ravines called nullahs. The hills were pocked with caves and faceted with cliffs steep enough to be challenging but rough enough to be inviting to a light and nimble girl.

In addition to rock climbing, Ahmednagar had some other points of interest for non-Baba-lovers. It was a paradise for herpetologists, with six species of poisonous snake: four types of vipers whose bite causes gangrene if it doesn't kill, the small but deadly striped krait, and the king cobra, the Raja Naag of Kipling's tales, whose neurotoxic venom can kill a child in minutes.

And though true iguanas, whose splendid scientific name is iguana iguana iguana, are not native to India, iguana-like lizards were everywhere. They were easy to catch, as long as I held them by the nape of their spiny necks so they couldn't turn and bite me. The huge-eyed gray geckos were faster and more of a challenge. But the blue-bellied skinks were the biggest prize of all, being both the rarest and the fastest of all the lizards. I had a craving to capture a skink.

As if in answer to my desire, I heard a rustle. Animals fled if you moved, so I froze.

A head peeped out from a pile of dead leaves. I recognized the black snake-like head of a skink. Ever so smoothly and quietly, I edged up until I was less than a foot away. As soon as more of its body was out, I'd stoop and grab it behind the head.

It poked its head further from the pile. It had an awfully long neck for a skink. In fact . . .

In one smooth motion, a king cobra slithered out of the leaves.

It was close enough to strike the second I moved to flee or attack. The nearest antivenom was twenty minutes away, and the bite of a king cobra could kill in ten. I remembered what Grandpa Artie said about dangerous animals—"If you don't bother them, they won't bother you"—and breathed more softly.

I could have touched it with my sandaled foot. It was six feet long, black, and shiny as a beetle. I could see the folds of its hood. The cobra lay sunning itself, then slid into the bushes. I heard footsteps. A band of pilgrims was approaching.

I had my orders regarding the sighting of a poisonous snake near anyone's house, and for once I agreed with them. The cobra was sleek and elegant, but so is a well-polished gun. I dashed up to the pilgrims.

"I just saw a cobra!" I exclaimed. "Quick, you've got walking sticks, come and kill it."

The pilgrims stared at me, then laughed. "A cobra, huh? Was it a biiig scaaary cobra?"

"I'm serious. It was right by Zireen's bedroom."

"Suuure it was. I hear cobras looove bedrooms."

"It was! It went into those bushes over there!"

"Uh-huh. Those biiig scaaary bushes."

I gave up on them and ran back to Meherazad proper, where I found Harry Carroll, who was willing to come hunt it. By then the cobra was long gone.

A week later a six-foot cobra was found and killed in Zireen's bedroom. The servants burned the body, believing that if they left it out, its mate would find it and seek revenge. A month later, a second, smaller cobra was killed near Paribanu's porch. In all the years I was there, I only once saw a cobra in the wild.

Undaunted by the cobra incident, as time went on I continued my study of the local ecology. Though Ahmednagar was usually drought-stricken and some years the rainy season failed to occur at all, the monsoon made a spectacular appearance near the end of my first year there. It came not as gentle pattering rain but as a city-

wide waterfall. Land that had cracked in the heat by Saturday night was under a foot of water by Sunday morning. Rainwater filled the valleys and interlocking nullahs. The plains became strips of mud between rushing rivers and lakes the shape of puzzle pieces. The streets flooded silver, the hills turned emerald, and frogs hopped away from every step I took.

The Meherazad creek became an ecosystem overnight, populated with silver fish the size of trout, minnows, crayfish, snails, waterweeds, tadpoles, frogs, crabs, and transparent ghost shrimp. I coaxed my parents into buying me an aquarium, which I stocked with my catches from the creek and reservoir.

The reservoir was a vast water tank near Meherazad. Sometimes I saw water snakes in it, pale shapes floating vertically below the surface and gently writhing, dancing to an aquatic piper. Water crept up the concrete stairs leading into the reservoir and coated them with moss. Finger-long walking catfish clustered on the damp steps above the waterline, clinging with the fins near their heads and bobbing gently when a wave lapped over them. The air smelled of fresh water that is still but not stagnant, a green smell touched with blue.

The walking catfish almost provoked a servant's strike at the Compound. A few days after I introduced eight of them to the aquarium, I returned from Holy Wounds to discover that they were all gone. I was baffled. Had a goos eaten them? Had a servant swiped them? After prolonged mulling produced no sensible explanation, I took off my patent leather shoes and wandered barefoot toward the bookcase.

Squish.

There, stuck dead and damp to my sole, was the solution to the mystery.

I searched for the remaining seven, but I couldn't find them. Figuring they must have died under furniture where they'd dry up peacefully and never be found, I decided not to mention the matter to my parents.

For the next week, one catfish per day emerged from hiding, walked to a part of the floor where a barefoot servant would step on it before she saw it, and died. The servants were outraged. Mom was annoyed. Dad was amused. I got a lid for the aquarium.

Except for such brief moments when circumstances brought us together, my parents and I lived in separate worlds. Dad wandered the periphery of the spiritual life, Mom lived in Baba-land, and I bolted for the least sacred places I could find the instant I was released from Holy Wounds.

If I had been more extraverted, I might have befriended every single pilgrim kid who ever showed up for a two-week stay. If I had been less independent, I might have stuck closer to Mom or Dad. If I had been less stubborn, I might have embraced Baba and the Baba scene. And if I had been the reincarnation of Martin Luther King, I might have gotten the local kids to accept me.

But I was only me.

I was lonely at school, at home, in the town, and in the Baba places. But I wasn't lonely in the country. I wasn't even alone. I was surrounded by life.

I wouldn't wish my childhood on even the most overscheduled and overprotected American kid. But no amount of video games can make up for growing up without ever climbing a tree or cliff, without mapping out the nullahs with a gecko in your pocket, without learning how far a solitary shepherd's cry can carry across the plains.

Ahmednagar did have some there there, after all.

17

Fourteen at Holy Wounds

Much as I enjoyed exploring the countryside, I was only able to do so on weekends when I visited Meherabad and Meherazad. The Compound was in the middle of the town and every time I ventured alone outside of its walls, the local kids greeted me with a chorus of "Mani Mao!" and a shower of hurled rocks. So my weekdays were mostly spent indoors, and most of that time was at Holy Wounds.

Though the nuns had told my parents that they did not attempt to convert the students, a Catholic indoctrination class was mandatory but was cunningly disguised with the title "Moral Science." I spent my weekdays being lectured on Jesus and my weekends being lectured on Baba, and though Mom insisted that they were the same person, I felt a definite sense of whiplash.

Some of the Moral Science lessons were perplexing all by themselves. Reading the textbook one night, I grew more and more puzzled. I no longer have the book, but its text is burned into my memory:

"Maria was a good little girl who loved Our Lord Jesus Christ the Savior with all her heart. She lived next door to a bad boy named Alessandro. Alessandro did not believe in Our Lord Jesus Christ the Savior. Maria often begged Alessandro to take Jesus into his heart, but the bad boy would not listen to her.

"One day Alessandro came to Maria's house when her mother was not home.

" 'Good morning, Maria,' said the bad boy. Then he asked Maria to do a bad thing.

"Poor Maria was horrified!

" 'Oh, no, Alessandro,' she said. 'I will not do that bad thing. Our Lord Jesus Christ the Savior says we must not do bad things.'

"When Alessandro saw that Maria would not do the bad thing, he grew angry. He drew his knife and cut her in fourteen places. Maria fell down dying. Then the bad boy ran away.

"When Maria's mother came home she found her beloved daughter lying on the ground, bleeding from fourteen wounds.

"Maria's mother screamed in horror. Then she knelt beside her beloved daughter.

" 'Oh, Maria, what has happened to you?' asked Maria's mother.

" 'Alessandro cut me with a knife,' said Maria. '"He did it because I would not do a bad thing. But do not be angry with Alessandro. I forgive him. I am going now to join Our Lord Jesus Christ the Savior in heaven. Goodbye, mother!'

"Then the good little girl died.

"We must be like the good girl Maria. We must forgive those who harm us. We must not do bad things, even if it costs us our life. If we die because we will not do bad things, we will be blessed for-

ever and go to heaven to be with the angels and Our Lord Jesus Christ the Savior."

I have no idea why the characters in Moral Science parables always had names like Giuseppe and Lucrezia, unless the books were imported directly from the Vatican. But once I finished boggling at Gopal and Rupali learning morality from Alessandro and Maria, I got stuck on the bad thing Alessandro had wanted Maria to do. As in, what bad thing was it?

Telling lies? Throwing rocks? Robbing a liquor store? I reread the story, but there were no clues regarding the nature of the bad thing. How was I supposed to avoid doing it when I didn't know what it was? And what was the significance of the number fourteen?

I took the story to Mom and asked her to explain it. She read it leaning precariously against one of the pencil-thin iron bedposts that supported the mosquito netting, now bundled atop the frame for the day. Then she sighed and gave me back the book. Her round face sagged with distress, presumably due to the tragic death of Maria.

"Do you get it?" I asked. "Do you know what the bad thing is?"

"Yes, I know," said Mom sepulchrally.

"Well, what is it?"

Mom looked even more pained. Maria's bloody demise must have really gotten to her. "It's . . . um . . . you see . . . well, you know what the fourteen cuts mean, right?"

"He stabbed her fourteen times?"

Her voice dropped to a dramatic whisper. "They mean rape. Alessandro raped Maria."

"Oh." I knew what rape was, thanks to a novel Dad had borrowed from The Goldberg. It was called *The Dice Man* and was about a man who made all his decisions by rolling dice. "If I roll a twelve, I'll rape Arlene," shrieked the inside cover in thirty-point type.

"What's rape?" I'd asked Dad.

"Er . . . sex by force," he'd said, his hands twitching in apparent indecision over whether or not he should yank the book from my innocent grasp.

"Huh. *Did* he roll a twelve?" I asked, demonstrating at one blow my ignorance of both sex and narrative structure.

"Er . . . yes."

To Dad's relief, I'm sure, that satisfied my remaining curiosity.

But I was a long way from puberty and sex, let alone rape, was not the first thing that came to mind when I thought about sin. "But what was the bad thing Alessandro wanted to do?"

"I told you. It was rape."

"Oh."

"I have to disinfect the vegetables now," chirped Mom and bolted.

We really did disinfect the vegetables. They were soaked for hours in a pink solution of potassium permanganate, a process known imaginatively as "pinking."

I mulled over Mom's interpretation after she took off. If rape was the bad thing, why did Alessandro ask Maria if he could do it? If something was, by definition, done by force, why ask permission? I gave up, added it to my growing list of inexplicable things, and hoped we wouldn't be tested on it.

For some time afterward, I was under the impression that "fourteen" was a euphemism for "rape." This made a number of conversations and newspaper articles both intriguing and mystifying, as references to rape seemed to appear in stories about everything from birthday parties to the Indian national debt.

But then, I was used to being confused. Not long after I quizzed Mom about Maria and Alessandro, I was approached by the Compound's resident hermit, Shinork. He had often seen me dashing from the ashram library with a book of fairytales

clutched in my hands, pursued by howls of fury from the mad librarian Ratanji, and so had figured out that I liked stories of myth and legend.

"Psst," he said, beckoning to me conspiratorially. Shinork did everything conspiratorially. "Firoze told me a good Khizir story today. Want to hear it?"

Khizir is a holy spirit from Islamic folklore, something like a guardian angel, who pulls drowning men from rivers or guides lost travelers in the desert. Khizir is always dressed in green, which is the sacred color of Islam. Some say that he is not a single spirit, but one of many: Any spirit doing the job of Khizir is called Khizir.

"Hey, Shinork," I said, "What is Khizir, exactly? I know he rescues people, but what is he?"

The explanation I gave above would have satisfied my curiosity. But Shinork was not used to talking to children. Or, for that matter, adults.

"Khizir isn't a person," he explained. "Khizir is an office."

"An *office*?" I had never heard the word "office" used to mean "job" or "role." As far as I was concerned, offices were buildings or rooms in buildings with desks and typewriters and telephones.

"Yes, that's right."

"Khizir isn't a person. Khizir is an office," I repeated, sure that I'd heard it wrong.

"Uh-huh."

"But . . . it dresses in green . . . and it helps people . . . and it's an *office*?" I asked, thoroughly bewildered.

"Yes."

"But . . . how can that be?"

"Anything is possible for God."

For years after that, every time I heard a story about Khizir, I pictured that rescuer of lost travelers in the Arabian desert as a flying green office building. With swivel chairs.

It didn't seem any more implausible than divine faces on trees, magical chocolate poop, or God banging his head against the floor till he knocked his teeth loose. Or than the terrible true meaning of the number fourteen.

18

The Adolescent Girl

At the end of my first year in Ahmednagar, I got my first break from ashram life. Grandpa Artie the Communist remarried, and I acquired Grandma Anne. Mom refused to leave India, but that spring Dad and I flew back to America to visit them.

The Grandpas A, as I dubbed them, had moved to Santa Barbara, a resort town near Los Angeles. Grandpa Artie hadn't changed at all. He and I were watching a nature show on TV when it was interrupted by a special bulletin. "Ronald Reagan, the President of the United States, has been shot," said the pale-faced announcer.

Without missing a beat, Grandpa Artie snarled, "That son of a bitch, I hope he dies!"

I had never heard a grown-up say anything like

that before. I was shocked and disapproving. And amused and perversely proud. Grandpa Artie kept no silences.

Grandma Anne was a plump little woman with curly hair and a passion for blackjack. She was kind and generous, and told me she loved me within ten minutes of meeting me. She seemed to mean it too.

The entire set-up had to be too good to be true.

I found out how my first night there. They had given me a room of my own and after dinner, I'd gone in, shut the door, briefly savored the privacy, then stretched out on the bed to read.

Thirty seconds later: knock-knock. Grandma Anne poked in her head. "What are you doing?"

"Reading."

"Reading what, dear?"

"*The Jolliest Term on Record.*"

"What's it about?"

"Boarding school."

"Do you like it?"

"Uh-huh." I pretended the conversation was over and went back to reading.

"Well, good night, dear."

"Good night."

She retreated, leaving the door open. I got up and closed it.

Five minutes later: knock-knock. Grandma Anne came back in. "Oh, are you still reading?"

"Yes."

"Why do you keep the door closed?"

"I like it that way."

"Why, dear?"

"I just do."

"Your Grandpa and I are playing cards in the living room. You could come watch."

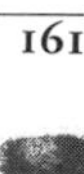

“Thanks, but I’d rather read.”

“All right, dear.”

She went out, leaving the door open. I closed it.

Five minutes later: knock-knock.

“I’m going to wash my hair,” I said, concealing *The Jolliest Term on Record* inside my blouse and hastening to the bathroom. Ensconced where no one would dream of knocking, I would shower first, then leave the water running while I read in peace.

I was luxuriating in the free-flowing hot water when it happened: knock-knock.

I turned off the shower. “What?!”

“Are you okay in there?”

“Of course I am.”

“Can I come in?”

“No! I’m in the shower.”

“Do you need any help?”

“I’m eight!” I shrieked. “I can wash my own hair!”

“All right, dear.”

Five minutes later: knock-knock . . .

What good was a room of my own when someone was always peeking inside? What good was a door that had to be left open? I knew that Grandma Anne meant well, and I liked her. But I was not accustomed to moment-to-moment supervision, while she couldn’t rest unless she knew what everyone was doing, thinking, and feeling, twenty-four seven three-sixty-five. And I loved reading more than anything else, but she insisted on having a conversation with me every time I tried to open a book. We got along fine for a visit of an hour or two, but as housemates, we were doomed.

I also disapproved of her taste in art. Pre-Grandma Anne, Grandpa Artie’s walls had featured Ansel Adams prints, Mexican folk art, and a watercolor depicting the woods at Nature Friends. Grandma Anne added several modern paintings that I didn’t appreciate, though she tried her best to convince me that it took more skill to paint a duck that didn't look like a duck than one that did, and the Adolescent Girl.

The Adolescent Girl was a life-size statue of a naked girl with breasts like sliced ping-pong balls, standing with her legs spread, her hands clutching her crotch, and an expression of agonized tension on her horsey wooden face. Grandma Anne thought she represented a sensitive young girl's ambivalent feelings about her inevitable passage to womanhood. I thought she was about to wet herself.

Grandma Anne and I had a lot of arguments over the artistic merit of the Adolescent Girl. To my annoyance, she once suggested that my own ambivalent feelings about my inevitable passage to womanhood were affecting my response to the monstrosity.

Dad did not get along with Grandma Anne either, but for different reasons. She badgered him to return to America and sometimes even hinted that he was an irresponsible parent to bring me up in a Third World backwater. That suggestion must have struck home, for it never failed to send him into a rage. I was torn about those arguments. On the one hand, I agreed with her. On the other hand, go Dad!

"But *why* won't you come back to the U.S.?" she nagged. "You've had your fun. Now it's time to come home."

"I didn't go for fun," snapped Dad, "and I'll come back when I damn well please."

"You should at least let little Mani come back. Poor thing. What kind of life can she have there? What sort of education is she getting?"

"None of your goddamn business!"

"She's my granddaughter, so it's very much my business. You're not giving that bright child the opportunities she deserves. What are colleges going to think when she hands them a transcript from Holy Wounds of Jesus Christ the—"

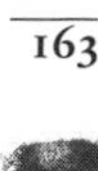

Dad leaped to his feet. Towering over Grandma Anne, who cringed back into her chair, he thrust his hand into her face, middle finger first. "FUCK YOU!" he bellowed. "JUST SHUT THE FUCK UP!"

Then he sat back down, smiled, and said, "Were we having steak tonight?"

Dad prided himself on such lightning changes of mood. As he would often say afterward, "I was never angry. I just wanted to make a point." And laugh. Other people, myself included, tended to find this unnerving in the extreme.

There was a long silence. Then Grandma Anne said, beginning meekly but quickly gaining in confidence, "All the same, Joe, you need to consider the child. I don't think she's happy in Ahmednagar, and I must say, I don't think it's any place to raise a sensitive young . . ."

Between the daily Dad versus Grandma screaming matches, the impossibility of reading without being interrupted every few pages, and the equal impossibility of getting one-on-one quality time with Grandpa Artie, I was somewhat relieved when Dad and I got on a plane to return to India.

Dad leaned back in his aisle seat as we reached the coast of India. "Can you see Bombay?"

I put down *Cherry Ames, Boarding School Nurse* and peered out the window. "Yeah, we're almost at the airport."

"So," said Dad with a mischievous grin. "Do you miss Grandma Anne already?"

I laughed. "You know, Mom would say Grandma was Baba's way of making me appreciate India."

"I think she was Baba's little joke on you."

The plane circled above the airport, then dropped like a stone. Passengers yelped and clutched at their seats. The plane climbed upward and began circling again.

The intercom crackled. "This is the pilot speaking. We are unable to land in Bombay at this time. All runways are occupied. Please be patient during this delay."

The plane dropped again, rose and circled and dropped, rose and circled and dropped. I became uncomfortably conscious of the location of my stomach within my body. I could feel it bouncing and lurching against its moorings and making tentative internal heaves.

I looked to see if Dad was also feeling sick, but he wasn't there. Typically, he had disappeared at the first sign of trouble and was presumably hiding in a bathroom. I started to get up to find one for myself.

A stewardess stopped me. "You must stay in your seat now. We will be landing soon."

I sat back down. The plane circled, then dropped. I swallowed. Maybe I should take out the barf bag, just in case. I eyed the passenger in the window seat to see how embarrassing it would be if I threw up in front of him. He was purse-lipped and elderly, with pince nez, sitting primly upright with his hands folded precisely in his lap.

It would be very embarrassing.

The plane climbed, then circled. My seatmate turned to me and proffered a small metal box. In an incredibly English voice, he said, "Lemon drop?"

The airplane plummeted. I threw up all over him, me, and his lemon drops.

Maybe Dad was right about Baba's little jokes. It did feel as if someone up there was laughing.

19

Bat Family Brown

When I was in America, I missed India's countryside and my freedom to explore it, but once I was back in India, I missed America's lack of rock-throwing kids and ruler-wielding nuns. But there wasn't much to choose between my female relatives in each country. Both Mom and Grandma Anne were loving yet annoying, and both were given to repetitive chatter. I mused upon those similarities as Mom, Dad, and I ate dinner at the Compound dining room under the watchful eyes of nine painted Babas. Eleven if you counted the ones on Mom's locket and brooch.

"And then that Darlene swept up to me," said Mom, leaning over her plate of curry and rice, "And she smiled at me as if she were my friend."

Dad winced but said nothing. I wasn't sure if he

was speaking to Mom or not. He sometimes went for weeks without exchanging a word with her, but they spent so little time alone together that it was hard to tell when he was giving her the silent treatment. Though dinner was not literally silent when the movie theatre had an early show.

"Aaa aaa aaa aaa aaa aaa aaa aaa!" sang the actress ecstatically. The hairs inside my ears flattened down at the blast of music. "Aaa aaa aaa aaa aaa aaa aaa!"

Mom waited a moment, perhaps for the ringing in her ears to subside, then went on. "And Darlene said, like she was talking to a child, 'Now, now, Da-nonna, I hope you're not upset. You know Paribanu chose me to serve the tea to be extra-specially sure that no mistakes were made, because we all remember how last time you forgot to set out the ginger biscuits, and Paribanu had to interrupt the story of Baba and the Burnt Toast to have you go fetch them.' "

It was one of the rare occasions when we had the dining room to ourselves, as the other residents were on vacation. It was also one of the equally rare occasions when Thaki made a dish I liked: curry with whole hard-boiled eggs that absorbed the flavor of the sauce all the way through to the yolks. Usually it was rice and dal. The other alternative was rice and Toxic Waste Curry.

Mom was still in full swing. "That was a complete lie—Darlene forgot them herself—but I felt that taking the blame would be embracing humiliation in the service of Baba, so I did, and I endured Paribanu *and* Zireen's scolding for Darlene's carelessness, and then she had the nerve to use that to curry favor and get assigned to serving tea instead of me."

"Aaaa aaa aaa aaa aaa aaa aaa!" added the actress.

Mom swallowed a spoonful of egg curry and continued without taking a breath, "And then Darlene said—"

"That's enough!" roared Dad.

Water sloshed out of my steel tumbler and over the front of my shirt.

"I'm sorry!" yelped Mom. "Joey, I know you hate hearing about my petty little life, and I know that Baba would want me to bear my cross and not complain, but I—"

"I said, that's enough!" Mom and I sat quivering, but Dad wasn't even breathing hard. "There's a name I never want to hear again: Darlene. I forbid you—either of you—to ever mention her in my presence again."

I was annoyed that Dad included me in his order, as I rarely had cause to mention Darlene anyway. I cast about for a way to defy the spirit of his order without breaking the letter of it.

"Okay," I said. "Let's talk about someone else. I heard a funny story about Andy Moores today."

Andy Moores was a pilgrim who had convinced a number of residents to invest in a pyramid scheme. Dad had retrieved his investment by threatening to report Andy to the Securities and Exchange Commission. Harry Carroll had gotten his money back by brandishing his fist and asking Andy if he wanted to meet the Five Perfect Masters. All the other investors had lost their money. Except for Carla the ex-witch. Carla had made a small but definite profit. She had a sixth sense about financial matters.

"Two names I never want to hear again!" said Dad. "Darlene and Andy. And that includes everything associated with them," he added, as I opened my mouth to ask if I could use the phrase "pyramid scheme."

I dug into the egg curry. Mom's eyes brimmed with tears. Dad picked up a copy of *India Today* and browsed it with every appearance of peaceful enjoyment. I wondered if I could get a book myself—I was forbidden to read during dinner—but decided not to push my luck.

One thing I'd liked about staying with the Grandpas A was that they talked to each other. Sometimes Grandpa Artie yelled at Grandma Anne, but she yelled right back, and ten minutes later they'd be chatting like nothing had happened. They didn't operate like my parents, who either ignored each other completely, batted sarcastic comments back and forth like tennis balls, or had unequal fights in which Dad bellowed and Mom wept. Sometimes I wondered if my parents even liked each other.

"*Aaa aaa aaa aaa aaa aaa aaa aaa!*," sang the actress. "*Aaa aaa aaa aaa aaa aaa aaa aaa!*"

"*Aaa aaa aaa aaa aaa aaa aaa aaa!*," sang the actor. "*Aaa aaa aaa aaa aaa aaa aaa aaa!*"

No one else spoke. Silence, so to speak, was restored to the table.

Mom devoted herself to being Firoze's secretary, a banal job transfigured by her regard for him. She saw him as the equivalent of St. Peter, her link to Baba, and a saint in his own right. Every letter she typed was an act of worship, every reprimand for filing errors was a blessed opportunity to obliterate her ego, and every flimsy blue aerogramme she read to him was a joyous communion of souls.

Dad played volleyball, debated with The Goldberg, bought antiques in the bazaars to sell in America, and complained that he was bored.

Mom was so obsessed with Baba and spent so much time urging me to love him more and more that I laid the entire responsibility for our move on her shoulders. No matter how many cakes she baked or paper dolls she cut out for me, I could never forget that she was the reason I was at Holy Wounds instead of a gifted magnet school in LA.

Dad was so detached from our Baba-laden existence that I was convinced that Mom had talked him into our move. He took no responsibility and accepted no blame. If Mom's philosophy was "Everything is Baba's will and therefore good," Dad's was "We will

not discuss anything involving negativity or conflict." I believed that he was willing but unable to help me out. This made me prefer him to Mom, whom I thought was able but unwilling.

Dad further confused the matter with occasional but vehement proclamations that he was an agnostic, that he didn't follow any religion, and that while he thought Baba was probably God, he really couldn't be sure. The ashram folk thought he was a free-thinking rebel. I thought he was one of Coconut's great mysteries.

The only sign Dad gave of passion for Baba, other than his presence at the ashram, were the hymns he composed.

FORGIVE ME FOR SPEAKING SO INTIMATELY

TO YOU THIS MUST ALL SEEM A BORE

TO LISTEN TO ME TALK ABOUT MY STRUGGLES TO DROWN

WHEN WE BOTH KNOW I'VE GOT ONE FOOT ON THE SHORE

The theme of disciples trying to lose their identities in God but being held back by their own weak wills was omnipresent at the ashram. I regarded it, as I did reincarnation, with secret horror. Even when I hated myself, I preferred being say-the-wrong-thing, cry-when-I-want-to-be-brave, grubby-faced, scabby-kneed Mani to being obliterated. When people talked about merging with God, I pictured being devoured, shrieking, by The Blob.

Everyone I knew was struggling to drown, and I was struggling to get the hell out of the water.

I could not fathom why Dad wanted to erase himself, or what he was doing at the ashram. I speculated that Mom had made him move there. Or that he wanted to be a big fish in a tiny pond, to rebel against his atheist father, to seem a dashing nonconformist by gently ribbing Baba-lovers in the center of all things Baba. He did genuinely love Baba, but there were many Baba-lovers, and very few moved to Ahmednagar. Maybe once he got there, the realization that the cold war between him and Mom would go nuclear if he tried to move us back made staying seem like the better option.

But we never talked about any of this. Not talking was something my family excelled at, though we seemed voluble. Dad told amusing stories about his idealized childhood and engaged in erudite discussions. Mom spoke eloquently of the joy and pain of erasing the self in the service of God. I chattered about funny things I'd seen and books I'd read.

But we didn't talk about emotions, other than the love of God. We didn't talk about whether we were happy, for happiness is meaningless when you're on a grand spiritual quest. Our words bounced off each other like a bat's sonar, and instead of replies, we received ghostly images of the other person.

For all the impact my words had on anyone, I might have been a ghost myself, mouthing silently from the spirit realm. Baba said that people who died suddenly sometimes became ghosts who didn't know they were dead and hung around the world wondering why they couldn't communicate with anyone or affect anything, and were unable to move on until they figured it out.

That would explain a lot.

20

A Hero at Holy Wounds

Reluctant as I am to give Holy Wounds any credit for anything whatsoever, one facet of its curriculum was not only educational, but entertaining and even inspirational. And I would have never encountered it in America.

Year after year, the Indian history class provided stirring tales of rebels and tyrants, heroes and villains, dismemberments, disembowelments, disinterments, last stands, daring escapes, woman warriors, and giant lizards. Some of it was as apocryphal as George Washington's cherry tree. But several of the least likely stories turned out to be absolutely true.

The textbooks had a peculiar style that combined a lively sense of narrative with an antique vocabulary larded with inappropriate British idioms and a fondness for gore. Phrases like "rent his bowels asunder" were not uncommon, and Indian commanders might alternate shouting the Marathi war cry "Har Har Mahadeo" with addressing their troops as "my plucky young lads." "Baji Prabhu and the Memorable Battle of Ghodkhind" was a typical chapter title.

We started studying the seventeenth-century folk hero Shivaji when I was nine, the year after I returned from visiting the Grandpas A. I still have my textbook on him.

A typical chapter title is "The Discomfiture of Shaista Khan," referring to an episode in which Shivaji snuck into the Khan's bedroom at midnight and sliced off part of his hand. The illustration tastefully depicts Shivaji looking heroic, the pajama-clad Khan impersonating *The Scream,* and a thumb flying through the air.

Shivaji was a significant Indian historical figure and also a local hero in Ahmednagar. His connection to the town was that he had been born a mere two hundred kilometers away and had a tenuous legal claim to the even-then-defunct Ahmednagar Kingdom. But I can't blame the town for snatching at his glorious coattails.

The statues portrayed a small dapper man with a clipped beard and moustache, turbaned and with one hand resting on his sword. Even in his most heroic poses, riding a rearing pony and brandishing that sword, he never looked ferocious or battle-crazed, but thoughtful.

In Shivaji's time, India was ruled by the Mughal Emperor Aurangzeb. The Mughals were Muslims who swept in from Central Asia in the 1500s and conquered most of the country. After a few generations of rule, Aurangzeb's predecessors avoided unnecessarily enraging their mostly Hindu subjects. Aurangzeb's great-grandfather, the Emperor Akbar, had been so broadminded that he created a religion that combined Hinduism and Islam. (It didn't catch on.) Aurangzeb's father, Shah Jahan, built the Taj Mahal.

Aurangzeb imprisoned his father, executed his older brother, and seized the throne. While previous Emperors had been patrons of the arts, Aurangzeb loathed art and music as heathen frivolities. He also instituted a tax on non-Muslims and imposed Muslim religious law on the entire population. This did not go over well.

Shivaji's family were Marathas—people from Maharashtra who speak Marathi. They were of the Sudra (peasant) caste but warriors and courtiers by occupation. Shivaji's father abandoned his family when Shivaji was a baby. Shivaji's mother, a remarkable woman by all accounts, decided to raise her son to be the one who would to free his people from Aurangzeb's rule. And he did.

("Ji" is an honorific, like "sir" or "mister." The female equivalent is "bai.")

Shivaji was a guerilla fighter, a trickster, an Indian Robin Hood. He specialized in surprise attacks in the dead of night, finding the weak points of supposedly invulnerable forts, and running away to fight another day.

And he was real.

It may be a legend that he once tied torches to the horns of a herd of cows at night to mislead the enemy into thinking that the lights were those of an army.

But it's fairly well documented that when Shivaji and his young son were put under house arrest in Aurangzeb's capital, he pretended to be sick and started sending immense fruit baskets to temples in the hope of a miraculous recovery. The day after the guards stopped searching the baskets, he concealed himself and his son inside them. Aurangzeb's army ransacked the countryside searching for a Maratha nobleman and his son heading northwest but missed the pair of wandering sadhus traveling east, then north, and finally southwest and home.

And nobody knows who was planning to assassinate who when Shivaji met with Aurangzeb's general, Afzal Khan, but the outcome of the encounter is undisputed.

Shivaji was besieged by Afzal Khan's much-larger army, so he sent word that he was willing to meet to discuss terms of surrender. Both men were supposed to be unarmed, but Shivaji's spies had warned him that Afzal Khan planned to kill him. When the towering Afzal Khan tried to stab the smaller man with a hidden dagger, the blade turned on the chain mail under Shivaji's tunic. Before the Khan could try again, Shivaji disemboweled him with a set of tiger claws he had concealed in his left palm.

Tiger claws, or waghnakh, are brass knuckles with blades. With your hand open and your palm down, you look like you're wearing connected rings. When you clench your fist, curved knives jut out from between your fingers. Ahmednagar blacksmiths still forge them for village toughs.

And though there is no proof that Shivaji conquered a fort atop a precipice with the help of a tame monitor lizard, or ghorpad, there are Indians today with the surname Ghorpade who claim to trace their lineage back to military lizard-trainers.

The man who invented and executed the alleged lizard tactic was Shivaji's commander Tanaji Malusare. Tanaji had been a boyhood friend of Shivaji's, and Shivaji nicknamed him Sinha, or Lion. The story goes that Tanaji and three hundred soldiers met at midnight and looked up at the fort atop the hill. The cliff they stood beneath was so steep that it had been left unguarded, for no man could climb it.

But Tanaji had a secret weapon: a ghorpad named Yeshwanti, or "The Means of Victory." He took her from her cage, patted her, anointed her forehead with red kumkum powder, and even hung a pearl necklace around her scaly throat. Then he tied a rope around her body. But when he placed her on the cliff face, she ran halfway up, then stopped and trembled.

Tanaji's men, waiting in the chilly night and no doubt wondering about their commander's sanity, pounced on Yeshwanti's hesitation.

"The lizard is frightened," whispered one.

"It is an omen of death," muttered another.

"Let's go ho—"

"I have given my promise," said Tanaji, and called softly up the cliff. "Move your feet, Yeshwanti, or I'll fry you up for a midnight snack!"

Yeshwanti bolted up the cliff. A slim soldier boy climbed the rope, secured it, and tossed down ten more. Within minutes, three hundred men were storming the fort.

In the midst of the battle, the fort commander Udaibhan met with Tanaji in single combat.

Udaibhan was a Rajput from the northern deserts of Rajasthan. The Rajputs were something like the samurai in that they were an aristocratic warrior caste who cultivated artistic as well as warlike skills and obeyed a rigid code of honor that sometimes required ritual suicide, individually or en masse.

Tanaji was a Maratha, whose warriors were often of peasant caste, were illiterate but possessed a rich oral tradition of ballads and storytelling, and fought guerilla-style. If Maratha warriors committed suicide, it was for personal reasons or to escape torture. Rajput tales of valor tend to end in tragedy, with honor upheld but the heroes dead and the kingdom lost; but the stars of Maratha ballads rarely sacrificed their lives to a losing cause, and often enough they died successful, contented, and in bed.

The duel of Udaibhan and Tanaji pitted one ancient warrior culture against another. It was a clash of high caste against low, aristocrat against soldier, defender of empire against freedom fighter. They were both skilled warriors trained in their native sword styles, and though I doubt that anyone paused to watch, their duel must have been a sight to see.

It was also a brutal fight to the death. Udaibhan hacked off Tanaji's right hand, but not before Tanaji fatally wounded him. Both men died as the battle still raged.

Tanaji's men wavered as they saw that their leader was dead, but his brother rallied them, and they took the fort. Yeshwanti survived the battle, and her descendants took part in many more, though with a higher mortality rate once people figured out the trick.

That's the story as I learned it, cobbled together from books, verbal accounts, and even a highly entertaining line of historical comics published by Amar Chitra Katha. (Another Amar Chitra Katha tale of a doomed royal dynasty contains a caption that I didn't appreciate until years after I first read it. It's against a pink background and reads, "Upon hearing the news of the fort's capture, the king became gay.") The Tanaji comic features the immortal line "Be sensible, the lazy reptile has no divine powers," but the illustrator was less inspired. Poor Yeshwanti looks like a sock puppet.

Exactly how Tanaji scaled the unguarded rear cliff to get into the fort is a matter of debate in historical circles, but he did it somehow, and he died doing it.

It is said that when Shivaji heard that Tanaji had been killed, he said, "*Sinha gada, sinha gela*." ("I have won Lion Fort but lost my lion.") But the fort Tanaji captured was called Kondana, and it was only named Sinhagad in his honor after his death. Another version of what Shivaji said is, "I have lost my right hand." Even as a gallows-humor tribute, that seems in bad taste.

More sober accounts have less pithy quotes, but they're all variations of "Tanaji's life was too high a price to pay for the fort." I don't suppose anyone knows what he really said, but it seems clear that he took it hard.

Sinhagad is a twenty-minute drive from Pune, Baba's hometown. It's rough and beautiful, with graceful ramparts and intricately carved temples and a formidable cliff labeled "Tanaji climbed here." Its pools are covered with floating round waterweeds, so still and green that you can imagine running across them like a water skater.

The fort has one monument to Tanaji and one to his right hand. The latter has a frieze depicting his battle with Udaibhan and a

nook with a life-size hand carved into it. The former has a bust of a man with bold features and a curling moustache, wearing the Maratha flattened turban. He looks fierce and proud and a little sad. He died before he knew if the fort was won. I imagine he fought one last battle after the final duel, to live just long enough to know, but he'd lost already, and lost again. And won.

As you may have noticed, I was obsessed with Shivaji and Tanaji.

And not only with them. I devoured the histories of India's woman warriors, of the Rajputs and their crazy-valiant last stands and honorable suicides, of the martial artists of the south and the warlike Sikhs of the north.

No one had intended for me to develop a passion for military history. I was supposed to be passionate about God. I bowed down at the holy sites, recited the prayers and sang the hymns, but none of it held any more inner meaning for me than reading a newspaper aloud.

The mandali, residents, and pilgrims told me how fortunate I was to experience the spiritual benefits of India. But the space in my brain reserved for obsession, which they gave to God, filled instead with dreams of history and heroism, of the bloody reality, the elegant legend, and the points where they intersected. Perhaps it was the gap between what people told me my life was like and how I actually experienced it that made me fascinated by the contrast between history and legend, between ideals and reality. Or maybe I just liked stories about undersized underdogs who kicked ass.

Mom and Dad brought me all the way to India to let me share in their enlightenment, and I perversely became a history buff instead.

Baba had claimed that in addition to being the reincarnation of Jesus, Mohammed, Zoroaster, Krishna, Buddha, and Rama, he had also been Shivaji. The latter had been one of Baba's "minor incarnations," in which he does not announce himself as God and does not found a religion.

I was put out when I heard this, though I felt obliged to say "Oh, wow." My life was so permeated with Baba that anything that had nothing to do with him automatically caught my interest. Shivaji the man was the one I found admirable, not Baba Mark Thirty-Nine. Of course God could conquer forts and fight empires to a standstill. It was only impressive if a human did it.

I reconciled the issue by deciding that Shivaji had not actually been Baba. Each incarnation, Baba said, made one mistake. Jesus' had been to wonder on the cross if God had forsaken him, Zoroaster's had been to strike dead the man who assassinated him, and Rama's had been to force his wife to undergo trial by fire. Baba's, I decided (if Baba had really been God), had been to think he had been Shivaji. It was excusable. Shivaji's career had been enviable by anyone's standards—even, apparently, God's.

Baba was not the only person to claim the Maratha hero for his own. The Indian independence movement saw his battle against Aurangzeb as a precursor to their own struggle; modern Hindu nationalists have celebrated him as well, though his policy of religious tolerance was antithetical to their bloody separatist campaigns; and one little girl adopted him as a role model.

If I couldn't go a weekday without being beaten, stoned, and humiliated, I needed a way of seeing myself and my life that lent me some scrap of dignity.

I was, I decided, a warrior.

If I was forced to stand in the sun, I was a prisoner of war, and I would stand and not collapse. If the teachers hit me, I would not pull back my hand or flinch away or make a sound. I would not cry. I would be brave. I would stand and fight when I could, and if I had to run because I was outnumbered, it would only be to fight another day. I would never forget how brutal and harsh my life really was. I would not let anyone brainwash me into thinking that what was done to me and the other children was right. I would not give up. I would not go crazy. I would not let them break me.

I would be silent.

INTERLUDE II: 2000

SHIVAJI'S FAITHFUL DOG

I couldn't keep all the vows I made when I was nine. I broke the ones about not screaming or crying or complaining on an almost daily basis, and no matter how guilty I felt or how quickly I renewed them, they broke again with the next beating. But I kept trying.

When I was a child, I imagined myself a soldier—sometimes fighting at the front, sometimes lost behind enemy lines, sometimes a prisoner of war. It was a strong clear metaphor that made sense of my chaotic life, like Mom's image of herself as St. Peter's assistant and Dad's as Ahmednagar's lone iconoclast made sense of theirs.

But when I moved to America and left my battlefield behind, I found that metaphors can have a life of their own. I jumped when doors slammed and ducked when people made sudden moves, and on one memorable business meeting over breakfast, a waitress reached over my shoulder with a cup of coffee and I slapped it out of her hand. When I paused automatically before entering the back room of a bookshop to survey it for hidden dangers, and another customer, a Vietnam vet in camouflage pants, asked me quite seriously what war I'd been in, I decided that something had to be done.

So when I was twenty-six, I returned to Ahmednagar. Again.

I hadn't been back or seen my mother since I was seventeen, but I was tired of obsessing about my wretched childhood and wanted to accumulate some new and pleasant memories of India to counterbalance the old and unpleasant ones. But I suspected that if I said that to any Baba-lovers, they'd say my childhood had actually been blessed and wonderful, and I was deliberately remembering it wrong because I was a masochist. So I told everyone I was researching a book about Shivaji. I was, in fact, still obsessed with Shivaji, and I thought touring his forts would be an excellent source of happy memories.

To avoid merely collecting newer bad memories, I decided to stay in a single room at the Pilgrim Center for ten days, then spend the rest of my trip traveling by myself. I figured those precautions would avert disaster, especially since I was now a sensible adult rather than a hormone-crazed teenager.

The trip started off promisingly. I had prepared cutting retorts for anyone who mentioned virgins, mummies, or midgets, but the residents and mandali were either cowed by the "Wanna make something of it?" neon sign hovering over my head or had mellowed with time. No one said anything insane or insulting, not even Coconut or Saraswati.

Ahmednagar itself had evolved since my last visit. It was still polluted, poverty-stricken, and ugly, but it had added a cybercafé with air conditioning. I was sitting in the café, e-mailing my friends about

how much things had changed, when the lights went out, the monitor went black, and the air conditioner spat out a fusillade of ice cubes, one of which hit me on the cheek.

Maybe things hadn't changed *that* much.

After my last visit, the mandali had offered Mom a house at Meherazad on the condition that she share it with her arch-rival Darlene. The two of them had eventually developed a civil relationship, which may have been the mandali's intent.

Mom had spent the past six months nursing the terminally ill Firoze, who had died shortly before my arrival. She was as gaunt and haggard as if she hadn't slept since he'd first been diagnosed.

"Mom, have you been sick?" I asked as we walked down the path toward Seclusion Hill. Dust swirled around our feet like ashes after a forest fire.

"I've been caring for Firoze twenty-four hours a day. And the dust gives me asthma." She coughed to prove it.

"Has anyone been taking care of *you*? What have you been eating?"

She waved her hand dismissively. "The cook only cooks for the mandali, and I don't have time to cook for myself. I grab a chapati sometimes."

"I don't think Firoze wanted you to martyr yourself on chapatis and water."

Her eyes filled with tears. "You don't understand. It's like I've been widowed."

"I'm sorry." It didn't surprise me that Mom had loved Firoze, no doubt in an irreproachably chaste way. He'd been her boss, her saint, and the love of her life. What do you do when the man who was everything to you is dead?

"Everyone's dead now," said Mom. "Firoze is dead, Zireen is dead, Paribanu's dead, Dari's dead, even Ratanji's dead."

I'd never been able to muster more of a reaction to reports that yet another mandali had died than the vague regret one might feel at the death of a likable neighbor. Since Mom's letters seemed to expect me to be devastated, I thought my unbroken heart proved that I was shallow and cold. Then Grandpa Artie died, and I discovered that I was quite capable of grief. I just hadn't loved the same people Mom had.

"Are you still going to stay here?"

Mom eyed me as if I'd asked if she intended to launch herself into orbit any time soon. "Of course."

"But with everyone dead . . . "

"It doesn't matter. This is my life now—here, with Baba. Which reminds me, have you been to his tomb yet?"

"Uh-huh."

She eyed me sharply. "Really?"

"Yeah, Mom, *really*." My emotional age had been devolving since I'd first greeted her. I calculated by the snotty note in my voice that I was now about thirteen.

"But did you—"

Since the next logical question would have been "But did you bow down?" I moved to distract her. "I'm going to the Daulatabad fort the day after tomorrow. Want to come with me?"

"Of course, sweetie-pie." She hugged me, sweaty cotton to sweaty cotton. "It'll be just the two of us, mother and daughter. Remember how much fun we had at Kandala?"

"Yeah," I said. "I remember Kandala."

"It's so wonderful seeing you after all these years," said Mom, keeping a wary eye on the enormous beehives stuck to the cliffs beside the fort.

A salesman popped out as we walked through the fort's first gate. "Beautiful earrings!"

Mom shooed him away. "I feel so sad about how distant we've been. I only wanted the best for you, but I know it was difficult being the only foreign child here."

Difficult? There was so much I wanted to say that I choked on it. *It nearly ruined my life*, I wanted to say. *If I tell dates about my childhood, they never call me again. What the hell were you and Dad thinking?* I settled on, "It was beyond *difficult*. The kids hated me, and the Holy Wounds teachers beat me."

Mom began to cry. "*Beat* you?"

"Yeah. You knew that."

"No, sweetie. I had no idea. Oh, how awful. Why didn't you ever tell me?"

"I did tell you. I told you and Dad over and over, but it never helped, so eventually I gave up."

"You never told me anyone hit you."

"Sure I did."

"Sweetie, I know you think I was a terrible mother, but surely you don't believe I could have been so callous that I could have known that my own child, whom I loved, was being beaten and not have cared."

If I insisted that I had told her, I'd be agreeing that I thought she was callous and a terrible mother. Which would make me a callous, terrible daughter. "I think you wanted to believe that I was happy."

"Of course I wanted you to be happy," said Mom.

"That wasn't—"

"I didn't have a happy childhood, so I wanted you to have one, in Baba's home with Baba's mandali and—"

Fast as an earring salesman, I pounced on the opening. "Did your father abuse you when you were a child?"

Mom's tears stopped like I'd turned a handle. "He was a very controlling person," she said cautiously.

An old man leaped out at us with startling energy, a fan of postcards in his hand. “Fifty rupees! Beautiful pictures!”

“No!” snapped Mom and I, dodging him.

I lowered my voice. “But did he abuse you?”

Mom peered into the tunnel in the hill ahead of us, then enunciated her words with legalistic precision. “He never touched me,” she said, and marched into the darkness.

I trailed behind her, wondering if she meant he had made her touch him, or if he'd made her do stripteases while he looked but didn't touch. Or maybe I had a perverted imagination, and Mom meant that he had put her down and tried to control her life, but that was all. But then why wouldn't she just say so?

According to the guidebooks, the unlit tunnels leading up to the castle had trapdoors that opened to the moat, retractable iron doors that could be heated red-hot and slammed down in front of invaders, and chambers that could be piped full of smoke or poison gas, but it was too dark to see any of that. Invisible bats chittered in the sooty darkness.

“Baba, Baba, Baba,” murmured Mom in counterpoint.

I pointed my camera straight up and set off the flash.

“Eeeeeeee! Eeeeeeee! Eeeeeeee!” shrilled the bats.

Whoosh! A gust of air buffeted my face, and something clipped the side of my head. I yelped.

“Baba, Baba, Baba!” exclaimed Mom.

“Eeeeeeee! Eeeeeeee! Eeeeeeee!”

Bats were ricocheting all over the tunnels, dive-bombing my head and shoulders. Mom and I grabbed each other's hands and scrambled out. A few brave bats, the last defenders of Daulatabad, pursued us until we emerged into the white-hot afternoon sun.

A trio of young men were waiting for us. “Hello, madam. Hello, missy. Take our picture.”

“No,” said Mom. “Sweetie, I want you to share your life with me.

I want to know what you care about. You're so fascinated by forts—what is it about them that interests you?"

"Uh . . . " At that moment, what interested me was Mom and her mysterious childhood and how it might have made her who she was. But our conversation of ten minutes ago seemed to have been erased from her memory, just like she'd forgotten all the times I'd begged her to help me when I was a child.

"Shivaji was just a Maratha kid." I couldn't get my mind off childhood. "But by the time he was nineteen, he'd made his buddies into a band of guerilla fighters and was leading them against the emperor."

"Shivaji was never just a kid, honey," said Mom. "He was one of Baba's minor incarnations."

"Uh . . . yeah. But his friends were ordinary teenagers, and they did amazing, heroic things. See, if a bunch of kids could just decide to be brave, then . . . uh . . . " I trailed off. Nobody confessed to wanting to be a hero. Even real heroes didn't: They said, "God gave me strength," or "Anyone would have done what I did." But if anyone could be a hero, then I could too. All it took, I hoped, was choosing to be one.

"Firoze was a very heroic person," said Mom, proving that I wasn't the only one who didn't really have forts on her mind. "He gave up everything to follow Baba."

A man emerged from the gate ahead of us. "Don't go there," he said. "There's trouble. Come with me."

"That's an original sales pitch," I remarked to Mom. The man hurried away, but Mom and I kept walking.

Hundreds of tourists stampeded out from the gate, rushing toward us in a mad panic, clutching their cameras and screaming, "Bees! Bees! Bees!" We turned and fled, pursued by the mob, who were in turn pursued by a ravening swarm of bees. We dashed through all seven gates and into the parking lot, piled inside our car, and slammed the doors. Bees hurled themselves against the windows and windshield.

Our driver, Khan, had been napping in the front seat. He sat up and blinked at us. "Bees," he remarked wisely.

A week later I took off to tour Maharashtra with Khan. He was a Baba-lover from Ahmednagar, a wiry little guy with enough machismo to put Hemingway to shame.

"So you will write book about Shivaji." Khan skidded around a curve, hurling me into the side of the car.

"Uh-huh," I said, unpeeling my face from the window.

"My ancestors were great warriors."

"Really? Who were they?"

"My great-grandfather fought with . . . ah, some king . . . in some battle. He died very bravely." Khan stomped on the accelerator, knocking me back into my seat. "You must put him in your book!"

"Okay, Khan."

Like siege warfare, driving with Khan consisted of long stretches of discomfort punctuated by brief moments of terror. My head bounced when I leaned it back, my hands bounced in my lap, and my teeth clicked together when I tried to sleep. Khan honked when he passed another vehicle, which he did at least every five minutes, or when he went around a blind curve, which meant that he often leaned on the horn for minutes on end.

When an accident occurs in India, and they often do, the drivers of both vehicles are supposed to place a circle of rocks around them and leave them where they are until the police arrive. Even if they're in the middle of the road. Even if the police don't come for days, and they generally don't. When they do show up, they're reputed to sort out whose fault it was by arresting and beating everyone in

sight. As a result, the only accidents that aren't hit-and-runs are the ones in which both vehicles are disabled.

Car crashes figured prominently in the life and legend of Baba. He had been involved in two serious wrecks, one in India and one in America. Baba said they had been his will and were his equivalent of the Crucifixion in taking on the pain of the world. Anyone who's spent much time driving in either country will probably agree that a car crash is an appropriate way to suffer for their collective sins.

Khan and I often drove on mountain roads, or ghats, which are hairpin curves joined to hairpin curves. They're so narrow that cars driving in opposite directions or stuck behind a slow vehicle have to go partially off the road to pass each other. This often put us on the wrong side of the road. There was a thousand foot drop on the cliff side and no rail or wall, but the occasional helpful sign read, "Fatal Accident Zone," or "The demon king Ravana had ten heads. You have only one. Drive carefully."

Despite the signs, everyone drove like maniacs, and nobody ever got out of the way. When faced with a honking, exhaust-belching car bearing down on them, neither people nor cows nor dogs nor cats nor chickens would move until it was inches away. And then they strolled away slowly. Even the chickens.

Our first fort was Raigad, the site of Shivaji's tomb. It lacked the elaborate defenses of Daulatabad, because it didn't need them. It was atop a three thousand foot hill. The fort guide pointed out the sheer black cliffs with the comment, "Even a ghorpad couldn't climb those."

Access to Raigad was via a ski lift. Khan eyed the creaking machinery and said, "There is a road. We will drive."

"No, I'm taking the lift."

"It is not safe."

"You can drive yourself if you like." The ghats were making me carsick, and I preferred possible death to certain nausea. "Or stay here. I don't care."

Khan bristled. “I am not afraid.” He settled into the gondola as if he was taking his position in the shield wall at Thermopylae.

The fort guide sat beside me and Khan. With a rumble and clunk, the gondola jerked into the air and began its ascent. The brown and yellow plains spread out beneath us like a quilt.

“What happens if there’s a power failure?” I asked.

Khan’s lips tightened.

“Not to worry,” assured the guide. “There is a back-up generator. If the back-up generator fails, there is a diesel engine. If the diesel engine fails, the lift can be operated by hand. And if hand operation fails, there are rescue ropes.”

“What are rescue ropes?” I asked.

“They are ropes, madam. For rescuing.”

“But how do they work?”

The guide gazed up at the distant hilltop. “You know that my people, the Sikhs, also fought against Aurangzeb. I will tell you one story from that time.”

“Okay.” I was more than willing to be distracted from the image of people atop the cliff hurling ropes at a stalled gondola.

“After one battle, a Sikh water bearer was seen giving water to the wounded and dying men of both sides. Other Sikhs who saw this became angry. They reported him to their leader, Guru Gobind Singh. So the Guru called the water bearer to stand in front of everyone and asked him if it was true. The water bearer said yes, it was. The men who had reported him waited to hear if he would be executed, or only flogged or exiled.

“Instead, the Guru gave the water bearer a box of healing ointment. ‘Take this,’ he said, ‘and tend to all the wounded soldiers, no matter which side they’re on.’”

“That’s a great story,” I said.

Khan gave the guide and me a hostile, airsick glare.

We set down at Raigad, a square mile of ruins atop a dusty red

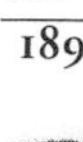

hill. Shivaji's tomb was a domed building somewhat similar to Baba's tomb, but in place of Baba's pet cemetery was a pillar topped with a statue of a hound dog. A nearby plaque was inscribed, "Waghya (Tiger-like), Shivaji's faithful dog." It described how the loyal Waghya had followed Shivaji everywhere, saved his life several times, and, when Shivaji was being cremated, leaped on the pyre and burned himself to death.

"How much of that stuff about Waghya is true?" I asked the guide.

He burst out laughing. "This fort used to be in very bad repair. Lokmanya Tilak, the great freedom fighter, was very interested in Indian history and wished to preserve it. But no one would give money. People were not interested then in old dusty forts. But Tilak was very clever. He knew that people wanted a story. So he invented a heroic dog and asked for funds to make a statue of him. He would say, 'Waghya gave his life for Shivaji. Can't you give a little money for him?'

"Then people gave money, and Tilak used it to restore the fort. But he also had to make the statue. And so you see it: Waghya, Shivaji's faithful dog."

"You take turn driving," Khan ordered. He had been sulking ever since the ski lift.

I said, "I'm not used to driving on the left."

"I teach you," he said.

"And I've never driven in India."

"It is time you begin."

I looked down and saw my trump card. "Khan, this car is a stick shift. I can only drive an automatic."

"Yes. You learn all."

"Forget it, Khan. I'm paying you to drive, so drive."

"Ah. You are afraid of trying new things."

I decided not to dignify that with a reply.

Then Khan played his own trump. "Soldiers in Shivaji's army did not refuse to go to battle because they were afraid."

I stifled the impulse to shriek "You son of a bitch!" and grab him by his scrawny throat. "You can think whatever you like," I said. "But I'm not driving this car!"

When we stopped for dinner, he loosened up enough to tell me a long and hard-to-follow story about how his stepmother had tried to poison him when he was a boy.

"That's terrible," I said.

"Life is struggle," said Khan. "So you must be strong!"

I removed a long sharp bone from my tandoori fish.

"Brave people eat the bones," said Khan ferociously.

"I don't want to be so brave that I end up in the hospital with a bone in my throat."

Khan lifted the spine from his fish and dropped it whole into his mouth. Crunch, crunch, crunch.

It occurred to me that Shivaji's peasants-turned-soldiers had probably been a lot like Khan, pushy and hostile and always jockeying to prove their manhood. If Tanaji could meet me, he would despise me as a poseur. Depressed, I slunk off to my grubby hotel room, where I spent the night in pitched battle against an army of bedbugs.

After a week of tramping around sunny forts, the car began to smell like a badly maintained locker room. I took to riding with my head stuck out the window, like a dog. That was why I saw it: a motor scooter lying broken by the side of the road. An old man was sprawled facedown beside it with the rear wheel over his legs. He wasn't moving.

"Stop!" I said.

I'd taught first aid and CPR, and I knew how to evaluate an accident. You can tell how much force has been applied by the way the bodies lie: battlefield photographs look like everyone's been flung down by a giant hand, while people who trip only look like they've fallen. The old man lay twisted, like he'd been thrown. The scooter wheels weren't spinning, so he had been unconscious for long enough for them to stop. None of the signs looked good.

Khan didn't even slow down. "Hey," I said, "Pull over. Didn't you see that accident?"

Khan sped up. "I saw."

"Then stop. Stop the car!"

He stepped on the gas.

"Turn around," I said. "There's a man hurt. Go on, turn around."

"There is nothing to be done."

"Yes, there is! I—" I doubted that Khan knew the terms first aid or CPR. "I'm a doctor. Go back. I can help."

"No."

"What do you mean, no? Turn around! We're wasting time!"

Grabbing the wheel would be suicidal. I had nothing but words, and a man might die if they weren't good enough. The trees swept by, markers of precious seconds ticking away.

Khan said, "Why are you shouting?"

"Because that man might die if we don't help him!"

"If we go back, police will think we hit him. They will arrest us and beat us."

"No, they won't. Come on, Khan, you think they'd beat an American tourist—a woman? Anyway, the police aren't there."

"Fine!" The car swerved violently. "We go back! They will arrest *me*, and beat *me*, and *my* life will be ruined! You say word, I go back! I pick up man, I *throw* him in car!"

But he didn't turn around.

It wouldn't help the old man if Khan handled him roughly, and if I explained why he shouldn't, he might do it just to spite me. If the police came before an ambulance did, my word might not be enough to shield him. I had no right to force him into risks he didn't want to take.

We'd gone so far by now, pedal to the floor, that by the time we got back, it might already be too late.

Khan said, "Why are you crying? Do not cry."

"Hey!" I said, "There's a truck stop. Quick, stop, maybe they have a phone."

The unexpected appearance in the roadside café of a tearful American woman made all heads turn. I understood enough Hindi to catch Khan telling everyone that his sheltered client had gone hysterical over the sight of an accident.

I said, "Goddammit, Khan, ask them if they have a phone, and if they do, call an ambulance!"

Khan made the call. Then he and the café owner hovered over me, offering me tea and importuning me to be a big girl and stop crying. I wanted to kill them both. Instead, I pulled myself together and got back in the car.

I wondered if Khan would have pulled over if I'd been a man. Me, a hero: What a joke. He had seen right through me. I was a fake, like Shivaji's faithful dog.

Mom showed up at the airport to see me off. "Jai Baba, Rachel," she said. "Jai Baba, Khan. How was your trip?"

"It was very funny," said Khan. "She cried!"

"What? Why?" asked Mom.

"Never MIND, Khan," I snapped, wondering if it would be totally out of line to withhold his tip, no matter how many starving children he was supporting.

"We saw an accident," said Khan happily. "She wanted to stop. You know we cannot stop, madam. She became very upset."

Mom's eyes narrowed. She didn't glare at Khan as if he were an enemy, like I had been doing; she curled her lip at him as if he were a bug. "If it had been Baba who had been hurt, would you have thought it was funny to leave him there?"

Khan shook/nodded and scuffled his feet. "No, madam. But it was not Baba. It was only a man."

"How do you know?" retorted Mom. "Baba said we should treat every stranger as if he were Baba himself, because you never know if one really might be him in disguise."

Khan looked abashed, so I decided not to argue that people deserved decent treatment on their own merits, not because they might secretly be God.

"Khan, go outside," ordered Mom. Her years in India had taught her the tone of voice that says, "You are only a servant, and you must obey." Khan went.

"I think you did the right thing," she said to me. "Did you call an ambulance?"

"Yeah, but . . . "

"That's why Baba put you there, then."

For an instant, I wished Mom was right about Baba. If she was, then the old man had lived, for what was the point of arranging to fetch an ambulance for a corpse? But that was Mom's Baba. Khan's Baba didn't care about the fall of a sparrow.

Mom and Khan and I had all grown up knowing that no one would protect us, but we had taken different messages from the same lesson. Khan learned that the hard survive and the empathetic are crushed. Mom learned that all suffering is for a reason, and the greater the pain, the greater the purpose. I learned to see every injured stranger as a fallen comrade.

I might not be Shivaji's brave commander, but perhaps I was Guru Gobind Singh's water bearer. Or maybe not a soldier of any kind, but a war correspondent keeping the stories from going untold: a publicist for India's ruins, like Shivaji's faithful dog.

21

Night Train to Bombay

I planted my feet on the train platform. It was gray concrete, like every building in Ahmednagar that wasn't a cow-dung hut, and splattered with scarlet paan spittle and other stains less identifiable by color but easily distinguished by smell: spilled curry, spilled tea, coconut oil, engine oil, hair oil, pee.

"NO!" I shrieked. "Don't stuff me through the window."

Mom and I and several other residents were going to Bombay for a brief vacation. Dad, who was staying in Ahmednagar, had accompanied us to the train station to see us off. We had planned to leave the night before and had even bought tickets, but there had been such a huge mob of people trying to get on the train that we had been unable to even get close to it, let alone board it.

"Calm down," said Dad. "You and your mother need to get on the train, so you're going through the window."

I burst into tears and instantly hated myself for breaking the no-crying vow for about the two-hundredth time that year.

"Oh, Mani," said Mom. "You used to like going through the window."

"I never," I blubbered.

I wished people would stop insisting that I enjoyed things I hated or that I used to enjoy things I had always hated. I respected Dad's position more. Just as being hit with a stick was better than being made to stand in the sun, overt force was preferable to force pretending that it was my own idea.

"Think of it as an adventure," said Mom.

Since half my loathing for the window trick was for its indignity, I decided not to add to the humiliation by going through kicking and screaming.

"Fine," I said. "Give me the luggage."

The Bombay train pulled up with a whoosh of air and a clatter of gears. Long before it came to a stop, the mob on the platform flung themselves at the doors. An impenetrable wedge of seething, shoving, thrashing humanity sealed the train like a cork in a wine bottle.

I clutched the luggage as Dad grabbed me around the waist and hoisted me in the air. All around me, parents were thrusting their children aloft. I panicked, violated the solemn vow I'd made the day before, and shrieked like the train whistle.

"Watch the bananas!" yelled Mom.

My shoulder scraped against a rusty bar as Dad stuffed me through the window. I tumbled to the floor and landed on a bag with a squish. The starchy-sweet smell of crushed bananas filled the compartment. I plopped the bags on one bench and threw myself across the other.

An Indian family dashed inside.

"Taken!" I yelled, and they moved on.

Tickets were purchased in advance but possession was nine-tenths of a reservation. The favored method of securing a seat was with a child, but riders could also reserve seats by hurling their luggage onto a bench. They usually used cotton bags or suitcases, but now and then they got creative and pitched cricket bats, plaster statues, or live trussed chickens through the windows.

Mom moseyed inside, along with The Goldberg, homeopath Dr. Chris, and Carla of the New Age curse. They passed around fruit and ginger tea. I declined the pulped bananas and took a pink guava and a sweet lime, which had the pure taste of citrus without any sourness.

With a lurch that made me grab for my book (*Warrior Queen of Jhansi*), the train began to pull out of the station. A boy of seven or so dashed after it, trying to pass a lunchbox through a compartment window, his sooty bangs bouncing in and out of his eyes. He was much too far away to catch up in time. Someone would have to buy dinner at the next station.

The boy put on an extra burst of speed, hit a slippery patch on the platform, lost his footing, and fell under the train.

I froze. The train kept moving. I looked around the compartment to see if anyone else had seen what I had. In the second before their fixed expressions told me that they had, I knew that if they had not, I wouldn't have said anything. My automatic response to anything terrible was silence. I wished the others hadn't seen or hadn't seen me see. If only I could have kept it a secret. Having everyone else know meant they would talk to me about it and make me say how I felt about it. The awfulness of that hung on a scale, in balance with the awfulness of the event.

A woman on the platform screamed.

"Oh, Baba," said Mom. "Baba take the poor boy's soul."

The train ground to a halt, and men in uniform jumped out. The woman fell to her knees on the platform, keening and ripping at her hair. The three-tiered lunchbox had popped open on the concrete nearby, spilling rice and curry and a neatly folded chapati.

"Don't look," said Mom.

I looked.

An exultant shout rang out. Men bent down to pull someone up from the tracks. It was a conductor, cradling the boy in his arms. He was alive and completely unhurt.

The mother pounced on her dazed son and began alternately kissing and shaking him. Three men leaped out of a compartment to embrace him. Passersby clustered to help the family congratulate the boy on his lucky escape. He had been so small that he had lain flat and let the train pass over him.

"Oh, thank Baba," said Mom. "Baba saved him. Jai Baba!"

Every time the train stopped at a station, the air rang out with the cries of food sellers who hopped on and off board or passed their wares through the windows. "*Chai chai garum chai!*" was the treat of the evening. The hot tea was sweet and milky and flavored with cardamom, but what made it truly special was its packaging. It came in a sun-dried clay pot, ridged and red and graceful. The pots came free because they cost almost nothing to make. They were highly fragile and considered disposable. I liked to collect them, but most people drank the tea, then tossed the pots out the window to shatter into cinnabar dust.

As the train sped toward Bombay, the parched plains gave way to a greener landscape.

"Look!" Carla pointed out the window. "A great blue harem!"

I snickered, picturing a troupe of indigo-clad maidens undulating across the rice paddies.

“That’s an egret,” said Dr. Chris. “Great blue herons are blue.”

“I know that,” said Carla. “I was talking about the big blue bird that was flying, not the regrets on the ground.”

Long after night fell, I was too wired to sleep. I visited the bathroom, which was a room with a hole in the floor. As this was the standard setup for railway toilets, the tracks were often unimaginably revolting. When I returned, Mom and Carla were out cold, and the men were gone. I crept toward the bridge compartment, a small common area between cars. As I had suspected, The Goldberg and Dr. Chris were standing there chatting. I lurked at the door, unseen.

An Indian businessman stepped into the bridge compartment. He wore a suit and tie and carried a briefcase and seemed taken aback by the presence of three foreigners. “Good evening,” he said in English.

“Good evening,” said Dr. Chris.

“Hey,” said The Goldberg.

The businessman looked out the window beside the door that led outside. Then he put down his briefcase and opened the door, letting in a whoosh of cold air and a deafening sound of wind. He stood framed in the darkness for a moment, then stepped out.

The door slammed shut behind him. Rat-a-tat-tat, rat-a-tat-tat, sway right, sway left. There one instant and gone the next. A man had been alive a second ago, and now he must be dead.

Had I imagined it? Did the door really lead outside, or to another compartment? Had he committed suicide? Could he have thought the train was stopped?

“Did you see . . . ?” asked The Goldberg, for once at a loss.

Dr. Chris said, “Maybe we should stop the train.”

“We’re miles away, bro,” pointed out The Goldberg. “Anyway, there’s no cord.”

The conductor who had pulled the boy from the tracks walked in, making his rounds.

“Excuse me, sir,” said Dr. Chris. “A man just walked off the train.”

The conductor eyed him quizzically.

"He stepped right out that door," said Dr. Chris. "Look, he left his briefcase."

"Ah," said the conductor, and picked it up.

"Are you going to stop the train?" asked The Goldberg.

The conductor shook/nodded his head: In a moment, I'll ask my supervisor, we can't make two stops in the same night. "I will see to it." He moved on.

I returned to my berth ahead of the conductor's beat. Was the businessman dead, or lying in a field with a broken leg? Had Baba saved him like he saved the boy? Why should a child be more worthy of life than a man? Children were vicious creatures, and the man had seemed nice—polite, anyway. I had barely seen his face, and now he was gone. I should have looked closer.

I waited for the train to stop, but it ran on and on, rat-a-tat-tat, rat-a-tat-tat, until I fell asleep.

Mom shook me awake. It was dark outside, but everything was still. The train had stopped at last. "Is he alive?" I asked.

"The little boy?" asked Mom. "Yes, don't you remember? He wasn't even hurt."

"Not the boy—" I started to say, then wound down. I wasn't supposed to know about the businessman yet.

"She must have heard us talking about the man who jumped off the train," said Dr. Chris helpfully. "I don't know what happened to him. The train never stopped."

"It *is* stopped," I pointed out.

Mom patted my shoulder. "That's because we've arrived. Wake up! It's two in the morning."

We disembarked and piled into a taxi. I had to sit in Mom's lap. Life would be so much more dignified if I weren't so small.

"Indra Hotel," ordered The Goldberg.

"Baba, Baba, Baba," began Mom.

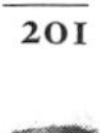

The taxi swooped through the streets, reveling in the lack of traffic, and screeched to a stop at a vacant lot.

"Where's the hotel?" I asked.

"No hotel," said the driver.

"What do you mean, no hotel?" said The Goldberg.

"Hotel is gone only," explained the driver.

The lot, upon closer inspection, contained remnants of masonry that might once have been a hotel.

"Why didn't you say so before, bro?" asked The Goldberg. "We can't sleep in a construction site."

The driver shook/nodded his head: you didn't ask, I'm as surprised as you are, I thought you wanted the construction site. "You want hotel? I know good hotel. Green Diamond, best hotel."

"Well, guys, what do you think?" asked The Goldberg.

"I vote for the Green Diamond," I said immediately.

"Fine with me," said Dr. Chris.

"Oh, Baba," said Mom. "I guess the Green Diamond will have to do. I hope it has a phone, so we can call Joey."

"Carla?" asked The Goldberg. "What's the Carster say?"

Carla shrugged with one shoulder.

"Green Diamond," ordered The Goldberg.

To my relief, the Green Diamond indisputably existed, a silver spear against the cloudy night sky. We marched up to the front desk and demanded rooms for the men, and Carla, and me and Mom.

The desk clerk said, "Rooms on thirty-ninth floor."

Mom was afraid of heights. "Don't you have any lower down?"

"Sold out," said the clerk. "Thirty-ninth floor only."

The men and Carla went to the hotel restaurant to get a drink, and Mom and I hauled our luggage to the elevators. Their wood floors were warped and the sliding fretwork of the inner doors was rusty, but that was standard for bottom-of-the-barrel Indian hotels.

Mom eyed them unhappily. "Those don't look very safe. Maybe we should walk. Do you see any stairs?"

"The hotel has forty floors," I pointed out. "If there was anything wrong with the elevators, nobody would be staying in any of the higher floors."

Armed with that logic, we stepped inside—Mom gingerly, me with a leap and a thump to the floor, which shook ominously—and I slapped the button labeled 39.

"Baba, Baba, Baba, Baba, Baba," began Mom preemptively.

The elevator hurtled up, slowed radically at the nineteenth floor, then got a second wind, leaped to the thirty-ninth floor, and stopped. The doors did not open. I looked for an "open doors" button. There was none. I punched the 39 button again, and the doors reluctantly slid open. I dove out, just ahead of Mom. I was starting to think that she had been right about the elevators.

We stashed our luggage and went to join the men and Carla at the downstairs restaurant. I pushed the down buttons on both elevators. We waited. I started to pull *Heroic Tales of Maharashtra* from my book bag. Then I heard a noise.

"Do you hear something?" I asked.

"Hear what?"

I didn't want to sound like a lunatic, but . . . "Voices," I admitted. "And a sort of thumping or banging sound."

Mom listened. "Maybe it's people talking in another room."

I heeded a paranoid impulse and put my ear to the elevator door.

"Hellllp! Hellllp! We're traaaaapped!" The elevator vibrated: Thump! Thump! Thump!

"Uh, Mom . . ."

Mom put her ear to the door. "Baba! There's people in there!" She yelled through the crack, "We hear you! We're getting help!"

The thumps and pleas for rescue continued. Either they hadn't heard us, or they didn't understand English.

"We're walking down," said Mom. "I knew I didn't want to be this high."

We walked down thirty-nine flights of stairs and informed the clerk that people were trapped in the elevator.

"Ah," he said wisely, as if we had confirmed his own suspicions, and rang a bell to summon workmen.

"I'm not staying on the thirty-ninth floor and walking up and down those stairs," said Mom. "I want another room."

"Do not walk," said the clerk. "Take lift."

"I'm not getting in that elevator. You've got people stuck in it."

"Lift will be repaired."

"I don't care. I want a room on a lower floor."

"Rooms are on upper floor only."

"Are you the manager? I want to talk to the manager."

"Manager is out of station."

"Then you give me another room!" shrieked Mom.

The clerk smoothed his moustache. "We have one—one room on third floor."

"Great. We'll take that."

"But you will not like. That room has . . ." He paused. His tone had been so doom-laden that I expected him to say, "cobras under the bed," "live wires sticking out of the walls," or "part of the floor missing," all of which were realistic possibilities. "Indian toilets," he concluded anticlimactically.

"This is India," Mom pointed out. "We're used to Indian toilets. We *prefer* Indian toilets. We have Indian toilets at home!"

The clerk shook his head darkly. "You will not like."

Mom put her hands on her waist. "We want the third-floor room."

Reluctantly, the clerk handed over the keys. It was then that we remembered that our luggage was in our room on the thirty-ninth floor.

Rather than tackle the climb immediately, we went to the restaurant and regaled our fellow travelers with the Tale of the Elevator. But eventually the time came when we had to mount those stairs. When we finally dragged our feet onto the thirty-ninth floor, we saw what had happened to the elevator. It was stuck between floors, with a three-foot opening about seven feet above the corridor.

The doors and part of the wall had been hacked open, exposing the elevator and much of the shaft. An axe lay on the floor. Two workmen and a boy assistant steadied a ladder spanning the gap between the elevator and the corridor. A party of irate and portly Sikh businessmen were squeezing through the gap, swearing in Punjabi and trying not to look at the gaping shaft below.

I had often thought that nothing could be worse than being an American schoolgirl in Ahmednagar, but Indian businessmen also seemed to have it rough.

Mom and I collected our luggage and started down the stairs. "Oh, Baba," sighed Mom as we reached the first landing. "Baba certainly gave us an adventure tonight."

"Yeah," I said, "Those men would've been stuck there all night if we hadn't heard them. We're heroes!"

I could see the statue: me in bronze with my ear heroically pressed to the wall. It would inspire girls for generations to come.

"That's how Baba works, sweetie," said Mom. "It was Baba who led us to them."

She had attributed the little boy's rescue to Baba too. What was the point of doing anything if God always got the credit?

"Oh, Baba, my feet," groaned Mom on the fifteenth landing. "Why couldn't that stupid clerk have given us the third-floor room in the first place?"

"Baba didn't want him to. Because then we wouldn't have rescued the men in the elevator." I gave her my most sugary smile. "That's how Baba works."

22

A Shared Delusion

The ashram party line, of which Mom was a vocal proponent, was that everything was Baba's will and Baba was perfect. Therefore, everything that happened was good and supposed to happen. But after my trip to Bombay, my doubts began to crystallize. Why had Baba saved the boy who had fallen under the train but not (I suspected) the man who had stepped out the door? If the boy had died, wouldn't Mom have said that was Baba's will too? If every aspect of my life was Baba's decision, then why did he want me to be bullied, lonely, and miserable? Why did he pick some people to be leprous beggars and others to be Prime Minister? If I, an ordinary little girl, could have arranged the world in a more just way than God, then what sort of God was he?

And if Baba wasn't God, then who had he been?

Well, I thought blasphemously, we all know what to call regular people who think they're God. The trouble was, my idea of what was crazy often clashed with the ashram's ideas. But every now and then a pilgrim went so spectacularly berserk that no one tried to explain it away as an overdose of divinity.

Sometimes these pilgrims read the rule banning illegal drugs, ignored the clause stating that prescribed ones were allowed, threw out their medication, and arrived at the ashram two days before the purple demons descended. Sometimes, they decided that they'd had such a life-changing spiritual experience that they no longer needed their pills. And sometimes they just spontaneously went bonkers.

Bill-Dan was one of the pilgrims who achieved such an advanced state of spirituality that he tossed his meds. His name was Dan Conway, and the first sign that he should have kept taking his pills was when he started telling everyone to call him Bill.

A resident named Lou was the first to notice that Bill-Dan, as the residents dubbed him, was losing it. But instead of advising him to consult a doctor or telling anyone else what was going on, he invited Bill-Dan to move in with him. The idea, apparently, was that Lou could keep a close eye on him and would be available at all times for counseling. This might have worked better if Lou, a trust fund baby with an MBA, had any qualifications to treat mental illness.

One evening Lou showed up at the residents' dining hall with Bill-Dan in tow. An important carom game was underway in the back, a grudge match between the residents' four best players: Dad and The Goldberg on one side, and Dr. Chris and Harry Carroll on the other. This was the big event of the week, so most of the residents were there.

As Dad lined up his shot, a gust of wind blew through the badly fitted window frames. The light bulb hanging from a string from the ceiling swung like a pendulum, casting dancing shadows across the board.

Dad looked up, exasperated, and pointed at the light. "Stop!" he commanded.

The wind died. The bulb shivered to a stop.

"Check out my main man!" exclaimed The Goldberg.

Harry Carroll and Dr. Chris chuckled.

Bill-Dan let out a long, piercing shriek of absolute terror. As everyone turned to stare at him, he leaped up and, flailing his arms and caterwauling, hurtled across the room, out the door, and away over the fields.

Lou glared at Dad. "Why'd you have to do that? He was making such good progress."

"Do what?" asked Dad.

"Well, he's gotten the idea that the residents have psychic powers. He thinks you're all reading his mind and mentally spying on him. So I brought him here to show him that you're just nice, normal people."

In the silence that fell as everyone contemplated the dubious wisdom of that plan, the light bulb once more began to sway in the draft.

"Stop!" I commanded. But it kept on swinging.

About six months after the abrupt departure of Bill-Dan, Dante Ludovico flew in from Italy. The pilgrim's hair was black and appealingly tousled, his eyes were pools of melting brown, and he had a sexy cleft in his chin. He was 6′ 4″ and gloriously muscled from his broad shoulders to his silken-haired chest to his finely sculpted thighs. Also he had a large and well-shaped penis.

I knew this because of the afternoon that he emerged from Pilgrim Place in a slow-motion jog, stark staring naked. I had been sitting on a bench outside, reading *Well Played, Juliana!*, but even the most spirited all-girl lacrosse team couldn't compete with a splendid nude man. I dropped my book.

Dante jogged in place at the gates, grinning so widely that I could see the flash of his perfect teeth as he turned his head back and forth. He wasn't grinning at me, or at least not at me in particular; he seemed delighted with the entire world and all of creation. His penis went bouncy-bouncy-bouncy in rhythm with his feet.

I was dying to run into Pilgrim Place to see if anyone else had seen him, but I didn't want to abandon my front-row view of the action. Dante solved my dilemma by slowly jogging away. I noted his course and dashed inside.

Dad was with a group of men listening to Coconut expound on the dangers of reaching a fourth-plane state of consciousness.

"You see," Coconut was saying, "Yogis have these powers. And yet they must not use these powers. You see how it is."

"Dad," I announced, "I just saw a man run out of here, completely naked."

He didn't react. Neither did anyone else.

"Sometimes it is that yogis misuse their powers," continued Coconut. "They will be reincarnated as a rock. Then they must work their way back to humanity over millions of years. You see how it is."

"*Completely* naked," I repeated, in case Dad had missed that part. I was irritated at everyone's failure to appreciate this new and spectacular diversion.

"Well," Dad said calmly, "What are you going to do about it?"

"I'm going to follow him," I said. "He was heading for Darlene's, and I'd like to see her face when she sees him."

Coconut said, "It takes five hundred years merely to reach the reptile stage."

I ran back out. Dad followed me at a more leisurely pace. But Dante never reached Darlene's house. When he hit the volleyball court he sat down and began scooping up handfuls of dust and pouring them over his head.

It turned out that Dante, like Bill-Dan, had decided that now

that Baba had entered his heart, he no longer needed his medication. Two weeks later aliens ordered him to take off his clothes.

I'd never spoken to Dante before his freak-out, and I wasn't inclined to after it. But he stayed in my memory as the finest specimen of the masculine body that I'd ever seen, proof that some people don't need airbrushing to be perfect. And proof that not all imperfections are visible. Even when it looks like it's all hanging out.

But the most spectacular lunatic to visit Ahmednagar was an American of Hungarian descent whose first name was Vladimir. So was his last name. My family had known him for years via Baba meetings in Los Angeles. He had made no particular impression on anyone and was probably only remembered because of his unusual name.

Years later he arrived in Ahmednagar with a new wife, Rosalita, in tow. He was a big muscular man and had grown his hair into a wild approximation of Baba's flowing locks. He wore a white robe and looked quite striking, I'm sure, when he strode into Baba's Hall and announced, "I am Baba. At last, I have returned!"

Without missing a beat, Firoze shouted, "Get out, or I'll call the police and have you thrown out!"

Vladimir got out. But only as far as the less favored of Ahmednagar's two commercial hotels, the cockroach-ridden Chandra, which was mostly notable for a menu featuring Uncle Chips, Happy Chips, Plane Chips, Cronchi Chicken Ball, Veg Ball with Cronchi, Tomato Soap, Chicken Soap, Veg Soap, Chicken 65, Roast Leg of Lamp, and Leeches with Ice Cream. There he stayed with Rosalita, who claimed to be a witch and also claimed to be Paribanu. I was curious as to how they explained the existence of the real Paribanu. Did they say she was an imposter? But despite my repeated suggestions, no one ever got around to asking.

The claim that no one seemed to doubt was that Rosalita was a witch. She had maggot-pale skin, black hair falling past her waist, scarlet lips, and glittery green eyes. She looked like Snow White's evil twin. I was dying to approach her and inquire, "Are you a good witch or a bad witch?" But Mom dragged me far away every time she saw them coming, so I never got the chance.

The Vladimir situation took on immense proportions in everyone's minds. At the ashram the tiniest events were seized upon and wrung out for the last drop of entertainment value. It was the talk of the town for months when a local goat gave birth to a stillborn mutant, and it provoked more than one fiercely argued debate on the subject of "That Two-Headed Kid: Random Freak of Nature or Baba's Warning of the Coming Apocalypse?" Now imagine the effect of a genuinely dramatic situation.

To provide further juicy complications, Vladimir had a hanger-on, a young American who alternated between explaining to the residents that he had been touring India when he happened to meet up with Vladimir, only now he thought Vladimir had lost it, and hanging out with Vladimir at their hotel. The residents decided that the young man was a double agent. Thereupon, some refused to talk to him, some tried to pump him for information while withholding any of their own, and some fed him disinformation.

As a tactic to make Vladimir even more paranoid, it probably worked pretty well. If it was intended to de-escalate the situation, it backfired.

Word came from Vladimir's minion that he was willing to negotiate with Dad, presumably because they'd known each other in Los Angeles.

Dad showed up at the Chandra and got down to business immediately. "Listen, Vladimir, I have to tell you that nobody here believes what you've been saying about you being Baba and Rosalita being Paribanu."

"But it's true," said Vladimir. "I am the Avatar of the Age. I am the Messiah come again. I am—"

"Vladimir, it doesn't matter whether it's true or not. Nobody believes it. I don't believe it. You'll never convince anyone here that you're Baba; it just makes trouble when you say you are. You have to either stop saying that stuff or leave Ahmednagar."

"I'm going to Los Angeles," said Vladimir. "I must spread my message."

"When are you leaving?"

"I'm not," said Vladimir calmly. "I'm sending one of my replicates."

The conversation grew even less coherent from that point on. Dad left the Chandra without even obtaining an explanation of why Vladimir had wanted to talk to him.

Through his henchman, Vladimir announced his intention of making an appearance at Amartithi. Firoze called in a squad of police to wait for him.

Amartithi was the biggest Baba-related holiday of the year, a week-long celebration climaxing on the anniversary of Baba's death. Fifty to sixty thousand pilgrims, mostly Indian, streamed into Meherabad to celebrate it. They were housed in immense tents. (For reasons that were never articulated, Indians and Westerners had separate tents.) Pavilions were erected, special prasad was given out, and Baba-related live entertainment—singing, dancing, skits, lectures, and bull sessions—went on around the clock.

Most of the festivities took place at Meherabad, but on the second day of Amartithi, thousands of Baba-lovers poured into Baba's Garden at Meherazad to behold The Tree with the Face. Dad was assigned to prevent souvenir seekers from pulling off the bark and to show them the face. This was difficult, since he couldn't see it.

Luckily, he had assistance. One of the Meherazad servants, a devout and batty old lady, used to toddle up to point out the face to the gathered pilgrims. She not only showed them the location of the former face, but many other faces on other parts of the tree. To Dad's amusement, the pilgrims were often able to see those faces as well.

(Spotting Baba's face was a common hobby at the ashram. Urmila saw it in the black-and-brown mosaic of a burnt chapati and kept it in a box until it fell to dust. Harry Carroll crushed a scorpion against the wall with his shoe, and lo! Baba's face appeared in the smear of arachnid guts and tread marks. He wanted to preserve it as a memorial, but his wife Grace, who said she could see a face but it didn't look like Baba's, removed it from the wall with a disinfectant-moistened sponge.)

On the second-to-last night of Amartithi, it's a ritual to stay up all night, observe silence at quarter to noon the next day, and then exclaim "*Avatar Meher Baba Ki Jai!*" ten times at noon, the exact moment of his death. That night, Firoze sat with Dad, The Goldberg, and a squad of cops, drinking thermoses of tea to ward off the chill.

As night slipped into early morning, a ball of white light appeared in the sky. It was like a comet without a tail, shining steady and bright. It appeared over the horizon, rose over the tower and proceeded with slow majesty across the sky, until it vanished over the hills.

"Far out," whispered The Goldberg.

Vladimir Vladimir stepped out from behind a pavilion.

Firoze rose to his feet, and they faced off, a looming apparition in flowing white and an old man squinting through Clark Kent glasses. It should have been no contest, but Vladimir hesitated before the fury in Firoze's eyes.

"Police!" shouted Firoze. "The madman is here! Take him away!"

The police lifted their long wood lathis and charged. Vladimir spread his arms wide, as if in welcome.

Lathis raised and fell until Vladimir was on his knees and blood stained his snowy robes. He made no sound, nor did he move to protect himself. He took the beating like a peaceful protestor. Or a madman. Or a saint.

The police began to drag him away.

Vladimir reached into the folds of his robes, pulled out a letter, and held it out to Dad. "Give this to Rosalita," he begged.

Dad took a step forward.

Firoze spoke in tones that compelled obedience. "We touch nothing from that man!"

"Sorry, Vladimir," said Dad.

Vladimir and Rosalita were shipped to a mental hospital in Pune where they were held and medicated for a while, then deported to America. That was the standard procedure for lost-it pilgrims. The psychiatrist in charge of their case, a South Indian woman named Dr. Menon, was fascinated by them and would have preferred to keep them in the asylum for her to study at her leisure.

"They're a rare case of folie a deux," explained Dr. Menon. She had come to Ahmednagar to visit relatives and had stopped by the Compound to meet the people who kept sending her such new and unusual cases. The residents plied her with tea and quizzed her about Vladimir.

"It's French; it means a shared delusion. It's very unusual for two psychotics to believe each other. In an entire asylum of mental patients, with each one convinced that they are someone or something they are not, I have never before seen a case in which two patients shared the same fantasy. Always before, each one thinks that they are sane, and everybody else is mad." Dr. Menon sipped her tea. "I think I will write a monograph about them."

Not all the strange pilgrims who came to Ahmednagar were Baba-lovers. Every two to three years, Ahmednagar was visited by the Holy Roller. He was a man who had made a vow to roll across the entire length of India. No one knew why, or where he'd started, or why, having once completed his task, he started over again. All we knew was that every few years, a man rolled into town.

He lay on the road in his filthy rags, rolling over and over with his arms at his sides, not even moving his face out of the sewage and pig shit and pools of fetid water.

Locals gave the Holy Roller food and asked for his blessing. Dad spoke to him once and reported that he seemed truly holy and not like a madman or a con artist. But we thought Dante was crazy because he stripped and rolled in the dust in the volleyball court.

Nobody who has talked to a schizophrenic whose ability to form a single coherent sentence has unraveled, or suffered through a depressive episode in which suicide seems preferable to the pointless drudgery of getting out of bed every morning, can believe that mental illness is a purely cultural phenomenon. But a short step from the sharp edges of biochemical disaster areas is the borderland in which behavior that would get a person institutionalized in one country or era is sanctified in another.

Mom's constant Baba-chant was a mark of extreme eccentricity in Los Angeles, but one of enviable devotion at the ashram. Malik the Mast would have been a street-person if he'd been American. Baba-lovers thought Vladimir was crazy because he claimed to be Baba, but they didn't think Baba had been crazy because he had claimed to be God.

Had Baba been nothing but Vladimir with superior charisma and a larger following? During the Vladimir situation, I slyly asked the mandali how one might tell the difference between a madman who thought he was God and a genuine incarnation. They re-

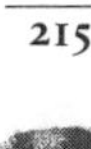

sponded that it was obvious when you met them. Madmen seemed mad; Gods seemed Godly.

I couldn't deny that Vladimir had, in fact, seemed crazy. Even from a distance, he and Rosalita evoked the sinking feeling you get when someone who had previously seemed normal mentions that the transmitter in his head is, even as he speaks, beaming his thoughts to Jupiter.

But Malik the Mast also gave me that feeling. Although he had been plucked from the crowd and labeled holy, he seemed no different from any victim of mental illness, at once frightening and pathetic, obsessively pacing out the boundaries of his cramped interior world.

Still, the residents sensed a unique aura of spirituality about Malik as he scuttled around Meherabad, eyes fixed on the ground lest he miss an invisible object to add to his invisible collection. A pilgrim woman who had a close encounter with him was quite vocal about how blessed she had been to have been pissed on by a fifth-plane saint.

And though Baba's younger days had been marked by bizarre behavior, the old man projected onto the sheets we used as movie screens, blessing the crowds who bowed at his feet, seemed no more or less deserving of such adulation than the Pope, and certainly no more mad.

If a man seemed sane, and a hundred thousand people believed that he was sane, did that prove his sanity? But if Baba wasn't insane, did that mean he was God? Could a person be wrong about something as monumental as his own divinity and be considered sane but mistaken? Was Malik the Mast holy or just a scary old crazy man? How can you tell?

The last question was the only one I ever asked aloud, and it had a simple answer: Baba, being God, just knew. Masts, said Baba, only existed in Asia. Western people who seemed insane were insane. After Baba's death, this rule was the key for classifying Americans like Bill-Dan and Vladimir or Europeans like Dante. But it gave rise to confusion when frothing, gibbering Indians came to town.

On the whole, Baba-lovers were inclined to give Indians the benefit of the doubt. They might howl at the moon, hoard invisible objects, or channel eleventh-century saints, but India was more mystically advanced than the materialistic lands the Westerners had fled, so whacked-out Indians were probably just *differently spiritual.*

After all, as I was often reminded, the sun rose in the east and set in the west.

23

On the Road with the Grandpas A

Three years after I moved to the ashram, the Grandpas A decided to visit us in India. I thought of them as ambassadors from the life I ought to be living and hoped Grandpa Artie would get in a heated religious argument with someone, lose his temper, and denounce Baba as a fraud. Unfortunately, that thought had also occurred to my parents, who spread word in advance that no one was to ask the Grandpas about their religious beliefs.

Before they arrived, I had noticed a welt on my thigh—a scratch or an insect bite. I knew how dangerous even the tiniest break in the skin could be in Ahmednagar's foul air, but I had no intention of telling anyone about it. The last time I had reported a medical problem, an infection under my thumbnail, Mom had taken me to the head of the ashram's free clinic, a mandali woman named Dr. Ambika. The doctor had prescribed a folk remedy—sticking my thumb in a ripe lime.

"For how long?" I asked.

"Until the infection is drawn," she said, rummaging in her desk drawer for the fruit. "Only a few days. A week at most."

"I won't go around for a week with my thumb in a lime!"

Dr. Ambika pushed aside a stack of Baba pamphlets, a framed Baba photo, and a bottle of penicillin. She held out the lime. "If you won't use this, the only alternative is to stick a needle under your thumbnail."

"Gimme the lime," I said.

I spent the next three days with a bright green lime hanging off my thumb, to the loudly voiced amusement of everyone I met. It worked, but I wasn't sure the cure had been worth the embarrassment.

So when I noticed the pink lump on my leg, I secretly doused it with antiseptic, put a band-aid over it, and forgot about it. The day before we were to leave with the Grandpas A, I peeked under the band-aid. To my alarm, the dime-size welt had evolved into a nickel-size bluish-red boil.

Uh-oh.

Maybe I should tell someone before we went off into the wilderness. But what if they didn't let me go? What if Dr. Ambika had worse things than limes up her sleeve?

In any case, by then I'd have hit myself over the head with a hammer before I'd have told anybody anything. I wiped down the boil with antiseptic, covered it with a fresh band-aid, and hoped it would go away.

The next day, the complete Brown family piled into a rented white Ambassador, a bulbous vehicle of limited reliability and extreme clunkiness. Because of a protected trade agreement, at that time every car in India was a white Ambassador.

"Oh, this is exciting!" exclaimed Grandma Anne. "Isn't this exciting, Mani? Are you excited? You don't look excited. Is there some reason why you're not excited?"

I surreptitiously poked at the boil. Had it gotten bigger? "I'm excited."

"This is a real family road trip," proclaimed Grandpa Artie. "It's about time we had one."

The driver started the car.

"Baba, Baba, Baba," muttered Mom.

"Are you still doing that, Dan-Anna?" asked Grandpa Artie.

The car leaped forward, throwing us all back against the seats.

"Not so fast!" exclaimed Mom.

Maliciously, I said, "*Zorsay chelao!*"

That meant "drive furiously," or at least that was what the Hindi phrasebook said it meant. I enjoyed saying it, not for its effect on drivers, who drove furiously whether you requested it or not, but for its effect on Mom.

Like clockwork, Mom said, "Baba! Don't say that! Driver, go very slowly."

The driver screeched out of the driveway, gravel flying out from beneath the tires, and sped out onto the main road.

An adorable little puppy wobbled into the street.

"Look out!" shouted Dad and the Grandpas A.

"Watch the puppy!" I screamed.

"Baba!" shrieked Mom.

The driver accelerated over the puppy.

"Oh, no," said Dad.

"Oh, Baba," said Mom.

"Poor thing," said Grandma Anne.

"Jesus H. Roosevelt Christ!" exclaimed Grandpa Artie. "Why the hell didn't you swerve?"

"Stop!" I said. "Go back. Maybe it's still alive."

The driver sped up. "It is dead, madam," he said. "Nothing to be done."

The family road trip had not gotten off to a promising start.

As we drove across India, we stopped at least once a day at some marvel of architecture or sculpture. I was bored. I didn't care for temples, and we didn't visit the less aesthetic but more historical forts that I would have appreciated.

We skipped Sinhagad and its monument to Tanaji's right hand in favor of a temple with an unusual depiction of a *standing* Buddha; and we passed by the site where Shivaji had disemboweled Afzal Khan with one blow of his mighty tiger claws to spend three hours at a temple devoted to the rarely-depicted Creator God Brahma.

I was sick of Gods. Gods were the indirect cause of all my problems. If we had to look at statues, I wanted to see the statue commemorating Rani Lakshmibai, the queen who died fighting the British in the war that is known in England as The Sepoy Mutiny but in India as The First War of Indian Independence. Or to the Maratha queen Tarabai, Shivaji's daughter-in-law, who carried on the fight against Aurangzeb (by then extremely old and extremely frustrated) after her husband's death.

I resented everyone's insistence that I look at the pretty pictures instead of staying in the car to read about how Baji Prabhu and a few hundred soldiers had fought a vast army to buy Shivaji time to escape their doomed fort. The wounded Baji Prabhu had held on to life long enough to hear the cannons sound from Pratapgad, the signal indicating that his king had reached safety. And then he had died, his task complete.

Even when faced with impossible odds, one could still go down fighting. I wanted to make a valiant last stand in Ahmednagar. No

one would ever know whether I had been brave or not. But I would know.

I made that vow often, a solemn little girl chewing on the end of her braid and dreaming of a noble death.

"You are so adorable!" people would exclaim and pinch my cheeks. I ignored them. I was a tragic hero, a valiant warrior. I was tough and brave and doomed, but I was not adorable.

I amused myself as we drove by counting camels and car crashes. By the second week of the journey, I was up to fourteen camels and thirty-nine wrecks, most of the latter on ghats. But the most memorable wreck we encountered was not on a treacherous mountain road but on a smooth stretch of highway. It seemed unlikely to have much in the way of wrecks or camels, so I stared out the window, populating the fields with mounted armies and filling the air with the sound of clashing swords.

I was a woman warrior. Not a general, not a queen, just an ordinary cavalrywoman in Shivaji's army.

A servant woman once told me that Maratha women wrap their saris around each leg, unlike the non-Maratha styles that let them fall like a skirt, in honor of the women who fought in Shivaji's cavalry.

"They had to be ready to fight at any time," she explained. "No time to pull up their saris—they had to jump on their horses and go. So they kept them wrapped tight so they could ride."

I asked another servant about that later. "Women cavalry?" she exclaimed, laughing. "I never heard of such a thing. We wrap our saris so they don't get in the way when we sweep the floors."

I have never found any other evidence for female cavalry in Shivaji's army. But it seemed plausible. I had seen that dainty little women like Mrs. Joshi could be capable of horrifying violence. Girls stood their ground under the punishing sun while bigger, stronger boys passed out.

Indian history was filled with accounts of women who fought. Tarabai, Rani Durgavati, Chand Bibi, even Phoolan Devi, the bandit leader who became a member of parliament. According to eyewitness accounts on both sides, the rebel queen Rani Lakshmibai had women in her army as support staff, gunners . . . and cavalry.

My horse had stumbled on the field of battle, breaking her leg and throwing me. The cavalry had ridden on ahead and been slain in that last desperate battle.

So it was that I, a cavalrywoman without her horse, had come late and yet just in time, the highest-ranking officer yet living, to rally the troops and hold the breach. Fighting on though mortally wounded, I had kept my feet until the enemy had retreated. Only then allowing myself to fall, I sank to my knees in that bloody field, and said—

If it hadn't been for Mom, I would have kept on daydreaming, oblivious to a sight even more dramatic than the one before my mind's eye.

"Oh, Baba!" Mom exclaimed. "Mani, don't look! Cover your eyes!"

Jolted back to reality, I leaned over her lap and stuck my head out the window.

A car was partially off the road, on its side with its windshield shattered. A man lay sprawled on the road in front of the wrecked Ambassador. His head was also on the road, but several yards away.

Once we'd driven far enough that neither car nor corpse nor head could be seen, I broke the silence.

"That man was decapitated," I announced, pleased with the once-in-a-lifetime opportunity to use the word in casual conversation. "That means his head was cut off. I've never seen a decapitated body before. Have any of you?"

I guessed from their non-response that nobody had. I was dis-

appointed by their lack of interest in such an unusual sight, not to mention their lack of enthusiasm for my vocabulary.

"Did you notice that the head was still wearing a hat?" I inquired. "A green stocking cap? I wonder how that happened. I would've thought the hat would have come off when the head came off, wouldn't you?"

"Mani?" said Dad.

"Uh-huh?"

"Let's not talk about it."

I subsided. Being decapitated in battle wouldn't be a terrible way to die, although I would prefer to have time for stirring last words. But to be hurled through a windshield and have your head roll to the side of the road would be undignified, pointless, and depressing.

I wished our car had seat belts.

I prodded the boil on my thigh. It seemed bigger, and the flesh around it swollen. Death by infected bug bite would also be undignified, pointless, and depressing, not to mention painful and gross. Maybe I should tell Mom.

"Baba, Baba, Baba, Baba, Baba," she chanted. Dad and Grandpa Artie looked ready to strangle her.

I'd wait and see if it got worse.

We stopped at a hotel run by Baba-lovers and had dinner with the family. The patriarch had a lump like a lime sliced in half in the precise middle of his forehead and another on his left temple. I couldn't stop staring at his protuberances. Had his skull grown outward, or had he been born that way? They couldn't be contagious . . . could they?

After dinner, Mr. Lumpyhead picked up a book. "Baba said that three-quarters of the world will be destroyed. This book explains how it will happen. It was written by a famous psychic who foretold many disasters."

He began to read aloud with lip-smacking relish. "The sun will swell, and the air will become like molten metal. There will be no relief, for all water will be warm and then hot, until even the seas begin to boil. All people will burn, their skin will blacken and burst in the heat . . ."

As Mr. Lumpyhead read on, sounding as if he couldn't wait for it to start, the room grew hotter and darker. "The sun's hideous heat will cause great blisters to form on the bodies of the wretched men, women, and children of the earth. They will long for water, but it will be boiling hot and will only add to their agony and thirst."

Everything was dim except for the glint of the old man's glasses and his shiny deformed head, and all was quiet except for his voice ringing out to describe our fiery deaths. My head swam, and I felt as if I were trapped in a nightmare.

"Birds will drop from the sky, and fish will be boiled alive in the rivers and lakes. And it will happen in the year 1989, as it was foretold. In that year, the summer will never end, and we will burn in it, yes, we will burn."

What if it was true? The famous psychic had been right about everything else. And the sun *was* going to expand. My book on astronomy said so. It would turn into a red giant, and then a white dwarf, and then a ball of ash. Nineteen-eighty-nine was only six years away. It was getting hot already.

I whimpered. Mom touched my forehead.

"I'm taking Mani to bed," said Mom. "I think she has a fever."

We visited floating palaces and ancient abandoned cities, camel fairs and wildlife preserves. I have a snapshot taken at one of the latter. It shows me standing in front of a sign reading, "WARNING. Visitors, your attention is drawn to a man-eater tiger operating in close vicinity. Do not go on foot beyond campus. It is most dangerous." I'm wearing a white sweater and a huge grin.

I kept the secret under my band-aid until we reached Nainital, a high-elevation hill station, crystal-aired and bitter cold. The lake at the center of town was iced over around the edges.

We took a pony ride up a mountain that offered a view of the Himalayas at its peak. The ponies were not the spirited prancers I had hoped for, but placid creatures who plodded up the gentle ascent. Grandma Anne perched uneasily atop her pony. When it bent down to crop a bit of grass, she fell off.

The guide leaped to her side, apologizing profusely. She picked herself up and, though obviously shaken, remounted. My plump, blue-rinsed Grandma proceeded up the trail, not quite undaunted but back in the saddle. It hadn't taken any courage for me to ride, but then I wasn't likely to fall or to break bones if I did. Grandma Anne was a busybody, but she had nerve.

That evening, I locked myself in the bathroom and ripped off the band-aid on my leg. I had been able to feel through the plastic that there was no swelling, and it didn't hurt much, so I wasn't expecting anything awful.

There was a hole in my thigh. It was the width of a quarter and about an inch deep, an inverted cone with pus at the bottom. The sides of the cone were raw pink flesh. While I had waited and crossed my fingers, my leg was being eaten away.

I should have taped a lime to my thigh.

"Uh, Mom?" I tapped her shoulder. "I, uh, just noticed this thing on my leg."

Either my parents were too freaked out to dispute my account, or they were so used to Ahmednagar's rampaging infections that it seemed plausible.

A conference was held. They made no attempt to find a doctor in Nainital. Instead, Grandpa Artie took his flask of vodka and filled the crater with it. After a week of the topical application of vodka, the hole slowly began to close. By the time the Grandpas A left India, it was visibly healing. After a few months it closed, leaving a circular scar.

Years after I left India, I would show people that mark. I felt like it proved that my childhood had really happened.

"You see!" I would say, "There's the scar."

It was high on my thigh and difficult to display without dropping my pants. My victims would peer at the dot on my leg, shrunk by time to the size of a bb pellet, and try to muster an appropriate response. A few of them claimed that they couldn't see it.

But even I knew it was proof of nothing . . . except the little-known healing power of Stolichnaya vodka.

24

Down the Wet Path

When I was ten my chest was still flat as a boy's, and all my hair was on my head. But though I looked the same as I had the year before, albeit a measly half-inch taller, my hormones were beginning to percolate. But I had no idea this was going on. I just figured that I'd learned enough about animals, and it was time to begin my study of humanity. Specifically, I wanted to know about sex.

When I was four years old, Mom explained the mechanics of how babies are made. When I was seven she told me that sex was a good and loving thing that men and women did when they were married. But by the time I had gotten curious about the subject, sex had become a forbidden topic. Mom seemed horrified if it came up in conversation, the nuns made vague references to undefined acts that would send you straight to Hell, and Baba's opinion was that celibacy was best. But forbidding anything from an idea to an apple just adds to its appeal. And I wasn't the only one sniffing around the base of that tree.

I was reading in a back room one day, hidden from view, when Shinork sidled up to Dad. "I had another one last night."

Dad spoke loudly, catching my attention. "Another wet dream?"

"Shhh!"

I put down *Born to Trot* and peeped through the almost-closed door. A pilgrim kid had recently abandoned Judy Blume's *Then Again, Maybe I Won't* in Ratanji's library. Its teenage protagonist had secretly washed his sheets after his first wet dream. But Blume didn't explain what a wet dream was, except that it wasn't the same as wetting the bed and had something to do with the pretty girl next door who undressed with the shades up. I wanted to know more but sensed that I shouldn't ask.

"Well, was it?" asked Dad.

"There were . . ." Shinork licked his lips. "*Women* everywhere. Not women I know. Just anonymous . . . beautiful . . . luscious . . . *naked* . . ."

"Did you get it on with those luscious women?" inquired Dad.

Shinork nodded, a manic light in his eyes. "*All over the room.*"

"Shinork, have you ever had sex?"

"Um . . ."

"Hey, it's okay if you haven't, I just wondered."

"Well, you see, I was very shy as a boy. And a teenager. And a young man. And then when I was twenty-two, I came to the ashram, and, well . . ."

Dad folded his arms contemplatively. "Listen, Shinork, according to Baba, the entire world is an illusion, right? Everything we think is real—the dirt under our feet, sex, luscious naked women—none of it exists. It's nothing but a cosmic lightshow."

"Sure."

"So last night, all the men who had sex and got their wives pregnant were just as deluded as you were while you dreamed. In the grand scheme of things, we're all virgins."

"Wow," said Shinork.

That was interesting, but still didn't tell me what a wet dream was. A few nights later I was bathing with Mom. The bathroom was a cold stone cell. We had no hot running water, so the servants heated a bucket over the kerosene cooker and left it steaming on the bathroom floor. We sat on plastic stools and used cups to mix the heated water with cool tap water. I disliked this method of bathing, because it left most of your naked wet body exposed to the cold. But since it was the Indian way, Mom preferred it, pointing out that showers wasted water, and bathtubs left you lying in your own filth.

"You're all wet," she said, playfully splashing me. "It's a wet evening."

I saw my chance. "Everything's wet. We'll put on wet shoes and walk down the wet path . . ."

"And go to sleep in wet beds with wet sheets," said Mom, falling into my trap.

"And have wet dreams."

A familiar look of dismay—the "Mani's indicated that she knows about something that she shouldn't"—fell across her face. I could see minuscule water drops on the tiny golden hairs on her face and body. She was soft and fuzzy as a ripe peach. "What did you say?"

"Wet dreams," I said innocently. "Wet beds . . . wet sheets . . . wet dreams."

Mom chuckled. "Yes, Mani . . . don't say that, though. It doesn't mean what you think."

"What does it mean?"

Her eyes jerked to the side, for inspiration, then back to me. "Wet dreams are nightmares. But it's a bad word for them. Don't say it."

"Okay." Mom, Shinork, and Judy Blume had all given different explanations for the same taboo phrase. I couldn't help feeling that I was missing something.

I delved into more books for further information, but Mom confiscated any that looked like they might contain so much as heavy petting. This just made me more curious, and I began reading on the sly. I read *Clan of the Cave Bears* in Ratanji's library, poised to drop it and pick up *Prefects of the Chalet School* at the sound of footsteps. The first Cave Bear book is an exploration of the society of early man, written in a style reminiscent of those explorations of the society of the idle rich that one finds in supermarket book racks. The sequel has the heroine Ayla and her Cro-Magnon beau Jondalar having sex, inventing everything but the Internet, and having more sex.

Despite my avid curiosity about the subject, after six hundred pages of Jondalar fooling with Ayla's nodule and plunging his immense manhood into her capacious woman's cavern, I was too bored to finish. The only part that was illuminating was the nodule bit, and though I was able to locate something that I guessed was mine, it didn't seem much like Ayla's. Maybe, like breasts, it grew at puberty.

The loophole in Mom's anti-dirty books campaign was that sexuality was allowed if the books also contained uplifting religious content. That was how I was able to get away with reading an account of a Roman orgy, complete with whores with gilded nipples, in Taylor Caldwell's novel about St. Luke, *Dear and Glorious Physician*. Caldwell's Biblical novels were hugely popular at the Ahmednagar ashram. The religion provided a guilt-free excuse for the sex, for everyone repented at the end.

Reading the trashy novels of various eras in search of sexual content gives one a skewed idea of the whole thing, but it's a time-honored tradition. The modern equivalent of what I was doing would be to search the Web, an exercise that would probably convey the

impression that one goes straight from zero to bestiality—a practice most familiar to people on remote farms without Internet access, anyway.

While any small-town library would probably have provided similar fuel for sexual misconceptions, the Compound library had more than its fair share of the bizarre and the outdated. Due to the predilections of the sort of people who go on pilgrimage, it was overstocked with peculiar New Age manifestos, gloating predictions of the imminent end of the world, and ranting tracts advocating political theories so out-there that they were neither left nor right, but something like *orange*.

These disparate texts followed an identical pattern of reasoning. They began with an indisputable statement of fact, like "India's ancient myth cycle, *The Mahabharata*, contains stories about invulnerable warriors," or "Carrots are good for you," and, once that launching pad of sanity was in place, took a flying leap into lunacy, like "Therefore, *The Mahabharata* was dictated by alien astronauts in space armor!" or "Therefore, if you eat nothing but carrots and drink nothing but carrot juice, you will become enlightened and immortal!"

A pilgrim tried the nothing-but-carrots diet. After two months, he turned bright orange.

Nobody cared what demented pseudoscientific theories I might absorb, but normal sex was off-limits. I wasn't sure if demented pseudoscientific sexual theories were also verboten, but just in case, I didn't let anyone catch me reading the book that explained that if a man refrained from sex for thirty years, the sperm would migrate to his brain and give him psychic powers.

Even the mad librarian Ratanji was affected by the sexual content of his library, though he never read the books. Perhaps the heaving bosoms on the covers gave him vague, disturbing intimations of sweaty secrets within.

One night he made a surprise appearance at the residents' dining room. We stopped shoveling down chapatis and dal to stare at the apparition. Ratanji lurked in the doorway, maddened eyes darting back and forth, hands twisting beneath his chin.

"The sex," announced Ratanji, without preamble. "Why is it necessary? I do not see why the sex is necessary."

"Ratanji, bro," said The Goldberg, "I hate to break it to you, but without sex, the human race would die out. No sex, no people."

Ratanji's fingers writhed like sea anemones. "But why is it necessary? Why is the sex necessary?"

The Goldberg tossed the question back at him. "How are people supposed to have babies if they don't have sex?"

Ratanji thrust his scabby head forward. "They can walk into the forest and pluck the babies from the trees." With that, he departed in triumph.

Dad said, "I think Ratanji is a little Mast-like."

"He's nuts," I corrected.

"Oh, Mani," said Mom. "He was very close to Baba."

"He grunts outside my window every night," I said.

"He's not grunting," said Carla. "He's praying. There's a picture of Baba on that wall, and he's praying to it."

Out of all the Baba pictures on all the walls, he had to grunt at mine.

Shinork remarked, "Baba said this is Ratanji's final incarnation. When he dies, he'll become God-realized."

I rolled my eyes.

Dad said, "Sometimes I think three-quarters of everything Baba said was just to play with people's minds." Baba, who was all things to all people, was envisioned by Dad as the Divine Joker.

"How long did Baba say it takes to get God-realized?" asked Shinork.

"Eighty-four lakhs of years," said Mom.

Indians count large numbers in lakhs (one hundred thousands) and crores (ten millions.) When "Who Wants to Be a Millionaire?" was replicated in India, it was called *"Kone Banega Crorepathi?"* ("Who Wants to Be a Ten Millionaire?")

The Goldberg counted on his fingers. "Just think, bro. Eight point four million years of incarnations, all for the purpose of refining and perfecting a single soul, and the end product is Ratanji. God really does work in mysterious ways."

25

Harold Birmingham's Noxious Rays

"Your house is infested with noxious rays," announced Harold Birmingham.

Dad didn't ask how he knew or what they were. We had all learned that Harold should be given as few conversational openings as possible. He and his family arrived on pilgrimage when I was eleven. His wife and son were sane, likable people. Harold was a mutant.

"No kidding," said Dad.

"Oh, no!" Harold's eyes gleamed. "Noxious rays are deadly! That's why they're called noxious rays. When noxious rays invade a house, the inhabitants become fretful, anxious, prone to nightmares. Their immune systems weaken, and they—"

Dad crossed his arms over his chest. "Are you telling me this for a reason?"

Harold's voice lowered dramatically. "I want to rid your home of noxious rays."

"Do I need to pay you?"

"No, no, Baba would want me to do it as a favor."

"Do *I* have to do anything?"

"No, I'll do it all myself."

"Sounds okay so far," said Dad. "Do you have to come inside the house?"

"No, just the yard."

"All right," said Dad, losing interest. "Knock yourself out."

"What are you going to do?" I asked hopefully. "Are you going to sacrifice something?"

I took malicious pleasure in things that freaked out Mom. It was nothing personal. I would have also enjoyed things that freaked out Dad, except that nothing ever did. I hoped Harold would ritually disembowel a chicken on our doorstep. If he didn't mutilate it too badly, we could cook it afterward. Meat was a luxury in Ahmednagar.

"No, of course not!" said Harold. "I'm going to hammer three iron stakes into your front yard."

"That's it?"

"Uh-huh."

"Are we also infested with vampires?"

"Iron rebalances the flow of energies, which are misaligned in a hexagonal formation, and need to be—"

I edged away. Dad had already fled. "Cool. I'll come take a look when it's done."

Harold was as good as his word. He came by the next day with three iron stakes. The trouble was, our "yard" was a dirt walkway in front of our house. So he hammered them down there, in a small and hard-to-see triangle.

Mom tripped over it when she came home that night. "Baba!" she exclaimed. "How'd that get there? Get rid of it, Joey."

"Nope," said Dad. "It's warding off noxious rays."

Harold approached Dad a few weeks later, breathing heavily. "How did the triangulation work? Have you noticed a difference?"

"Harold," said Dad solemnly, "I haven't detected a single noxious ray since you put in the stakes."

"Good," said the irony-impaired Harold.

Despite Mom's protests and the stubbed toes of pilgrims, Dad thought it was funny to have a noxious ray protector in front of our house. So the triangle remained, a hazard to passersby, until I left India.

It's probably still there.

Harold stayed in Ahmednagar for several months. His son Walter was nothing like his demented father but an easy-going and inventive boy. Every weekend and afternoon after Holy Wounds, once he and I had gone through the routines of greeting the mandali and performing prayers and prostrations before the hallowed chairs, pictures, beds, bus, and marble slab, we quietly vanished into our own private world.

We became inseparable, a skinny girl with skinny braids and a stocky boy whose blond bangs were always falling into his eyes. We had fencing matches with the rattling brown seedpods of the Gul Mohr trees, netted crabs and minnows from the rushing creeks when the rains came, and went rock-climbing, geode-collecting, and lizard-catching in the hills and valleys of Meherazad.

The residents took note of our friendship and began saying things like, "You've got a little crush on Walter, don't you?" and "Walter and Rachel, sitting in a tree, K-I-S-S-I-N-G," and "There's nothing wrong with being in love—don't be ashamed of it," and "Come on, admit it, you like him *that way*."

"I'm NOT in love with him!" I'd scream. "Walter's my FRIEND! I don't KISS him! I don't WANT to kiss him! I just LIKE him! Why shouldn't I like my friend?!"

To which they'd respond that if I wasn't in love with him, I wouldn't deny it so passionately.

In fact, I didn't want to kiss him. For all my sex-laden sneak reading, the feelings the books roused and fed were just floating around, as yet unconnected to any actual people. I was on the brink of puberty, but I hadn't yet fallen in. All that being said, I can now reply to everyone who asked: Yes, in retrospect, I guess I did love Walter. What's it to you?

I never told him what my life was like when he wasn't around. I liked pretending that I was a kid, an innocent, like him. He thought I was brave and cool. He'd never respect me again if he knew that I ran more often than I fought, that kids threw rocks at me and teachers beat me and townsmen terrorized me for an afternoon's fun, or that almost every day I cried and wished I were dead.

Walter gave us code names, and I provided our mission: He was Cloak and I was Dagger, and we were secret agents who had infiltrated a conspiracy of global proportions. We planned missions, spied on everyone, and reported back to each other. Sometimes we worked as a team, and sometimes I came up with ideas and sent Walter to execute them.

"Dagger is the mind," he said, our heads close together beneath the flaming canopy of a Gul Mohr in bloom, "Cloak is the hands. One's no good without the other."

Alternately, we did the same sort of things with different genre trappings. Walter's luggage was mostly Dungeons and Dragons paraphernalia. But we ignored the dice and rules of play in favor of co-creating interactive stories set in the D & D world. When we were Barak and Laiena instead of Cloak and Dagger, we hid from mandali who were dragons, spied on residents who were ogres, and tricked pilgrims who were trolls.

Ahmednagar made a lot more sense as a monster-infested dungeon than it did as a holy city of God.

Our headquarters at Meherabad overlooked the flower dump atop Baba's Hill. That was where they tossed the used flowers from the Tomb, the holy pictures, and the mandali's graves. It was emptied weekly, so the day before pickup we perched above a foot-high pile of coiled marigold garlands and woven nets of jasmine, overblown roses, stiff zinnias, and orchids spotted like leopards and intricate as microchips. The flower dump exuded a complex aroma of perfume and greenery and luscious decay.

A pipal tree grew beside the dump and a broad wall bordered it. Our hideout was where the branches passed over the wall. We sat comfortably atop the sun-warmed concrete and used the books and boxes of dice we had stashed within hand's reach in the pipal's forks and hollows. We even had hats and coats hanging from broken-off branches.

The Amartithi festival occurred during Walter's visit, and the volume of the flower dump quadrupled overnight. We were sitting on the wall, slightly dizzy from the fumes emitted by the fermenting flowers, when an Indian boy leaped into view. As we blinked down at him, he pointed dramatically at us and shouted in Marathi.

Walter and I exchanged puzzled looks. We'd never seen the boy before and had been sitting on the wall for hours.

The boy cursed—I understood that part—grabbed a marigold garland from the heap, and flung it at us. It hit me in the face. "Stop that," I said in Marathi, spitting out a petal.

"Give me that," he said, pointing to the Styrofoam box that held our pencils.

"What's he saying?" asked Walter.

"He wants the box."

"Tell him he can't have it."

"You can't have the box," I said in Marathi.

The boy went into a frenzy. He dug both hands into the blossom pile and started hurling roses, garlands, and daisy chains at us, so frantically that most of them didn't even come close.

Walter was laughing so hard that he had to clutch at the wall. A white rose hit him in the mouth and almost went in. He and I leaped off the wall, intent on beating up the lunatic rose thrower or at least rubbing some flowers in his face. But the boy fled and was never seen again.

Walter and I dubbed the boy Flower-Flinger, but we couldn't come up with a better reason for his behavior than "He thought we'd give him the box if he threw flowers at us." Like many events in Ahmednagar, the obvious answer left more lingering questions than no explanation at all.

The fly in our ointment was another pilgrim boy, Kevin, who was two whole years younger than us but wanted to play. When we turned him away, he complained to our mothers, who ordered us to be nice to him. Before that, we had nothing against him except that he was too young and a third wheel. After he ratted on us, we took an active dislike to him.

So we devised a plan to make Kevin himself decide that playing with us wasn't any fun. We set a time to meet for our next game, and I primed him in advance with the belief that characters were determined by rolling the dice and by the Dungeon Master, in this case Walter, consulting the forbidden-to-players Dungeon Manual. This was, in fact, the way the game is supposed to be played, but Walter and I had created our characters, a swordfighter for him and a thief for me, by mutual agreement.

Kevin trotted eagerly to his doom. I eyed him with distaste. He had what Dad called "FLK Syndrome," which stood for Funny-Looking Kid and referred to the combination of jug-handle ears, buck teeth, and no chin. Also, he had a speech impediment that made him splutter his F's. Walter and I, who wouldn't have tolerated any intruders into our private games, much less this dorky little kid, had evilly kept this in mind.

"Okay, Kevin," said Walter. "You remember that once you roll the dice, the choice has been made. You can't decide that you don't like your character and you want to roll again."

"Uh-huh. Uh-huh. Let's roll the dice." Kevin bounced on his heels with excitement.

"Mani and I rolled the dice to decide everything, even the race of our characters. We're both human. But we decided, as a special treat for you, that you can choose your race."

"Oh boy!"

"But if we let you do that, you absolutely can't complain about anything else."

"Lemme do it! Lemme do it! I won't complain!"

"All right. Now, you can be a human, a dwarf, an elf— "

"I wanna be an elpth! An elpth!"

Walter and I leaned back to avoid the spit-spray.

"You sure?" inquired Walter. "I haven't even told you the other races . . ."

"Elpth! Elpth! Elpth!"

"Here's the dice." To amuse himself and me, Walter gave him the weird ones.

Kevin rolled. "What's it mean? What do I get?"

"Let's see." Walter pretended to consult the book. "Ah-ha. Two on the pyramid for an *elpth* gives you the name of . . . Flower-Flinger. Flower-Flinger the Elf."

"Thlower-Thlinger the Elpth," repeated Kevin happily. I ducked.

"Your power is that you fling flowers at your enemies. When you're in trouble, you take out a rose or dandelion or something and throw it right at that dragon, or orc, or whatever you're fighting."

Kevin looked puzzled. "Are they magic thlowers?"

"Nope. Fourteen on the octagons means you can't use magic. They're just regular flowers."

"But— "

"Uh-oh." Walter shook his head gravely. "Six on the hexagon. That's the flaw index—for character flaws—and a six is the very worst you can get."

"What does it mean?

"It means," said Walter brutally, marking his place in the book with a finger and leaning in to stare Kevin down, "Flower-Flinger is a coward. He's terrified of danger. In fact, he's such a coward that whenever he gets scared, he throws up."

"But . . . but . . ." Kevin's lip quivered. "I don't like my character. I don't want to be a coward."

"Too bad. That's the character you rolled. You can't change it now."

Kevin, who had better ammunition than daisies, said, "If you don't let me change it, I'll tell your mothers."

"Go ahead," said Walter. "Tell our mothers you don't want to play by the rules of the game."

"I will," said Kevin. "They'll make you change the rules."

It was a credible threat.

I said, in my honeyed Laiena the Thief voice, "Oh, but Kevin, Flower-Flinger is a *good* character. Just think—who wants to be thrown up on? If you throw up on your enemies, they'll run away. Or at least give you time to run away."

"Huh," said Kevin. "Okay. Let's play."

In an exaggeratedly bored voice, Walter rattled off, "You're in a dungeon. You turn a corner and see a troll. And you—"

"PUKE!" yelled Kevin. "I puke all over him!"

We ended up working out a compromise. If Kevin left us alone most of the time, he could play with us occasionally. Flower-Flinger the Puking Elf evolved into a craven idiot with absurdly good luck who accidentally saved the day and then pretended he'd done it on purpose.

Walter and I reserved the right to play tricks on Kevin, who was irresistibly gullible. Once we constructed a bird's nest, placed four large cream-colored berries in it, forbade him to follow us, and went to observe it. When he came out of hiding and pushed forward to see what we were looking at, we warned him that whatever he did, he mustn't touch the eggs.

"I won't break them," he promised.

"You can't even touch them," I said solemnly. "If you even brush them with your finger, they'll change color and shrivel up and die. You wouldn't want that, would you?"

Kevin shook his head. But he didn't believe us. A few days later, he ran up, conscience-stricken. "I touched them!" he blubbered. "I touched the eggs, and . . . and . . ."

We went to investigate. The berries had ripened to a rich crimson. Walter sadly shook his head. "That's it, then. First they turn red, then they wither and die."

"Now you'll never get to see the baby birds," I added.

"No," said Walter. "Because *you killed them*."

Kevin howled.

We tortured him with regular visits to the nest of shriveling berries until their decay exposed the seeds within. We disposed of the entire nest before it could give us away, and told him a wolverine ate it.

But despite ourselves, Walter and I came to enjoy playing with Kevin, or rather telling each other Flower-Flinger stories with interjections from Kevin. And though Barak and Laiena were just idealized and grown-up versions of Walter and me, Flower-Flinger turned into a genuine character. The adventure in which he accidentally invented gunpowder and blew up a dragon, and was elected mayor until an aggressive wasp and his weak stomach made him disgrace himself at his inauguration banquet, is a story I retain fond memories of to this day.

The summer after Walter left India, I visited the Grandpas A in America again. I also spent a week of the trip with the Birminghams at their small Kentucky farm.

The trip got off to a rousing start when Walter took me to visit the llama. Harold was a veteran of get-rich-quick schemes, from breeding chinchillas to breaking the bank at Vegas, and he planned to raise llamas for their fine cashmere coats.

I followed Walter through the lush wet grass. The last time I'd seen him, we'd been the same height, but now he was several inches taller. He marched up to the fence and extended his hand toward the llama. "Want to pet it?"

I hung back. "Don't they spit?"

"No, no," said Walter confidently. "It knows I'm a friend."

The llama leaned forward, looking hostile and superior, and spat a stream of gooey green liquid all over his face and shirt. I laughed until I fell down and rolled in the grass and stained my shirt as green as Walter's.

He and I were poring over the Dungeon Manual in his room that evening when his father stuck his head in the door. "Time for your enema!"

Walter groaned. "Dad, I'm in the middle of something. Can't I skip it tonight?"

"Now, Walter," said Harold, "You know that accumulated toxins—"

"Yeah, yeah. Mani, help yourself to any of my books. I'll be back in half an hour or so."

They left before I could pose the obvious question. I asked it when Walter returned, looking rather subdued.

"What's an enema?"

My friend's fine hair fell across his face as he turned aside. "Ah . . ."

I waited.

"Well . . ." He sighed and turned to meet me eye to eye. His were blue-gray. *Storm clouds over sea,* I thought dreamily. The contrast with his dark eyebrows and eyelashes made me notice them anew every time.

"Basically . . . there's a rubber bag filled with warm water, and a tube that connects to it. You put the tube up your butt and squeeze the bag, so the water goes in."

I knew by the effort it had taken him to tell me that, straightforwardly and face to face, that it was the truth. So instead of asking him if he was serious, I went straight to "*Why?*"

"It's supposed to be healthy." He shrugged, unwilling to either criticize or defend his loony father.

It sounded humiliating and horrible, and anything Harold Birmingham believed in had to be bunk. "Does it hurt?"

"No."

"But . . ."

"I'm used to it, I guess."

I dropped the subject, but I couldn't help picturing an enema scene: Walter draped over the toilet with his pants pulled down and a black rubber hose like a gas pump stuck up his bare butt. I tried to push it out of my mind. Even having the image there made me feel complicit in his shame.

This revelation of Walter's home life didn't knock him off the pedestal he occupied in my imagination. I admired his stoicism and his nerve and honesty in telling me the truth. If Barak the swordsman had been captured by orcs and tortured with tubes up the ass, that was how he'd have faced such treatment unbecoming to a hero.

Walter muttered something about looking for a book and spent an inordinate amount of time fishing around under his bed. I looked out the window at the darkening sky. My chest ached and pulled, as if something inside were scarring over. It had never occurred to me that I wasn't the only one of our duo who had trouble with real life.

I hadn't considered the implications of having Noxious Ray Birmingham as a father. Walter and I had more in common than I had ever imagined. I wished we didn't.

That night, Harold prepared alligator stew with Tofutti pie for dessert. The stew tasted like stew, but I was apprehensive about the dessert. I had never known tofu to taste like anything.

I coughed. I had woken up with a sore throat and figured I was coming down with a cold.

"You have a cough!" said Harold.

"No—"

"I'm a doctor of alternative medicine. Let me take you upstairs and diagnose you."

"I'm fine." I gulped water to stifle the tickle at the back of my throat. "Really, I don't need anything. It was just a little dust."

"I don't think so," said Harold jollily. "We must diagnose you!"

"It's a sore throat. It doesn't need a diagnosis."

Walter gave me a sympathetic look as Harold propelled me upstairs. "We'll just check that with the orgone box."

"What's that?"

"Ahhh." His eyes took on a dismayingly familiar fanatical glow. "The orgone box is the invention of the great thinker and healer Wilhelm Reich. It captures the power of—" He broke into a fit of coughing.

"Maybe *you* need the orgone box."

"Just a bit of dust. The orgone box captures the power of human energy. All the, ah, happiness everyone feels goes into the air, and it's captured in the orgone box."

The word orgone did not suggest anything to me at the time, but I looked it up later. According to the late crackpot Wilhelm Reich, an orgone box is a device which captures the energy created by human orgasms.

We stopped at an apparatus the size and shape of a grandfather clock.

It was polished wood and decorated with more dials than the control board of the space shuttle.

"The orgone box!" declared Harold.

I cast about for escape routes in case he tried to lock me inside.

"Hold out your hands."

I extended my hands toward the orgone box. "What's it do?" I couldn't see any cords extending from it. "Does it run on batteries?"

"It runs on orgones."

A crash and shriek came from downstairs. "Harold!" yelled Mrs. Birmingham. "The cat's in the Tofutti!"

"Stay right there." Harold trotted downstairs.

I examined the orgone box, careful not to alter the dial settings. The front of the box swung open like a cupboard. It was hollow inside. It contained no circuitry, no gears, and no machinery of any kind. The dials didn't connect to anything, but had twist-knobs that protruded into the inside of the box, as if they were intended to be manipulated from within.

Harold's big thumping footsteps began to ascend the stairs. I closed the box and extended my hands in front of it, which is how he found me.

"You can touch the dials," he said.

I tested one, then others. They didn't move.

"Now put your hands back out, close your eyes, and don't open them till I say so."

I heard a creak, a set of clicks, then another creak.

"You can open your eyes now. You see how the dials have changed positions?"

"Uh-huh."

"That's how they diagnose your illness. They say . . ." he studied them. "You have strep throat."

"I feel fine."

"The orgone box does not lie," declared Harold. "Now for your treatment."

He turned to rummage in a cupboard. If he took out a hose, I vowed to bite him and run.

He held up a vial filled with tiny white pills. "Take the first one now, and then one with each meal. Go on."

I recognized the homeopathic pills, as they were a popular treatment in Ahmednagar and one favored by Baba. Homeopathic medicine is made by diluting medicine until no trace of it can be detected, then using the chemically pure water to make sugar pills. The theory is that the energy left by the original substance not only remains but is strengthened by this technique. I knew the principle at the time and thought it was ridiculous.

Harold stood over me with his hands on his hips. He was built like a lumberjack, and I was eleven. I swallowed the pill, consoling myself with the thought that as it was chemically impossible for it to have any effect whatsoever, it couldn't harm me.

The next morning, I awoke unable to speak, squeak, or make any sound whatsoever. Harold said that his treatment had transformed my severe case of strep throat into simple laryngitis. Though I palmed the rest of his pills, it was days before I could even whisper. I wondered if the pill hadn't really been homeopathic, or if the laryngitis would have come on anyway. But I've never since been quite as convinced of the ineffectiveness of homeopathy.

I didn't have an alphabet board or system of sign language, but Harold didn't ruin my vacation.

"The door leads to a dark hallway," said Walter in his flat Dungeon Master voice. "It's so narrow that you'd have to go in single file. You can hear crackling noises, like people . . . or things . . . walking over dry leaves."

Shifting into impetuous Barak, he said, "'I think it's the ant-people.' I take a step toward the door."

I wrote on a legal pad as Walter read over my shoulder. "Laiena says, 'Wait, Barak. You'll need a torch to see, and then they'll know we're coming. But I'm used to working in the dark. I'll go first.'"

"My sword and I will be right behind you," said Walter/Barak. "Not even the Ant Queen and all her people can defeat the two of us together."

I wrote, "No one can."

26

101 Things to Do with a Baked Potato

Guidebooks didn't mention Ahmednagar, encyclopedia entries quoted disparaging proverbs, and the only people who moved there were Baba-lovers or in the army, but the neighboring town of Pune was a popular tourist destination.

Pune was Ahmednagar's doppelganger, complete with its own ashram. It was a two-hour drive from Ahmednagar, but it seemed like it was on another planet. The Sizzler served actual steaks, and the Kalyani Bakery's English-style ginger cookies had a devoted following. Pune had an English bookshop, movie theaters with sound systems on the inside, non-abusive schools, well-equipped hospitals, paved roads, cosmopolitan residents, live theater, and a newspaper. Even the weather was milder.

I never forgave Baba for not establishing his ashram in Pune.

But if Pune was Ahmednagar's good twin, the Rajneesh ashram was the Baba ashram's evil twin. The Rajneeshis, who like the Baba-lovers had an Indian guru but mostly Western disciples, dressed in orange robes and practiced strange sex rituals. Rajneesh's Pune ashram and its American offshoots were dogged by accusations of rape, profiteering, and the sexual abuse of children. Rajneesh was eventually indicted for tax evasion, and the woman who ran his ashram in Oregon was jailed for deliberately infecting local salad bars with salmonella.

Whatever else one can say about Baba's ashram, at least any sex was consensual and any food poisoning was accidental.

The Baba-lovers avoided the Rajneeshis, whom they regarded as the victims of a grandiose cult leader, but I loved Pune. Mom had some friends there whom we visited every few months. They were a household of elderly Baba-lovers, but were not notable cheek-squeezers. That alone would have made me enjoy the trips, but in addition, they were nice people, they served Kalyani ginger cookies instead of the dreaded glucose biscuits, and I got to read their collections of Modesty Blaise and Sexton Blake.

Modesty Blaise was the star of innumerable comic strips and eleven novels by Peter O'Donnell. She was a master of martial arts, a crack shot, a former child refugee, and a rape survivor. She had once led an international criminal cartel, but had gotten bored after her early retirement and become a secret agent. She rescued kidnap victims, went three rounds with a gorilla, dueled with exotic villains, and generally proved herself the coolest woman alive. Also, she had sex.

What lifted the stories above their faux-Bond trappings was Modesty's relationship with her partner, the cockney knife-thrower Willie Garvin. They both enjoyed affairs with other people, but

their true love was for each other, a passionate friendship that transcended sex. The partnership between the dark-haired woman who made the plans and the big blond man who provided the muscle reminded me of the lost days when Walter and I played spies. My visit to his farm was the last time I ever saw him.

I wonder if as many men have been disappointed in their boyhood hopes of finding a woman like Modesty Blaise as women have been of finding a man like Willie Garvin.

Sexton Blake penny dreadfuls were a horse of a different color. Their prose started at purple and shaded into ultraviolet, and they starred a detective who was a cross between Sherlock Holmes and James Bond and got hit over the head more than Wile E. Coyote at the ACME factory. They were printed in the 1920s in four-point type on newsprint, often written anonymously, and sold for twenty-six pence. I have no idea how they made their way to Pune.

Mimi flushed. “It was nothing.” She glanced with such a look of adoration at Splash Page that the young journalist blushed.

“I did it for m’sieu. You remember three years ago, in the Cafe of the Dead Rat—the fracas, m’sieu. At the risk of your life you grappled with that cocaine fiend and saved me from unspeakable horrors. He had designed for me a fate that was worse than death!”

While Mom listened to Baba stories in the kitchen, I curled up on the porch swing and breathlessly followed Blake’s escape from villains who plan to feed him to specially imported army ants, or Modesty’s duel to the death with a pair of athletic Siamese twins.

But the catch to the Pune trips was that we had to rent a car and driver to get there and back. Mom spent every trip there chanting Baba's name and begging the driver to go slower. When we arrived, she'd be so annoyed with the driver that she'd refuse to engage him for the return trip. Then she'd spend the trip back to Ahmednagar—I refused to call it "home"—chanting Baba's name and begging the driver to go slower. Since I was liable to spend the days leading up to the trip reading about historic warrior women who died fearlessly in battle and my time in Pune reading about Modesty Blaise, I felt that Mom was not living up to my minimum standard of female courage.

She seemed afraid of *everything*: sudden percussive noises, people touching her from behind, Dad, germs, bulls, snakes, heights, drafts, dust, cat hair, aggressive beggars, contaminated food, giant rats, feral dogs, loud voices, displeasing the mandali, and all forms of motor transportation. But it never occurred to me to ask her why she was frightened, or to consider how much courage it requires to get into a car at all when you're terrified of driving. Or that fictional characters like Modesty Blaise and famous heroes like Rani Lakshmibai might be a bit of a high standard to hold one's mom to.

But that's how I feel now. Back then, at the Pune taxi lot where decrepit cars were lined up for inspection under a sky the color of pencil lead, I observed Mom with a critical eye and wondered just how effective the anti-baby-switching precautions at American hospitals really were.

The driver whose lemon Mom was inspecting burst out, "But what is the problem, madam? Is very good car. I am good driver. You will be there soon. I drive very quickly."

She shuddered. "I don't want you to drive quickly. I want you to drive slowly, carefully, and safely."

"I drive very safely," protested the driver. "And my car is very fast!"

Mom moved on to the next Ambassador. None of them had seat belts, which undoubtedly contributed to the high fatality rate for car accidents in India.

One Ambassador's owner had overheard our last ten conversations with rejected drivers. "I drive very slow," he said. "I am very careful. No accidents."

Mom warmed to him. But when she pushed down on the back seat, it gave six inches under her hand. The springs on the left side were missing.

"Not to worry," said the driver, and stuffed in a pillow.

"Do you have windshield wipers?" asked Mom, sounding hopeless already. We had yet to see a rent-an-Ambassador that did.

"Yes, madam." He seemed offended by the question. "Of course have wipers. Vehicle is issued with wipers."

We got in and began bouncing down the road. The car, like all Ambassadors, had evidently not been issued with shocks. The sky dimmed, and the whitewashed rocks along the side of the road became hard to see.

"Baba, Baba, Baba, Baba . . ." Mom noticed that we were driving through a midnight not so clear. "Excuse me, sir, can you please turn on the headlights?"

"Lights are not needed."

I braced myself for a battle. Drivers only turned on their lights to flash other vehicles. They thought leaving them on wore out the battery.

"Yes, they are," said Mom. "It's pitch-black out there."

"There is light."

Conciliatory, Mom said, "I'll pay extra to make up for the wear on the battery."

"It is no use, madam," he said. "Lights are not working."

A sheet of lightning brightened the road like a million working headlights. Rain flooded down in an instantaneous deluge. Visibility went from poor to nil in a nanosecond. Even I became alarmed. I could see nothing out the windshield but splattering water.

"Turn on the windshield wipers," pleaded Mom.

"I can see," said the driver.

"I bet they don't work either," I remarked.

"They have to." Mom's hands twitched with agitation. "I only hired the car because it had them."

"I know," I said. "But you didn't ask if they worked."

The driver's lack of comment made it clear that my surmise was correct.

"Why didn't you say something?" shouted Mom. I wasn't sure who she was talking to.

I said, "I didn't think of it till now."

The driver said, "Not to worry, madam."

He fished under his seat with one hand. When it rained drivers would get a rag, roll down the window, and drive with one hand while hanging out the window and wiping the windshield with the other. Sure enough, he pulled out a bunched-up rag. He unwrapped it, revealing half a baked potato—his lunch, I assumed—and rolled down the window.

"You're not going to lean out the window and wipe the glass with that rag," Mom protested. "It's incredibly dangerous, and it doesn't help."

"Not to worry." The driver put down the rag and picked up the potato. As Mom and I watched, so astounded that even she fell silent, he stuck his entire upper body out the window and, without pulling over or even slowing down, began to polish the windshield with the baked potato.

"What are you doing?" shrieked Mom, after smears of potato put the level of visibility into negative numbers. "Are you crazy? Pull over!"

"Not to worry," said the driver. I could tell that Mom was getting on his nerves. He wrestled himself back into the car and turned to face her. "You see—"

“Watch the road!” yelled Mom.

“I am watching,” said the driver, not watching. “I am telling you, madam—”

An enormous truck hurtled into view, moving at such speed and ferocity that even the potato coating on the windshield couldn’t hide it. It was on the wrong side of the road and barreling straight at us.

“Look out!” I screamed.

“BABA!” shrieked Mom.

The driver, struck more by the honest terror on our faces than by our bothersome shouting, spun round, wrenched at the wheel, and missed the truck by three inches.

I sank back down. The seat sank with me. The pillow had come dislodged in the commotion.

The driver turned back around. “You see, madam—”

Mom slapped him across the face. “You almost got us killed!”

An emotional shockwave reverberated around the taxi an instant later. All three of us cringed with embarrassment and broken taboos. I sat staring at the silver flow of rain. Narrow escapes were much more enjoyable when they happened to Modesty Blaise. I wanted Willie Garvin in the driver’s seat. He could make a lethal weapon from a baked potato and use it on Mom. Or the driver. Ideally, both of them.

After a few minutes, Mom spoke. “I’m very sorry. I was completely wrong, and I apologize. Er . . . I’ll make it up to you. It was just that . . . well . . . you almost drove into a truck.”

“Yes, yes,” said the driver, recovering his aplomb and replacing the mangled potato under the seat. “Truck was on wrong side only. Those truckers are not understanding the importance of safe driving.”

INTERLUDE III: 2002

Family Portrait

When I was twenty-eight, Mom went on tour.

The Baba community sponsored her. Though she hadn't been out of India or on a plane for twenty-one years, she agreed to lecture at Baba centers around the world about the mandali and how she'd devoted her life to serving them.

While Mom agonized in India over the prospect of flying, I brooded over her intrusion into my Baba-free existence. I worked in TV development, which meant I read books for a living. I lived in a Hollywood apartment near Little Armenia and Thai Town with my two cats. I practiced karate, mentored at-risk kids, and had more friends than I could fit around my dinner table. I might not be Modesty Blaise, but at least I had a brown belt. And though I hadn't yet found my own Willie Garvin, I'd had a lot of fun road-testing men for the position.

I was living the life I'd longed for when I was a child, and I was afraid that if Mom contacted it she'd annihilate it like antimatter.

I had preemptively nixed the possibility of her staying with me for the week she'd be in Los Angeles by pointing out that my long-haired cats would give her the mother of all asthma attacks if she set foot in my apartment. So she was staying with Elaine, a fellow Baba-lover and old friend of hers.

"Your aunt Bobbie called me," chirped Elaine over the phone. "She's so excited to see her sister after twenty-one years. She asked about you too. Isn't that sweet?"

Several years before my trip to India in 2000, Bobbie had called out of the blue to ask me to have lunch with her. I hadn't even known she lived in Los Angeles, and I'd been a toddler the last time we'd met. At the restaurant, I approached the scarlet-suited businesswoman with caution. She looked more like Miss Corporate America than anyone related to my mother or me.

"You must be Rachel." She got up and hugged me. I gave her points for not calling me Mani.

As I pulled out my chair, she said, "Tell me, Rachel, how many years have you been in therapy?"

"What?" I squeaked, sitting down with a thump. "None! Who told you I was in therapy? Do I look like I should be in therapy?"

"I assumed that with your childhood, you'd have been in therapy for years."

"Well, I haven't!"

"It's nothing to be ashamed of," said Bobbie.

I grabbed the menu like a lifeboat. "I think I'll have the crab cakes," I said. "What are you getting?"

Bobbie drummed on the tablecloth with scarlet-tipped fingers. "Those things your mother told you. . . . They never happened."

"What things?"

"You know."

"No, I don't. What things?"

"Oh, nothing. So are you done with grad school now?"

What things? I began to babble. "Yeah, I got my MFA in playwriting, but no one's producing original plays anymore. They just do sit-down readings, but the reason I got into playwriting was because I wanted to collaborate with actors and directors and designers, so that defeats the entire purpose of—"

She cut me off at the pass. "Those stories your mother tells about our father aren't true."

"What stories?" *I've always wondered,* Dad had said. "What stories, Bobbie?"

"Oh, nothing. What were you saying about playwriting?"

"Um . . . " I had no idea what I'd been saying. I flapped my hand at the waiter. "I'd like the crab cakes, please."

Bobbie requested the chopped salad.

"I've heard that's good here," I offered randomly. "They put . . . olives in it."

Bobbie leaned across the table. "Despite what your mother may think, our father never did anything inappropriate to us. None of that stuff ever happened."

"What stuff are you talking about?"

She leaned back in her seat. "Nothing."

"WHAT STUFF?!"

"Your mother wrote me a letter," said Bobbie cagily. "She said she'd had . . . an unhappy childhood. I thought she'd written to you too."

"Nope. Mom never tells me anything."

"I wanted to inform you that my childhood wasn't like that. Nobody ever did those things to me."

"What things?"

"Nothing."

That was how I found out that Dad and I weren't the only ones who wondered about Mom's childhood. And that Mom wasn't the only one who didn't want to talk about it. It was also the last time I'd heard from Bobbie. Though I had eventually gone into therapy, and it improved my life considerably, I had never felt the urge to telephone Bobbie and tell her she'd been right about that.

Elaine said, "So Bobbie's meeting your mother at the airport with us."

Nuala threw herself at my feet and rolled over, mewing to have her belly scratched. I scratched it. She hissed, bit my hand, and ran away. I had sworn that I would be a better parent than my parents, but I'd still raised a neurotic cat. Mom had probably sworn to be a better parent than her parents too.

Good thing I'd had Nuala spayed.

Elaine and Bobbie and I converged at the airport. I was relieved to see that Bobbie's attire was less ferociously corporate. Mom came out, sturdily trundling her suitcase up the ramp, her dupatta fluttering in the air-conditioned breeze.

This is my turf, I reassured myself. *And she's so booked with lectures that our total time together is going to be about six hours. This could be almost painless.*

One of the benefits of having Bobbie present was that in the ensuing round of hugs and greetings, I wasn't the only one who responded to "Jai Baba" with "hello."

"Pull your shirt down, Rachel. I can see your belly button." Mom poked it playfully.

"You're supposed to see it," I said. "That's the fashion."

"To see women's bellies?" exclaimed Mom.

"Uh-huh," I said.

"Yep," said Elaine.

"That's right," said Bobbie.

Mom frowned. "Isn't it a bit . . . provocative?"

"Nope," I said.

"Not really," said Elaine.

"Kids nowadays don't seem to think so," said Bobbie.

"And your nails." Mom lifted my hand. "They're blue!"

"Yeah," I said. "These too." I extended my sandaled foot en pointe.

In addition to the ice-blue nail polish, I was wearing white Capri pants and a hot pink crop-top. It was my favorite summer outfit, but the thought of shocking Mom with flaunted skin had also entered my mind when I'd selected it. It hadn't occurred to me that my nails were startling too.

"Wow," said Mom. "How long has that been around?"

"Maybe ten years?" I hazarded.

"Mmm-hmm," said Elaine.

"Uh-huh," said Bobbie.

I buffed my blue nails against my belly-baring shirt.

The restaurant was a trendy Chinese place with a long wait list. While Elaine approached the maitre d', I went to the bathroom and brushed my hair for as long as I dared. When I returned to the lobby, the women were engaged in a serious conversation. "If I must, I must," said Mom.

"Must what?" I sat down in the chair beside her.

"Sweetie, seeing you wasn't the only reason I came to America," said Mom. "You know my father is very old now."

"So we're going to visit him before he dies," said Bobbie.

I looked from Mom to Bobbie to Elaine, wondering what

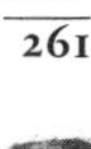

everyone knew, what everyone thought the others knew, and what would be safe for me to say aloud. "Really?"

Bobbie said, "He wrote to your mother that his last wish is to see her. He wanted to put past quarrels behind him now that he's old and dying."

"Does he have cancer?" I hadn't heard that he was dying.

"No," said Bobbie. "But he's very, very frail. He can't get around by himself. He's living with an aide. And he may have Alzheimer's."

I didn't see the point of showing up in person to forgive someone who wouldn't know what he was being forgiven for. "Is he even going to know who she is?"

"He'll know his daughter," Bobbie assured me. "He said himself that he wanted to see Dan-Anna before he dies."

"Da-nonna," corrected Mom.

"Wow, Mom. You're really going to see him?"

"Yes, sweetie." Mom straightened her back. Her hands stayed clasped tightly in her lap. "Baba wants me to forgive him. If I don't do it now, I'll be bound to him through all our incarnations until I do."

"Forgive him for what?" I asked.

"It's water under the bridge," said Mom.

Bobbie chimed in, "Your mother and I remember the past differently, and we've agreed to disagree about that. But I'll admit that he wasn't the world's most sensitive and considerate father."

I gave up on the hope of getting a straight answer out of either of them. "So when are you going to see him?"

Bobbie said, "I'm driving your mother out tomorrow. He lives in Rancho—"

"AIIIIIIIEEEEEEEEE!"

Mom leaped to her feet with a shriek. A small black object flew out of her lap. I screamed. Elaine screamed. Bobbie screamed. The maitre d' made a girly noise. Everyone in the lobby turned and stared.

The maitre d' retrieved the black object. "It's just the buzzer," he explained. "Your table's ready."

"Sorry, Da-nonna," said Elaine. "I forget to tell you what that was. It's a gimmick they have here."

"Baba," said Mom, panting a bit. "How strange."

The restaurant was so crowded that we walked to our table in single file, with me on point. A man at a table ahead of me dropped his cell phone. It skittered toward my feet. I stepped back and collided with Mom, who had been following two inches away.

"AIIIIIIIIIIEEEEEE!" she shrieked. "A scorpion!"

This so alarmed a man at another table that he leaped up and collided with Elaine. Everyone was staring at us again. I liked to pretend I was a Gap model in my tight pink shirt and tight white pants, strolling down the road and enhancing passing tourists' LA experience. But no matter how stylish I looked, right now I was just part of the crazy lady's party.

I picked up the cell phone and brandished it at Mom in all its rectangular silverness. "This does not look anything like a scorpion!"

"Sweetie, don't snap at me," said Mom.

"I'm so sorry," said Elaine to the room at large. "She's been living in India for twenty-one years."

"Everything's so strange to me," said Mom, smiling sweetly.

Everyone chuckled and told her to enjoy her stay.

"There are cell phones all over India," I muttered rebelliously. "You have one yourself."

"I've been gone for years and years, munchkin," said Mom. "Have some compassion for your old mother."

The crowd gave me the evil eye. Mom was an adorable immigrant in her salwar kamiz, bravely navigating a land that had grown up without her, and I was her ungrateful citified daughter.

Was I a shallow Hollywood bitch? Had I made myself strong, or was I only hard?

We sat down and ordered drinks: alcoholic for Elaine and me,

non- for Mom. Bobbie had disappeared and was presumably either hiding in the bathroom or fleeing into the night. Which was what I wanted to do.

Mom turned to Elaine and me. "I don't want to go on this trip," she confided. "I'm dreading seeing my father."

Elaine said, "It'll be tough, honey, but there'll be a big weight off your mind when it's over."

I said, "If you don't want to go, then don't go."

"I have to," said Mom. "Baba wants me to forgive him. Once I do it, it'll be over, and then I'll never have to see him again. I just don't *want* to go."

"Would it help if I went with you?" I asked. I didn't particularly want to meet my molesting grandfather, but it wasn't as if a helpless invalid could do anything to me. I was also hopeful that a trip with Bobbie and Mom might shake loose some family secrets.

Mom's face lit with a hopeful smile. "Oh, would you?"

"Sure," I said. "Count me in. I'm kind of curious to meet the molester, anyway."

Elaine smothered a chuckle. Mom glared. "Don't call him that."

"Well, isn't he one?"

"Just don't call him that."

"But he is one, isn't he?"

Mom sighed. "Look, Rachel. I have to forgive him, so please stop reminding me why I don't want to."

"You don't *have* to forgive him," I said. *I* didn't forgive him, and I'd never even met him. "Forgiveness is something you feel, not something you're forced into."

"I'm not forced," said Mom. "But Baba wants me to do it, so I can't say no. Anyway, it's healthier to forgive than to willfully hold on to anger. You yourself can never move on as long as you cling to the wrongs of the past." She gave me a meaningful look.

"I don't agree with that," I said. "I think first you have to admit that there were wrongs done and what they were. And the person who wronged you should apologize."

At that moment, Bobbie returned and my drink arrived.

"What *is* that?" asked Bobbie.

"Is that alcoholic?" asked Mom.

"Can I have a sip?" asked Elaine.

"It's a Bangkok Blue." I held it up for inspection. "Pretty, huh? Matches my nails."

Bobbie drove Mom and me into a desert bristling with windmills. The design was starkly functional, but the spin was cheerful as a pinwheel stand.

" . . . so I feel truly blessed to have discovered Baba and been allowed to devote my life to him," concluded Mom.

I yawned. Bobbie said, "Well, Da-nonna, I may not believe in what you believe in, but I'm glad you were able to explain it to me. And I do respect your life choices."

"Oh, Bobbie, I'm so glad," said Mom. "Isn't it wonderful for all of us to be together as a family?"

"So how old is the mo—my grandfather?" I asked.

"Ninety-two," said Bobbie. "He'll live forever. The old cockroach."

I remembered my sensei's advice to go for an opening the instant you see it, before it goes away. I went for it. "Wasn't he a con man?"

"Rachel!" said Mom.

"She may as well know," said Bobbie. "Yes, he and his brother sold land they didn't own. Then his brother took all the money they'd swindled and ran off with it, and nobody ever saw him again."

"Do you visit your father often?" I asked.

"Nope," said Bobbie, getting into the swing of the honesty thing.

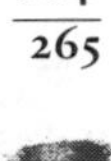

"Don't get me wrong, I like him. But he's a cold cold man. He never did anything to me, but he wasn't exactly what I'd call a loving father."

"That he was not," agreed Mom.

"Does he have any good qualities?" I had intended the question to be rhetorical, but it seemed a reasonable one to Mom and Bobbie.

"Oh, yes, absolutely," said Bobbie.

"Everyone has *some* good qualities," said Mom.

"Well, what are they?"

The sisters thought about this as the windmills flicked by. "He's *very* sarcastic," offered Bobbie.

"Always a plus," I said.

She exited the freeway and pulled up at a restaurant advertising the "World's Largest Selection of Draft Beers."

"Here we are," said Bobbie. "We're meeting him for lunch."

I'd thought he was bedridden, but I figured his aide could push his wheelchair around a restaurant. Whatever shape he was in, I was determined not to kiss him. I would say hello and maybe shake his (feeble or paralyzed) hand, but that was as far as I was willing to go.

"Baba, Baba, Baba," murmured Mom.

For the fifth time, I reminded them, "I have to be back in LA by six or I'll miss karate."

Mom flashed me a grin. "Are you kidding? That's my excuse too."

I walked into the lobby ahead of Mom and Bobbie. A spry old man dashed up to me with his arms flung wide, exclaiming, "How wonderful to see you again!" His gravelly voice couldn't have been stronger if he'd worn a clip mike.

Rather than make a scene, I let him hug me and kiss my cheek. "You're as beautiful as ever, Dan-Anna," he said lecherously. His hand slid down my back.

"I'm your granddaughter, Rachel." I extricated myself from his surprisingly strong arms. "Da-nonna's daughter."

"And as beautiful as your lovely mother," he said, even more lecherously.

Or was I imagining the tone in his voice, the touch of his hands? If I didn't believe that he had abused my mother, would I have thought him courteous and kind?

My grandfather and I both took a step back to size each other up. He had shrunk to my own height of five-foot-nothing, but his muscles hadn't quite melted away. His eyes were the same honey-touched brown as Mom's and mine, and lit with intelligence.

It was the most intense exchange of glances I'd encountered outside of a sparring match. He broke it with a jerk of his chin that I interpreted to mean, *Don't think I'm through with you.*

"Hello, Dan-Anna," he said.

I introduced myself to his paid companion, a hausfrau named Esther, while he gave Mom a long lingering hug.

Greetings done, we headed to a table. There was a brief commotion as my grandfather tried to sit beside Mom or me, and everyone but Esther tried to sit in whichever chair was farthest from him. As the youngest and strongest member of the party, I nabbed that prize seat.

I engaged Bobbie in desperate conversation while Mom told my grandfather about Baba.

Tears glowed in Mom's eyes. "I want you to know that I forgive you. Baba wants me to forgive you, and I want to forgive you. I want to leave the past in the past."

My grandfather smiled. His tongue flicked out and wetted his narrow lips. "I'm glad to hear that, Dan-Anna. And I want you to know that I love you very, very much."

The tension around the table lifted when he took off for the bathroom. Watching him stride energetically away, I said, "I hope I can move like that when I'm ninety-two."

Esther said, "Isn't it wonderful how vigorous he is? He was in a nursing home a few years back, but it didn't suit him. Actually, he got thrown out."

I said, "What can you possibly do to get thrown out of a nursing home?"

"He got in a fight with another patient," explained Esther. "It was over a woman at the home. He beat up the other man—who was over six feet tall, by the way."

Mom fidgeted. Her mission of forgiveness was accomplished, and she was ready to move on. When he returned, she checked her watch and exclaimed, "I'm afraid we have to go now. Rachel has to get to her karate class. She's almost a black belt."

"Not for a few more years," I said.

My grandfather's bright eyes shifted to meet mine. "I used to be a boxer. Bantamweight: 118 pounds. I wasn't supposed to bet on myself, but there's ways around that. I made quite a bit of money under the table. So you're a fighter too, eh? It's in the blood."

I pressed my back into the padded booth. I did not want to have anything in common with that creepy old man. It was bad enough being related genetically.

He leaned across the table. "Give me your hand."

Reluctantly, I did. He traced the lines on my palm. "This one here means you're a free spirit and you like to travel. Is that right?" He smiled with the practiced charm of the professional rip-off artist.

I looked into his eyes and thought at him, *You don't fool me, old man.*

He didn't back down. I got the message, *You don't scare me, little girl.*

We went outside. "A picture!" he exclaimed and began arranging us. "Esther, you have to photograph me with the lovely ladies. Dan-Anna, you stand here, Rachel, you stand here, wait, Esther, would that be a better backdrop—"

The instant everyone was looking away from him and me, he sidled up and grabbed my breast like he owned it.

I seized his hand and yanked it off. He continued directing traffic without missing a beat.

Did that really happen?

I looked at him. He smirked. "Dan-Anna, you stand by me, and Bobbie can go over there, and . . . "

He set up the whole photo shoot just to cop a feel off his own granddaughter. That son of a bitch.

"Okay, Esther, we're ready."

I should deck that motherfucker.

"Smile, everyone."

But he's ninety-two. And my grandfather.

Click! "One more, Esther dear."

I stole another glance at him.

He knew I'd be too shocked to scream. He knew I wouldn't hit an old man. That manipulative bastard sized me up perfectly. I should rat him out right now.

Click!

But everyone was already saying their goodbyes. If I said anything, he'd claim that he accidentally bumped me with his elbow. And it would ruin Mom's forgiveness if I informed her that her father had molested me ten minutes after she'd forgiven him for molesting her.

Now I could imagine what her childhood had been: the sly touches in public when all eyes were turned away, the clever cons played on a little girl until she began to doubt reality. How could she have withstood him? I was an adult and forewarned, and he'd still managed to molest me and get away with it.

At least now I knew.

I climbed into Bobbie's van, and we headed back toward my

home territory where no one could manipulate me into accepting abuse without a fight.

"Aren't you happy you went?" asked Bobbie.

"I'm happy that he's happy," said Mom, a bit doubtfully.

I didn't ask Bobbie why she'd given us the impression that my grandfather was disabled and senile. She must have thought the only way Mom would show up would be if she made him sound as non-threatening as possible.

Thanks a lot, Bobbie.

Bobbie dropped us both off at Elaine's house, where I'd left my car. "Good night, sweetie," said Mom. "Thank you so much for coming with me."

Do I have the right to ruin her peace of mind?

But Mom had made a career of silence, and all that had done was drive me crazy and her to Baba, and enabled an evil old man to keep on abusing people.

I blurted out, "He grabbed my breast."

She rolled her eyes, as if to say, *So the old dog was up to his old tricks.* I waited for more of a response, but none was forthcoming. So I drove to the dojo, where I trained as if every punch and kick was shattering the bones of the bantamweight bastard.

Afterward I went out with my dojo pals and told them the whole story over grilled fish and sake. "How awful," they said, and "I'm so sorry," and "It blows my mind that anyone believes in that Baba stuff," and "I'll buy your dinner, Rachel; you deserve it after that."

I called Dad the next morning.

"He's a pervert all right," said Dad. "Did you know he wrote a memoir? Unpublished, of course. The first chapter, which was all I could get through, was about how he lost his virginity to a prostitute at the age of ten. Aren't you glad we didn't let him babysit you?"

The next day I went to hear Mom speak at the LA Baba Center. Bobbie was also present, but I avoided her. Mom spoke with surprising eloquence of how Firoze had dedicated his life to obliterating himself and embracing suffering and humiliation in the service of Baba, and how she was trying her inadequate best to do the same.

Had her childhood made her wish she didn't exist? Had it so accustomed her to suffering that she couldn't imagine any other purpose in life? Her father, who should have loved her, had abused her. Her mother, who should have protected her, had turned her back. The entire world must have seemed treacherous underfoot. And what can offer more certainty, more pure and sexless love, and a better focus to concentrate on and drive bad memories away than God Almighty? What could be less threatening than a celibate God who didn't speak?

But maybe that's too easy. From cloistered nuns to Sufi dervishes to Jain ascetics, some people have always abandoned everything to go knocking on God's door. Disbelievers may accuse them of fleeing a world they can't cope with. But the devotees reply that it wasn't their choice: God called them.

All I know is this: Whether it was Baba or her own mind, Mom was always listening to a voice I couldn't hear.

Bobbie cornered me after Mom's talk. "How did you like your grandfather?" she asked.

"He grabbed my breast," I said.

"Oh," said Bobbie, taken aback.

"Uh-huh."

"When did he do that?"

"When we were taking pictures, and no one was looking."

"Oh."

"Uh-huh." I waited for Bobbie to deny everything.

She sighed. "I'm really sorry. He never touched me, but . . . I'm really sorry about that."

"Oh, good. I mean, I thought you were going to say I must be wrong or lying or something."

Bobbie shook her head. "No, Rachel. If you say it happened, it happened."

I drove Mom to a Thai restaurant after the meeting. Bobbie would meet us there.

As soon as the car doors closed, I said, "Mom, just so you know, I told Bobbie what my grandfather did to me."

"What?" exclaimed Mom. "You told Bobbie? Why?"

"She asked me how it went."

"But why did you have to tell her about *that*?"

"Why should I lie?"

"You could've just not mentioned it."

"Why should I pretend it didn't happen? It did happen."

"Well, please don't talk about it at dinner."

But though no one mentioned the molesting grandfather, Bobbie cracked open a different can of worms when she asked me how I'd liked growing up in Ahmednagar.

"I didn't," I said. "The kids hated me, and the teachers beat us."

"Oh." Bobbie clearly wished she hadn't asked.

Mom said, "I never knew you were beaten in school."

I said, "I think you really wanted me to be having a wonderful childhood, so it was hard for you to see anything else."

"It was Baba's will." Mom passed the coconut curry. "If you'd had a more pleasant childhood, you might not have become the compassionate person you are now."

"There must be better ways of teaching children to be compassionate than abusing them," I said.

"Maybe so," said Mom, "But that's how Baba chose to teach you."

I checked my watch. I was the stage manager for an organization that mentored kids from disadvantaged backgrounds by putting on plays with them, and I had a rehearsal across town that night.

Mom might never change, and the molesting grandfather sure hadn't. But Bobbie had, and I had. In an hour, I'd go change what I could.

27

The Sukiyaki Sisters

You might think that by the time I'd lived at the ashram for four years, I'd have gotten used to it. In fact, the longer I stayed, the more bizarre it seemed to me. I had no idea what I was doing there. But Baba-lovers were sure they knew.

A pilgrim woman once accosted me at Meherazad, as pilgrims were wont to do. This one wore a salwar kamiz embroidered with tiny mirrors, a Baba pendant, two Baba brooches with rhinestone borders, and rhinestone Om sign earrings.

"Hi," I said. I had become allergic to saying "Jai Baba." I didn't wish glory on Baba or think he had any already, and I resented having to lie every time I said hello.

"Jai Baba!" repeated the sparkly pilgrim.

"Jai Baba," I muttered.

"Are you Baba's little Mani?"

"I'm Mani," I admitted.

"I've heard so much about you," burbled the pilgrim. "You are so special to be living here, in Baba's own . . . "

Baba, Baba, bla-ba blah blah blah. I began to inspect the fuzzy green seed-pods of a nearby tree.

"So tell me, little Mani, what's the greatest spiritual blessing you've received here?"

Pilgrims were always asking me questions like that. They expected me to be a baby saint lisping precepts of innocent wisdom and were invariably ticked off when I didn't live up to expectations.

"I don't even know what that means," I snapped.

"Oh, dear, let me try again. Let's see. Well, I've only been blessed to have tea with Paribanu once, but a little birdie told me you're invited often."

"I get in every time I'm here." With any luck, I'd have bumped Glitter Girl off that afternoon's list.

"Then tell me, little Mani, what are some of the divine attributes of Baba's beloved Paribanu?"

I knew what she wanted to hear: Paribanu radiates purity and love, Paribanu's presence fills me with the light of Baba's divinity, Paribanu is a true saint and I am blessed to know her.

"Look," I said. "I like Paribanu. She gives me cookies. She tells good stories. But I have no idea what a divine attribute is, so I can't tell you about them."

"I must say, you don't seem very grateful to be living here in Baba's blessed ashram."

"That's because I'm not."

"Well!" The pilgrim fluffed her hair like a cat puffing up for a fight. "We have a little attitude problem, don't we?"

"I guess *we* do."

The pilgrim glared at me, then flounced away without even a parting "Jai Baba."

Pilgrims often told me I should be happy and grateful to live at the ashram, then got angry when I said I wasn't. But none of them ever asked me why.

They also often told me I was smart, to which I was prone to snap, "How do you know?" And most frequently of all, they told me I was special because I lived at the ashram. To which I would reply, "That doesn't make *me* special. If I'm special because I live here, then anyone who lived here would be just as special. You mean that I live in a special place." I hadn't yet heard of the derogatory meaning of "special," but if I had, I would have inwardly smirked every time I explained that I lived in a special place.

The residents, who knew me a bit better, called me "creative" or "artistic." I allowed that. I loved performing on Baba-related occasions, when the residents put on plays. I always snagged a role as "the girl" or "the boy."

Every year we celebrated Paribanu's birthday with a play about a female saint. In an inspired bit of typecasting, Mom was once cast as the Virgin Mary. But Dad stole that show with his depiction of the wise man Melchior as a mad scientist subject to fit-like visions.

Each play, no matter how unlikely it would be for such a character to exist within it, featured the ashram chef Herb Herman as a flatulent drag queen. This was partly because the audience included Marathi-speaking villagers, and Herb figured that fart jokes and men with walrus moustaches prancing around in ball gowns were funny in any language. The other reason was that being in a play gave Herb an excuse to wear a dress. He played a palace eunuch in *Yusuf and Zuleika*, a harem girl in *Rabia of Basra*, and a gossipy neighbor in *Esther*. His bold interpretation of the innkeeper in *Mary* was particularly memorable.

We also put on plays to celebrate Baba's birthday. These were supposed to be comedies with some spiritual content, but were usually manic farces that shoehorned in some Baba reference at a key

moment. One play, a murder mystery pastiche, didn't mention Baba until the very end. Then the detective's client said, "Happy Baba's birthday!" The detective, played by The Goldberg, exclaimed, "What a coincidence! I'm a Baba-lover too!" Then he ripped open his button-down shirt to expose a T-shirt silk-screened with Baba's face. Curtain.

But on the day of the performance, there was a fraught silence after The Goldberg tore off his shirt rather than the burst of cheers we had expected. As the curtain fell on a rising tide of whispers interspersed with half-hearted applause, we all looked at him. Then he looked down at his bare hairy chest. He had forgotten to put on the T-shirt.

Though Mom had been an actress, she only performed in the ashram plays when a mandali suggested that she do so. Perhaps she was seizing the opportunity to avoid Dad, who was always in them. Or maybe she was avoiding The Goldberg. He and Dad were joined at the hip, and at least twenty minutes of every rehearsal were devoted to The Goldberg arguing with the director or complaining about the script.

The mandali also had issues with Dad's friendship with The Goldberg. Coconut told Dad, "You and The Goldberg—Baba would never allow that. When two of the mandali became too friendly, Baba would always drive a wedge between them. He didn't like it when his disciples were more interested in each other than in him. If Baba was here, he would find some way to get between you."

Soon after his talk with Coconut, Dad suddenly became annoyed by the same traits of The Goldberg that had been irritating everyone else for years.

"He's such a prima donna," Dad complained. "The plays are for the mandali, not for us to sit around while he combs his duck-tail and argues about his motivation."

Dad was asked to direct that year's play for Baba's birthday, which was set in a circus. He didn't cast The Goldberg. After a period of moping, Dad began hanging out with Carla the ex-witch, who played a fortune-teller. She had only been in one other play, in which Dad had played a sultan and she had been one of his wives. Mom and I were relieved by this development, for Carla's quiet was a vast improvement over The Goldberg's bellowing.

The play featured me and a six-foot pilgrim woman as Siamese twins. I dangled from a harness on her back with a vast dress covering us. We were The Amazing Sukiyaki Sisters, in identical makeup and chopsticks in our hair, and we brought down the house when we sang "Tea for Two." I got along well with my twin, Nancy. She was a level-headed English professor who eschewed the usual pilgrim pastimes of lecturing me on obscure points of Baba doctrine, demanding that I agree that I was blessed to stay in Baba's home, or scolding me for failing to live up to their image of me as Baba's holy innocent.

A few months after she returned to America, she mailed me a box of books. Mom insisted that I reply to her with a real letter filling an entire page of notepaper. Thanking Nancy for the books and requesting more of them only filled a quarter of one page, so I drew a graph describing the staff of Holy Wounds. With footnotes.

NAME	SUBJECT	NATURE	BEAUTY*
Sister Perpetua	Moral Science	Nice but unfair. Only nice to Christians	5
Mr. Engineer	Hindi	Very mean	2**
Mrs. Joshi	History English	Meaner than Mr. Engineer	7
Sister Badger***	Scolding and Slapping	The very worst	8
Mr. Kar	Engineering	Nice but terrifying****	0

*1 being hideous, 10 being beautiful.

**Rat face

***Real name Barbara but looks like a badger

****Looks like a cross between Frankenstein's monster and a vicious water buffalo

I filled the second page with labeled drawings of Mrs. Joshi brandishing a club, "The Class Bully" with a spiked mace, and Sister Badger with a scythe in her right hand and a bladed whip in her left. The third page, labeled "What I would like to do to the class bully," showed me looming over a tiny Gopal, about to clobber him with a chain. To complete the wish-fulfillment, I depicted myself in pants.

I mailed the letter and forgot about it. Several months later, I received a tattered envelope that had been accidentally rerouted to Djakarta, Indonesia.

Dear Mani,

Thank you very much for your letter. It was hilarious. I don't know if I told you this, but I teach writing at a community college. My students are adults, but you're a better writer than any of them. I Xeroxed your letter and handed it out to them as an example of comic description and the use of detail. I want you to know that you're a real writer. You could do this professionally.

Jai Baba, and please keep writing!

Love, Nancy

That letter made a big impression on me. For the first time that I could recall, an adult had praised me in a way that I could believe. Nancy hadn't said I was blessed or lucky or unique; she'd said I was talented. And she'd backed it up with details.

I tucked away that treasured message that I had value as myself, apart from being a symbol. But I didn't decide then that I was a writer. I planned to become a veterinarian. Or a biologist specializing in white tigers. Something to do with animals, anyway.

That was *if* I grew up, which was seeming more and more unlikely to me as time went on. What Nancy didn't realize was that the only satiric exaggeration in my drawing of Mrs. Joshi was that in real life, she was not hunchbacked and did not have fangs.

A sense of humor can be a mixed blessing.

28

An Accident at Holy Wounds

I marched grimly under the mutilated heart. *Abandon hope all ye who enter here*, I thought. (Sister Perpetua read us excerpts from Dante's *Inferno* so we'd know exactly what circle of Hell we'd land in if we sinned.) It was another hot dusty morning at Holy Wounds, and I was in trouble again.

It had started with Sister Badger's dogs. Or possibly with Sister Badger's toilets. The two were inextricably entangled in my mind.

Like everything at Holy Wounds, the ashram, Ahmednagar, and India, the toilets had a caste system. There were six stalls in the staff bathroom: two for male teachers, two for female teachers, and two for nuns. They were forbidden to students, and we were caned if we were caught nearby and looked like we were thinking about using them. They were a great attraction because they were whiffy but clean. The students' toilets were permanently backed up, often to the point where the floor was indistinguishable from the contents of the hole.

This was because there were four stalls to be shared between several hundred students. Fights often broke out over who got to use them during recess. You could request a visit during class, but that was fraught with peril; the teachers might let you go, or they might mock you, hit you, and send you unrelieved and blubbering back to your seat.

One day the students' toilets were closed. When someone finally dared to ask, Mrs. Joshi informed us that Sister Barbara had become so appalled by the stench emanating from them that she had locked them up until we learned to treat them better. And no, we were not allowed to use the staff toilets. We'd simply have to exercise bodily discipline.

Soon after the bathrooms were locked up, workmen started building something in the playground. It was a cylinder with high mud walls, no windows, no roof, and a single door. Like the closing of the toilets, it was a special project of Sister Badger's. She stood in the shade of a doorway and shouted orders at the workmen as they toiled in the sun.

"Maybe it's new bathrooms," speculated the ever-optimistic Rupali.

"It's probably a garden," said fat Gita. "Sister Barbara must not want us to look at her flowers."

"I bet it's for solitary confinement," I said glumly, and then had to explain what that was.

We were all wrong, though I was closest. It was a cage, but not for humans. One morning we arrived at Holy Wounds and heard ferocious barking coming from the mud enclosure. It was Sister Badger's dogs.

The walls were too high to see over, so nobody knew what kind

of dogs they were, how many of them there were, or why they were there. For all we knew, they were a wolf pack that Sister Badger planned to feed us to.

There were two immediate consequences to the introduction of Sister Badger's pets to Holy Wounds.

One was that we all became immensely curious about those dogs. Like much else in Ahmednagar, Holy Wounds was boring when it wasn't painful or terrifying. It had no library, no playground equipment, no organized sports, no plants, no arts, and no music except for hymns. The dog enclosure provided a bit of (admittedly hideous) visual oomph to the dull gravel scene and a fascinating new thing to think about. Were there three dogs or six? Purebreds or mutts? Black, white, or spotted? We contemplated scaling the walls to see for ourselves.

The other consequence was that as there were still no bathrooms, the boys began pissing against the doghouse walls. They must have figured the pee would soak invisibly into the mud and blend in with the dogs' own smells.

Sister Badger announced at assembly that we were not to go near the doghouse or try to look at the dogs. Extreme penalties awaited those who disobeyed.

One might imagine that the students of Holy Wounds were incredibly obedient, given the sort of punishments that were routinely handed out, but we weren't. It may have been because punishments bore little connection with crimes. Girls were hit less and less hard than boys. I was hit less and less hard than the Indian girls. The entire school was often given group penalties with no explanation whatsoever. Obedient, polite, clever students were only beaten somewhat less than disobedient, sullen, stupid students, and everyone was punished arbitrarily more often than for doing anything in particular.

One day Mrs. Joshi was correcting papers when her pen ran out of ink. "Does anyone have an extra pen?"

I saw an opportunity to curry favor and leaped up to hand her mine.

She took it and began to write. A puzzled look crossed her face. It was a ballpoint pen, the transparent sort with a blue cap, and she was trying to write with the cap still on. Rather than looking at it to see what was going on, she turned the pen over and tried to write with the blunt end.

I cursed myself for my stupidity. Obviously I was supposed to have taken the cap off before giving it to her. Now she would punish me for my negligence. But, mixed in with dread, I experienced an increasingly rare moment of perspective.

This is ridiculous, I thought. *Who cares if I took the cap off? What kind of person thinks that's worth hitting an eleven-year-old for? What kind of place is this? What am I doing here? This is* ***insane.***

Mrs. Joshi lifted the pen and looked at it. "Come here, Mani," she said. "That was very rude; you must always take the cap off a pen before you give it to anyone. Six strokes."

They stung, but not too badly. I never got extra strokes for flinching at the original ones. It was the uncertainty more than the punishment that was unnerving. I could have just as easily received a caning for not offering my pen quickly enough (selfishness) or offering it too quickly (toadying).

A few weeks later Mrs. Joshi caned Shamim for giving her a pen with the cap off. She might, she explained, have gotten ink on her hands. I noted the discrepancy but didn't think much of it. Though the goings-on at the ashram still struck me as plenty weird, I had come to accept the brutality of Holy Wounds not as just, but as routine.

There were other teachers at the school, but in my memories it's always Mrs. Joshi, slapping us in a whirl of bright cotton, exhorting us to be brave and upstanding, and calling us horrid little toadies when we weren't.

Though there was not one British person at Holy Wounds, its slang and atmosphere were straight out of nineteenth-century

English boarding schools, the ones that left many of their students with masochistic fetishes for flogging, fagging, and Spotted Dick. Colonialism lived on in India long after there was anyone left to enforce it, like a veteran's dream of combat when everyone else has forgotten the war.

The prevailing mood at Holy Wounds was one of fatalistic tension. We were going to be beaten whether we peeked at Sister Badger's dogs or not, so we might as well get a look at them. At least, that's probably what the boys who climbed over the wall were thinking. Like many of the instances in which I got in trouble, I was not present at the time. I was poking around the periphery of the school grounds, looking for an unobserved area to pee in.

Sister Badger marched up and grabbed me by the ear.

"Ow!" I clutched at my hat and cringed. "What did I do?"

The plump little nun smirked. "You were throwing rocks at my dogs. You are a very bad girl."

"What? I did not! I've never even seen your dogs."

Sister Badger released my ear. "You are lying. Come with me."

I followed her to Sister Rotten Rose's office, protesting all the way. "I've never gone near your dogs. What makes you think I did?"

She didn't answer. I had to trot to keep up with the pace at which her black skirts swished along the ground. She marched me up to Sister Rotten Rose and declared, "She was throwing rocks at my dogs. And doing . . ." her voice lowered. "Dirty things."

I assumed she meant peeing. As I'd been guilty in thought if not in deed, I didn't dispute that charge.

"I never threw rocks at the dogs!" I said.

Sister Badger's eyes shone black with triumph. "She is a bad girl and a liar. I saw her do it."

"I didn't!"

Sister Rotten Rose's wrinkles deepened, and her sour mouth pursed. "Are you calling Sister Barbara a liar?"

I scowled. "No."

Sister Rotten Rose took out a long whippy cane and flicked its tip at me. I held out my palms.

"Cruelty to animals is a sin." CRACK! "We must be kind to God's little ones." CRACK! "They are innocent." CRACK! "They cannot defend themselves." CRACK! "Think of how they suffered for your amusement." CRACK! "We must not torment the helpless creatures." CRACK! "Now, are you sorry for what you did?"

I contemplated grabbing the cane out of her hands and jamming it through her eyeball.

"I'm sorry for what I did," I rattled off, doling out enough sarcasm to register but not enough to warrant another caning for insolence. "I'll never do it again."

"You may go," said Sister Rotten Rose.

Daring, I asked, "May I use the restroom?"

"No, no," said Sister Rotten Rose, and Sister Badger shook her head for emphasis. "Those are not for students. Hurry back to class now, I'm about to ring the bell."

I dashed to class and dashed home after it even more quickly. Every now and then I'd wet myself on the way and be forced to sneak into the Compound and stealthily wash my uniform before hiding it at the bottom of the clothes hamper for the servants to deal with. If people found out that a big girl like me was still wetting her pants, I would be humiliated for the rest of my life.

A few days after Sister Badger's accusation, word went around the school that three of the boys had climbed into the enclosure and petted the dogs. There were five of them, said the boys, fierce German Shepherds, but lonely and bored and eager to play.

I was certain that Sister Badger would hear the story and blame me. But something happened to deflect attention not only from me, but from the guilty boys and every other kid in school—everyone, that was, but Shamim, the Kashmiri refugee.

I didn't think Shamim was worse off than I was—Darshana of the infected ear (now Darshana of the infected knees, which dribbled pus down to her socks) was the only Holy Wounds kid I'd even consider putting in that category—but I felt sorry for him. He was a big boy and looked strong, but when we were forced to stand in the sun, he was nearly always the first person to throw up or pass out. That was considered its own punishment. But the penalty for crumbling under pain was more pain.

When he was struck, he'd flinch. And not only flinch—he'd cringe, cry, refuse to hold out his hand, try to pull it away if the teacher held it out for him, and even attempt to ward off the blows with his other hand. He was a ten-year-old who behaved like one, and the rest of us ten-year-olds despised him for it.

The Spartans would have appreciated the cult of stoicism adhered to by the students of Holy Wounds. Don't flinch, don't cry, don't faint, don't tell. We practiced Maratha endurance, the English stiff upper lip, and a silence worthy of Baba.

Mrs. Joshi settled herself into her chair, and we all opened our English texts. We each had to pick a poem from it to recite for our final exam. The day before we had read Lord Tennyson's "The Beggar Maid." I didn't think it would be a popular choice. It had only two stanzas, but not even Mrs. Joshi had known how to pronounce Cophetua.

I had chosen Wordsworth's "Daffodils." It was short, not embarrassing, and had no sentiments I violently disagreed with. But I had also memorized a poem from Rupali's big brother's textbook, so I could recite it to myself when I was being punished.

It was "Invictus," by William Ernest Henley. The rah-rah Mother India patriotism of the history books was undercut by the literature selections, which focused on dead British men and ignored all Indians but Rabindranath Tagore.

It matters not how strait the gate,

How charged with punishments the scroll,

I am the master of my fate:

I am the captain of my soul.

I'm less fond of "Invictus" now, especially since Oklahoma City bomber Timothy McVeigh quoted it as his last words before his execution. But it's tough to disdain melodrama when every morning you walk under a painting of a mutilated body part into Holy Wounds of Jesus Christ Our Savior Convent School.

"Open your texts to 'The Charge of the Light Brigade,'" said Mrs. Joshi. "Our first reader will be . . . Shamim."

Everyone cringed. With those words, Mrs. Joshi had set two trains in motion heading toward each other on the same track, full speed ahead.

He was the worst reader in the class. I could read Hindi better than he could read English. In fact, I could read Hindi better than he could read Hindi, and he read Hindi better than he read English. For one thing, I didn't have a nervous stutter.

Shamim cringed too. Unlike the rest of us, he did it visibly. Mrs. Joshi eyed him distastefully, as she might note the location of a cockroach before crushing it underfoot. He lifted the book between thumb and forefinger as if he were absorbing toxic chemicals through his skin, and gave it a horrified stare.

Mrs. Joshi slammed the end of her cane into the ground. Shamim jumped. "Read!"

"Eee . . . eee . . . eee-yintoo tuh-hee . . ."

"The!" snapped Mrs. Joshi. "Not tuh-hee. The! The! The! *The*

is *the* most common word in *the* English language, and you are *the* laziest boy in *the* school if you can't say *the* by now. Start over."

"Eee-yin-ta-ta-ta-ta . . ."

I was usually inured to seeing other children get hit. Sometimes it was even funny. Like the time Mrs. Joshi had left the classroom and Gopal had started dancing atop his desk, facing the windows so he'd see her approach. But she returned through the side door, tip-toeing and gesturing to the kids not to warn him. He continued dancing in the suggestive Bollywood style until she knocked him clean off the desk in the middle of a pelvic thrust. Even Gopal had laughed, once he'd picked himself up off the floor.

But Shamim was too pathetic to be amusing. I would have looked away when he was beaten, except that I would have been caned for day-dreaming.

"Ta-ta-ta-ta-ta-ta-ta-ta-ta . . ." He gave up.

"Did I say you could stop?" asked Mrs. Joshi. "Persevere!"

Shamim hung his head in wretched silence.

"Then come here."

He stood frozen at his desk. It always took him a while to get up his nerve to come forward.

"Three for being unprepared, and three for not coming when you're called. Come here."

"NO!" shrieked Shamim. This time, we all jumped. Even Mrs. Joshi blinked. "NO! NO! NO!"

I had always wondered if one day he would lose it completely. Apparently today was the day.

"If you don't come, I'll have to drag you. And that will be . . ." Mrs. Joshi had to think about it. No one had ever been dragged. "Ten more."

"NO! NO! NO!"

Shamim's face was red and twisted, his eyes bulging. It was as if he were possessed. The children next to him scrunched down into their seats.

Were Shamim and Mrs. Joshi going to get into a physical struggle? He was several inches taller than her and husky, but he was a kid and she was an adult. She had the authority, the willpower, and the personal presence, but he was desperate. I leaned forward eagerly. The entire class was agog. Nothing like this had ever happened before.

Mrs. Joshi marched toward him. She went unarmed, pointing out her lack of fear. I hoped he would deck her.

She grabbed his arm and yanked him out of his desk. It started to tip over as he clutched at it. The boy behind him grabbed and righted the desk.

"Thank you, Ravi," said Mrs. Joshi coolly. "Come along, Shamim."

He blubbered, wailed, and struggled ineffectively as she dragged him to the front of the class. I was disappointed. He might be big, but he was a big baby. No way was he going to punch the teacher.

"I'm going to give you one last chance to be brave," she said, picking up her cane. "Hold out your hands."

"NO!" He clasped his hands behind his back. I'd never seen anyone do that before, either.

Mrs. Joshi yanked out his right hand, palm down. He tried to tug it back, but she stretched it out, holding on to his fingertips. He jumped away, pulling her off balance. In a rage, she threw down her cane, grabbed him by the back of the head, and slammed his forehead into the wall. The crack was as loud as if it had been my head.

Everyone froze—the children, Mrs. Joshi, even Shamim. The rage and panic had left his face, and he looked blank and dazed.

I hope she doesn't go on hitting him after that, I thought. *That ought to count for sixteen. Or at least ten.*

Mrs. Joshi dusted off her hands and started toward the back of the class. I wasn't sure if she was going to fetch something or if she'd spotted some other troublemaker. I twisted in my seat to watch her.

There was a slither and a thud, and an uproar burst out from the front of the class. I turned around.

Shamim had collapsed. His eyes were rolled up, erasing everything but a sliver of white, and his body thrashed and jerked as if some invisible force was shaking him out like a dusty rag. His head beat against the flagstones.

I had never seen anyone have a seizure before. I was scared for him and scared to go near him.

Mrs. Joshi's mouth fell open, and her expression was one that I'd only seen before on the faces of her students.

She was in trouble.

"Ravi! Rakesh!" she shouted. They sprang up, the two biggest boys in class after Shamim. "Hold him down!"

They hurried forward and tried to pin him to the floor. Ravi held his legs and Rakesh leaned on his arms, but neither cushioned his head as it thudded into the floor, again and again and again. Mrs. Joshi ran out, across the playground, past the dog enclosure, and into Sister Rotten Rose's office, where they had a telephone.

A bottle of ink had tipped over on Ravi's desk. I watched it drip down into a slowly widening pool on the floor, black into black, black into black. The scuffling and banging noises abruptly stopped. Shamim had gone limp. Ravi and Rakesh scuttled back to their seats.

"Is he dead?" whispered Rupali.

Nobody wanted to get close enough to check. We all sat perfectly still, perfectly silent. Black into black.

Two men arrived and carried Shamim away. Mrs. Joshi came back with them. I had hated her for so long that I had stopped noticing what she looked like. But though she liked to use her stick, I had never thought she might actually kill a child. That new perspective made me see her as if it were the first time: a slender woman barely five feet tall, dainty in a rose-pink sari, who had committed the most shocking act of violence I had ever seen.

Mom was right: People never ceased to surprise you.

Shamim didn't die, although he was in the hospital for a week and kept home for a week after that. The class gossip was that Holy Wounds had claimed that he was epileptic and that his head injury had resulted from his seizure rather than the other way around. His parents were said to be furious but had no recourse except to write a letter requesting the teachers not to hit him on the head. For once, a parent's request had an effect. Mrs. Joshi never hit him on the head again.

If he had died, maybe she would have been arrested, but that wouldn't have resurrected him. The teachers weren't mere sadists, but potential murderers; our lives depended on their whims.

If Shamim had always known that, no wonder he had been afraid.

29

Not a Sparrow Falls . . .

Perhaps being tormented by the nuns, teachers, and kids at Holy Wounds gave me compassion for creatures even more small and helpless than myself. Then again, I'd been obsessed with animals since I was three, so maybe I'd have turned into a self-appointed rescuer of all creatures low on the food chain no matter where I was. Even in Los Angeles, I'd brought home injured toads and lost dogs. But Ahmednagar's plentiful supply of needy animals turned my hobby into a full-blown crusade.

I also had fewer official pets to focus on. I wasn't allowed to have cats or dogs, nor could I keep rats and toads and parakeets as I had in Hawthorne. There were no pet shops in Ahmednagar. Wild toads were available in abundance, but I didn't want to imprison them in aquariums and I had no outdoor space that would be safe from marauding predators, servants, or pilgrims.

But I got a pet eventually. Continuing my tradition of peculiar rabbit names, I called him Bun-buns. He lived in a hutch near the bathrooms, raised on stilts to protect him from the gooses, but I was allowed to play with him inside. He was a brown-and-white miniature rabbit, small enough for Dad to hold in one hand, and I loved him with all the passion that Mom turned on God and Dad turned away from.

For a year I had something to look forward to when I got out of Holy Wounds other than no more beatings for the day. Bun-buns wasn't as bright as Ratsy or as affectionate as the town dogs I befriended, but he was warm and furry and living, and he was mine.

Then Raju the servant boy came dashing up to meet me one afternoon as I walked up to the gate, bursting with news to share.

"Your rabbit's dead!" he exclaimed in Marathi, excited at the event and the chance to be the first to let me know.

I ran to the hutch. Bun-buns was stiff on his side. A trail of ants marched up a pole to swarm in his open eyes.

I got a shovel and buried him in the backyard. Then I hid in the library and cried.

I wasn't there ten minutes before Shinork poked his balding head inside to comfort me. "I'm sorry about Bun-buns."

"Thanks," I said thickly.

"Have you ever heard of a wake?"

I sniffled and shook my head.

"It's an Irish custom. After someone dies, they get together and have a big party, get drunk, and talk about his life. Now, you can't do the drinking part, but why don't I take you to the bazaar? We could get ice cream sodas and . . . er . . . talk about Bun-buns' life."

"I'm not going to drink an ice cream soda when Bun-buns is dead."

"I thought it might make you feel better." Shinork bowed his head humbly.

"Go away and leave me alone."

He hunched his shoulders and stared at me plaintively, his head poking out like a tortoise's. I stared at the floor. After a few minutes, I heard his retreating footsteps. Fifteen minutes later, he was back. "Coconut wants to talk to you."

Dragging my feet, I followed him into Coconut's office. The tiled floor, which alternated squares of black and white, gleamed in the fluorescent light.

Coconut hugged me to his jelly belly. "I am very sorry. Shinork says you were crying. Yes. You are crying. Do not cry. Here." He released me and thrust out a steel dish of anise seeds, which he chewed as breath fresheners.

Even apart from Bun-buns, I disliked the taste of licorice. I shook my head.

He popped a few in his mouth. "Sit down."

I sat.

"You are very sad now. But this is the will of Baba. Many sad things happen in this life. But your rabbit is very happy now with Baba. You know Baba loved the little animals. Even now, it is sitting in Baba's loving arms . . ."

I selected a black tile square as the center and four white squares to attach to each of its four corners. The tiles became a pattern of black on white. But if I saw a white square as the center, it became white on black, a completely different look. I could switch back and forth without even moving my eyes. The shift was entirely mental. Black on white, white on black, black on white . . .

"So you must be strong. You must love Baba. Baba sends us trials to make us stronger, better people. That is the purpose of suffering. Baba is the Great Jeweler, and we become gold in his furnace. Do you understand?"

I nodded.

"Stand up."

I stood. He hugged me again. "Yes. Very good. Jai Baba!"

I fled, but not to the library. Obviously that was the first place people would look for me. I went to the backyard and sat down beside the grave. Whatever Coconut said, I was not ashamed to grieve. Even the Rajput king Rana Pratap, who had been wounded nine times in battle and lost an eye, had mourned the death of his gallant warhorse Chetak. His memorial to Chetak, the *Chetak ka Chabutra*, still stands. And so, I vowed, would Bun-buns' tomb.

The next day after school, I found that gooses or feral dogs had dug up the grave, dismembered Bun-buns' body, and scattered the pieces across the weedy yard. I dug the grave again, deeper this time, jumped on it to pack the earth, and stacked bricks over it.

That was the last time I had a pet in Ahmednagar.

Like many prepubescent girls, I wanted to be a veterinarian when I grew up. Unlike most of them, I had the opportunity to practice veterinary medicine before I turned twelve. I often found injured animals, and Ahmednagar's only veterinarian didn't treat anything smaller than a goat.

Every time I visited Meherazad I made a circuit of its water tanks to see if any animals had fallen in. I often found lizards paddling valiantly and scrabbling at the concrete walls, occasionally a star-nosed shrew with a fringe of tentacles circling its snout, and once a baby bat like a soot-black mouse with delicate translucent wings. When I hung the bat upside-down on a bush to dry off it yawned at me, displaying its rose-pink mouth and tongue. If it wasn't for rabies, I would have kept it as a pet.

But though I came across many an injured bird, I did not have

good luck rescuing them. Even when they didn't go into convulsions or start dripping blood from their beaks five minutes after I nested them in a warm lined box, they invariably died in the night.

It was especially frustrating because Baba had been fond of animals and rescued many wild ones. The mandali often spoke of his pet monkeys, mongooses, and parrots. If they lived, it was by Baba's grace; if they died, it was by Baba's will, and they were blessed to have spent their brief lives in his care. But my parents wouldn't let me keep cats or dogs, let alone deer and foxes.

I had fantasies of nursing a broken-winged hawk back to health and setting it free, so the grateful bird would imprint on me, plunge down to perch on my outstretched forearm when I called it from the sky, and rip Sister Badger's eyeballs out.

But I never found any birds of prey in need of help, and every single injured crow, mynah, and hoopoe that I attempted to rescue died. I concluded that birds were too fragile to save without advanced medical technology and expertise or the personal intercession of God. But I stubbornly kept trying.

Mom said I should leave them where I found them, because they weren't suffering and it was Baba's will for them to die. Dad said it depressed him to have flocks of moribund birds expiring under the bed.

I argued that it was Baba's will that I do my best to save them, that they were too suffering and how would Mom like to die alone by the side of the road, and that it was my bed and Dad didn't have to look at them.

My parents caved. I kept bringing in doomed birds, figuring that at least I could give them a more comfortable death. Besides, maybe one day one of them would live.

One day, one of them did.

I found a young sparrow fluttering beneath the Compound's amber-studded neem tree. It had its adult feathers, but was so small and fluffy that I wondered if it had fallen from the nest. The sparrow was dragging one wing, and when I caught and examined it I could feel the break in one of its delicate bones.

I took it home, prepared a box for it, and splinted its wing with tape and half a tongue depressor. I was sorry it wouldn't live. It was a cute little thing, and I had done a good job of setting its wing.

To my surprise, the sparrow was alive the next morning and chirping to be fed. I dashed home from Holy Wounds that afternoon, certain that it would be dead. But it wasn't.

I kept the sparrow for a month and let it hop around the house under my supervision. Even Dad liked it. It became quite tame and seemed to enjoy perching on my palm. It weighed less than a mitten.

I kept it for several days after I took the splint off. But when it flew out of its box and spent an hour flitting from cupboard to bookshelf to bed to door, daring me to catch it, I knew the time had come to set it free.

I had intended to release it in the courtyard where I had found it, but Thaki's tabby cat was lurking beneath the neem tree. And cats were not the only hazard. There were servant kids running around, cars and rickshaws careening in and out, and sinister pilgrims on the prowl. I decided that my precious sparrow, the only bird whose life I'd saved, needed a safer area to test its wings.

I took it to the backyard where I had buried Bun-buns. It was a dreary expanse of gravel and weeds and rubbish heaps enclosed by concrete walls spiked with broken bottles, but it had the advantage of being so depressing that no one ever went there. The air of woe hanging over the place was so palpable that even I, with my craving for privacy, avoided it. But it held no hazards for a young and recuperating sparrow.

I checked the sky for hawks, then gently tossed the sparrow into the air. If it had any trouble flying, I'd recapture it and keep it for another week.

The sparrow spread its wings and flew. It circled twice over my head, then glided into a smooth descent and made a perfect landing several yards away.

A yellow tomcat dropped out of the sky and bit off its head.

Before I could move or make a sound, the cat gulped down the rest of the sparrow, hissed at me, and leaped over the wall.

I screamed then, a primal wail of shock and anguish, dashed after it, scrambled up the concrete, and peered over. The cat had vanished.

There was nothing left of the sparrow. Its blood and feathers had disappeared among the weeds. The cat, an evil-looking tom with scarred ears, was not one I'd ever seen before. It must have been lurking on the roof, then taken an Olympic-worthy flying leap.

The sparrow had gone from first flight to nothing left in thirty seconds flat. The bad-luck backyard, the manifestation of the demonic cat, the irony of having delivered the only bird I'd ever saved into the jaws of death by my misguided effort to protect it, the way *nothing* ever worked out right for me, the feeling that this was the latest proof that Baba or the universe was out to get me, and the sheer speed of events lent the episode a surreal symbolic value, like a Moral Science parable. It contained, I was sure, an important lesson that I was meant to learn.

But I had no idea what it was.

30

Carla's Dragons

Dad kept up his business ventures after we moved to India. When we lived in America, he had imported antiques and costume jewelry from Ahmednagar to sell at flea markets. At the ashram, he bought antiques and costume jewelry and exported them to America.

I often came along on his trips to hunt down treasures at the bazaar. We rooted through back rooms at the brass bazaar, pungent with old metal and polish and manure-crusted burlap sacks, and Dad taught me the difference between the hard glitter of new metal and the soft luster brought out by years of human touch. But though Dad had good business sense, he was fundamentally unambitious. His export business would have remained a one-man operation, earning just enough to keep his family in Ahmednagar, if Carla hadn't gotten hepatitis.

It wasn't my idea to visit her. Every time a mandali caught pneumonia or had a stroke, Mom hauled me to their bedsides. Though I wasn't hospital-phobic and used to hang out at the free clinic begging for lessons on bandaging, it was different when the sick person was someone I knew. I tended to hang back, gripped by the primal fear of illness and mortality, while Mom urged me to kiss them.

So I wasn't thrilled when Dad suggested that I accompany him to visit Carla, especially since I didn't know her well. But going on a sick visit with Dad would be a novelty. Also, I'd heard that hepatitis made you turn yellow, and I was curious to see if it was true.

Carla lay limp on her back in a blessedly unsmelly room. To my relief, Dad didn't make me kiss her. I warily approached the bed to inspect her color. I was disappointed to see that though she was indeed yellow, the shade was closer to dun than dandelion. Then I wandered out to play with her dogs while Dad sat and talked to her. He must have had a nice talk, because I accompanied him on more visits during her lengthy convalescence, and he went frequently by himself.

When Carla wobbled into the Compound several months later, she was so thin and wan that the mandali decided that she needed a vacation. They suggested Goa, a beach resort popular with leftover hippies. But they didn't think a woman should travel alone, especially one in Carla's weakened state. Since Dad was her closest male friend, he volunteered to accompany her as a bodyguard/chaperone.

"I could come too," I suggested.

Dad shook his head. "You have school."

I scowled. "But I've never been to Goa."

Mom said, "You and Rupali could have a picnic, just the two of you, like Dad and Carla in Goa."

I gave that suggestion the contemptuous silence it deserved. While I was busy sulking, I almost missed the funny looks Mom and Dad were giving each other.

"Just make sure you and Carla don't have a you-know-what," said Mom, and laughed.

"You never know," said Dad and laughed.

"What's a you-know-what?" I asked.

My parents gave me identical bland looks.

"Nothing," said Mom.

"Nothing," said Dad.

Dad and Carla returned from Goa tanned and happy. While they were there, they had decided to become business partners. Having had friends who burned down the Bank of America had not dimmed Carla's interest in finance, and their export business began to expand. She became a presence, albeit a quiet and unobtrusive one, around our house.

All her old energy was back when she beckoned to me a few months later. "Have you ever read a book called *Dragonsong*? I think you'd like it."

"No, but I like the title. Is it really about dragons?" I had been disappointed by Madeleine L'Engle's *Dragons in the Waters*, in which the dragons were boringly metaphorical.

"Yes. It's in the library. Not in the kids' section, in science fiction. By Anne McCaffrey."

"Thanks." I had browsed the science fiction shelf—I browsed every section, even the stultifying ones like romance and religion—but the covers I'd glanced were garish and forbidding, and the books I'd flipped through had upheld that impression, being filled with names with apostrophes and too many consonants, dry scientific descriptions, and no sex.

The cover of *Dragonsong* showed a girl holding a flute and surrounded by tiny dragons. I was enchanted. It's about a teenager on

another planet whose abusive parents won't let her pursue a career in music. Menolly runs away, adopts nine miniature dragons, and ends up with all her talents acknowledged and a bright future ahead of her.

Like Menolly, I was a misfit. I was a stranger in a strange land. And I wanted to read about people like me.

My life felt more dramatic and strange than the situations in realistic children's novels. It was hard to be gripped by first crushes and squabbles with parents when my everyday life featured madmen on the loose, decapitated corpses in the roads, and teachers with a license to kill. The metaphors of fantasy, in which a lover's heart might literally be made of stone, childhood might literally last forever, or your neighbor might literally be a monster, resonated with how my life felt from the inside.

Dragonsong introduced me to the concept of genre. Children's and young adult novels are shelved together regardless of subject matter, *Dinky Hocker Shoots Smack* beside *Little House on the Prairie* beside *So You Want to Be a Wizard?* But the McCaffrey experience taught me that if I wanted to read about wizards and robots, I could go to a section of the bookshop where any book I laid my hand on would contain magic or spaceships and sometimes both. A fan was born.

I was grateful to Carla for opening up this new world to me. I also wondered if she had recommended *Dragonsong* as a subtle signal that she understood that my life was just like Menolly's before she ran away, only without the dragons.

Could Carla be hinting that I could confide in her? Might she mean to help? Or did she just have good taste in literature?

I thanked her for the recommendation the next time I saw her and added, in a stumbling attempt at slyness, "I really liked how Menolly was so unhappy at first, and then she got away from all the people who were mean to her. Uh, you know, I really identified with her."

Carla cocked her red head. "We make our own reality, Mani," she said. "People can't *make* us unhappy. We choose how what they do affects us. If we're unhappy, it's because we're choosing to be unhappy."

"But don't you think situations can make people sad? Like how Menolly's parents wouldn't let her be a Harper even though it was the only thing she'd ever wanted to do?"

"Everything happens for a reason," said Carla firmly. "And everything that happens brings you closer to God. So you shouldn't regret or be sad about anything that you do or experience, because it's all part of Baba's plan to bring you closer to him."

I was getting annoyed. "So if you murder someone, you shouldn't regret it?"

"If it's already done, no, because it was part of God's plan."

"What about the person you killed? Should he be sorry?"

"No, because it's part of his karma."

"So everything is good?"

"Yes, basically."

"If everything is good, then there's no right or wrong. Then there's no reason why you shouldn't murder people."

My God, I thought, *I've turned into one of those free-will pilgrims.*

"Yes, there is," said Carla. "It's bad for your own karma. But the bad things that happen—I mean, things that *seem* bad—are part of God's plan, so it's all for the best. See, Mani, right now you're choosing to be sad. Don't do it. Choose to be happy!"

"Okay," I said automatically. "I guess you're right." And I thought, but didn't say, *And after I finish choosing to be happy, I'll choose to adopt nine miniature dragons.*

31

Will

My childhood was permeated by fear. I was afraid that Mrs. Joshi might bash my head against the wall. I was afraid that Sister Rose and Sister Badger might order me to stand in the sun. I was afraid that men might harass me, kids might pull razor blades on me, and Dad might turn his cutting sarcasm on me. But I wasn't afraid of any of them *personally*. I was only afraid of what they might do.

But Malik the Mast scared me purely with his presence. I don't know if it was his scuttling gait, his reaching fingers, his mechanical movements, his sudden bellows, or his gleaming eyes. Maybe it was a primal fear of madness. But though I was told that he'd never harmed anyone, he terrified me.

I would never have gone near him at all, except that he lived next door to Harry Carroll. Harry was so cool that I was willing to brave Malik the Mast to spend time with him.

Harry told me he had acquired the scar across his ribs when he had fought the leader of a street gang, mano a mano. He told me he had given a ride to a young woman who had left her coat in his car and that, when he looked up the address sewn into the collar, found that it was the graveyard where she was buried. He told me he had shot a lion in Africa, seen a guru resurrect a dead dog, and warned Jimi Hendrix not to take the drugs that killed him.

One afternoon when I went to visit him, Harry was on the porch, busy varnishing a chair.

"Can I help?" I asked.

He scowled at the jar of varnish. "No."

"Sure?"

"Yeah. Why don't you go climb a tree? I'm busy."

"I'm sick of climbing. Are you putting linseed oil on that chair?"

"You're bothering me, Mani. Get lost, or I'll tie you up and leave you for Malik the Mast."

I laughed. "Yeah, right. You know, Dad says you have to be careful what grade of linseed oil you buy. He says they all *say* they're pure, but most of them—"

He stopped brushing oil onto the chair and glared at me. "I'm not kidding. This is your last warning. Take off."

I leaned over and read the label on the jar. "Dad says '100 Percent Extra Pure' is *adulterated*. He says you have to use the '100 Percent Super Extra—"

He put down the brush and grabbed me, pinning my arms to my sides. I was so surprised that I didn't try to dodge.

"Hey!" I yelped. "Let go!"

Without a word, he dragged me into his house. Holding me tight with one hand, he used the other to open a tool chest and take out a coil of nylon rope.

"What're you doing?"

"I warned you."

I stared at the slick yellow rope, then twisted to check Harry's face. It wasn't contorted with rage or leering sadistically or otherwise transformed. He looked bland, brisk, and competent, like Mrs. Joshi did when she beat us. "What? About Malik? You're kidding, right?"

"Nope." He looped the rope over one arm so he could use both his hands to control me. I had started to struggle in earnest.

He scooped me up, crushing me against his chest, and marched outside, toward Malik's lair.

"Okay!" I babbled, trying to wriggle free. "I'm sorry! I shouldn't have bugged you when you were working! I was being a brat. I won't do it again. I'm sorry, all right?"

"You should've thought of that earlier."

Malik was outside, collecting deesh and muttering.

Harry dumped me on the porch and shoved me into an awkward sitting position, my legs stuck out in front and my back jammed up against a wooden pillar. I struggled, but that only pushed my skirt up to my waist.

I was directly in Malik's path. And I was starting to realize that Harry wasn't just trying to scare me.

I let out an ear-piercing shriek intended to alert everyone from here to Pune that something terrible was going on.

"You want to make Malik notice you?" asked Harry calmly. "Go ahead and scream. No one can hear you but him."

He was right. When I'd screamed, Malik had looked up, his neck curling awkwardly to focus his hollow gaze on me.

Harry crouched down over my legs and uncoiled the rope. The loops slithered about, and he let go of my left hand to wrestle with them. His legs were splayed, and his crotch was on my thighs and within my reach. If I grabbed or hit him in the balls, it might hurt him enough to give me a chance to escape.

If he was a boy, I would have tried it; but he was a man, and sitting there in his power with my skirt pushed up, I felt an entirely new kind of vulnerability. I didn't want to make him—or Malik—think about anything even remotely connected to sex.

I punched Harry in the stomach. But I had little strength and no leverage. And his belly, with a thick layer of fat over solid muscle, was one of the least vulnerable parts of his body.

He didn't even flinch. He just grabbed my free arm and wedged it into the pillar with his elbow. Then he yanked a length of rope tight around my waist.

"You can't do this!" I yelled. Malik's fingers ceased dragging along the floor, and his head twitched toward the sound. I subsided.

Harry wound the rope around and around, cocooning me to the pillar with my arms at my sides. I picked at it with my fingers, but the hard new nylon might as well have been rock for all it gave.

Why had I punched him? I should have bitten him. Why hadn't I thought of that when I'd had the chance?

Harry knotted the rope behind my back and walked away. Incredulous, I craned my neck until my cheek pressed tight against the splintery wood. I could just barely see him disappear into his house and shut the door. Until then, I hadn't really believed that he'd leave me for Malik.

The madman muttered and coughed, picking bits of nothingness from the ground and tucking them into the folds of his robe.

If I screamed, I would only attract his attention.

He shuffled forward, closer to me. Malik always moved in straight lines. When he encountered an obstacle, he'd turn aside and proceed at a right angle. I was in his path but maybe if I held perfectly still, he'd think I was part of the pillar and leave me alone.

But he knew the difference between people and objects. And the way he stared at women wasn't like the indifference with which he regarded men. He'd never attacked anyone, but no one

had been tied up and left for him before, like a goat staked out as a tiger's bait.

There were jokey rumors that he liked Western women. And I could see the sign that warned us to stay away.

I tried to flick my skirt down over my legs, but the bunched up part was out of my reach.

Malik tilted his head toward me. I froze.

He continued collecting deesh, slowly but steadily, coming closer and closer.

He was going to touch me with those long twitching fingers.

I clenched my jaws and squeezed my thighs together. I was not going to scream. I was not. If I kept silent, maybe he would ignore me and turn aside. If I screamed, he would definitely touch me.

He was going to reach up my skirt.

I was not going to scream. I would use my will to keep from screaming. Baba had been silent for forty-four years. I could be silent for ten minutes.

Shivaji wouldn't scream. Rani Lakshmibai wouldn't scream. A soldier wouldn't scream.

I was within his reach. If he stretched out his dangling arms, he could touch my legs. He could fondle my face. He could do anything he liked.

He was going to kneel down, thrust my legs apart, and rape me.

I would not scream. If I screamed, they would have broken my will. Will was all I had. It was what I used to stay on my feet when they made me stand in the sun. It was the only part of me that nobody could destroy without my consent. If they broke my will, I would have nothing.

The madman's fingers trailed over the ground, questing toward me.

I am the master of my fate. I am the captain—

He touched me.

I had thought that to have one's will broken was a metaphor. But something snapped like a small dry twig.

I screamed.

Once I started, I couldn't stop. I screamed over and over, thrashing hopelessly against the ropes, so consumed with terror that I had no idea what Malik was doing to me. I had fallen into a black hole of fear, and whatever was happening to me was on the other side of the event horizon.

There were hands on me. Harry, undoing the ropes. I don't know when he came out or how long he left me there or what Malik did. But the ropes were falling away.

I fled over the fields, into the lonely uncultivated plains, and hid in a dry creek bed. I sat in the dust with my arms locked around my knees, still as a field mouse waiting for the hawk to strike.

I hated Malik, I hated Harry, I hated my parents and the mandali and the residents and Baba. But most of all, I hated myself.

I had failed. I had nothing. I *was* nothing.

The sun set in a blaze of orange and gray, gorgeous and meaningless. I could lie down and sleep, but they'd find me. There was nowhere to run.

I went back.

Dad took me aside some time later. I don't know if I'd told him what had happened, or if Harry, worried that I might not come back, had confessed.

"I talked to Harry about what he did to you," said Dad. "I want you to know that I told him that I'd kill him if he ever laid hands on you again."

"Thanks," I said listlessly.

It didn't matter. I had failed.

32

The Way of the Warrior

I unlocked my front door and slid the deadbolt home behind me. I changed out of my uniform into a cotton dress and took off my shoes and socks. I picked up a chair and put it by the cabinet. Then I stood on it to take the knife from the top drawer. I moved the chair so its back was to the wall and sat in it, bracing the balls of my feet against the floor. I was too short to have my back against the wall and my heels on the floor at the same time.

My hands throbbed, alternately hot and numb. They felt clumsy and too big. I held them up to see if they were trembling. They felt like they were trembling. But the blade was still. I tilted it like a mirror, but I couldn't see my face.

It was a kitchen knife with a brass-riveted wood

handle. The edge was honed to slice garlic thin enough to read a book through each tear-shaped section.

I wanted to go to the bathroom. I wanted a drink of water. My feet were falling asleep.

I put the tip of the knife to the hollow of my throat. I could feel the pulse of blood against the blade as I settled it close. All I needed to do was shove it through. One quick hard stab should work even if I couldn't drag it all the way across.

Weren't my hands trembling? It felt like my hands were trembling.

Baba said suicide was wrong. Suicides became ghosts instead of reincarnating. I wasn't sure why that was bad, because I couldn't imagine anything worse than being reincarnated and having to go through my life all over again. If his story about ghosts who didn't know they were dead was true, maybe I'd killed myself already and my punishment was that nothing had changed.

But I didn't believe any of it anymore. Baba was love, they said, but no one who loved me and was all-powerful would have let Harry tie me up. Baba said life was a dream, but no dream-knife had ever felt as hard and cool or smelled as faintly of garlic and metal as the one I held in my hand. If life was real, then Baba was wrong, and if he was wrong, then he wasn't God and nothing he had said could be trusted.

The blade trembled at my throat. One thrust. Just because something frightened you didn't mean you couldn't do it.

If I didn't cut my throat now, I would have to get up the next morning and go to school, where they would throw rocks at me and beat me and make me stand in the sun and threaten me with razor blades and maybe break my head against the wall. If I failed today, tomorrow someone might tie me up and leave me as a madman's plaything.

There was no other escape. Where could I run away to? I was thousands of miles from home.

This was my last chance to redeem myself. My last chance to be a warrior. I pressed the blade into my flesh. Just a little deeper.

Rani Durgavati had stabbed herself in the heart when she was wounded and about to be captured. Rajputs had burned themselves to death or charged the enemy in suicide attacks. Had any Marathas committed suicide?

Shivaji had died in bed. Shivaji's older son, Sambhaji, had been executed by Aurangzeb. Tanaji and Baji Prabhu and Shivaji's younger son Rajaram had been killed in battle. I couldn't remember what had happened to Tarabai, Rajaram's wife. I started to get up to check *History of the Marathas*.

I sat back down. If I got up to do a fact check, I'd get distracted and start reading, and then I'd lose my nerve. I was distracted already. The knife had drifted from my throat. I put it back in place. If I stayed alive, eventually someone would start torturing me again.

Of course, no one was torturing me that exact minute. It seemed a shame to waste the time I had now, that I could spend reading a book or otherwise doing something fun, being dead.

LISTEN TO ME TALK ABOUT MY STRUGGLES TO DROWN

WHEN WE BOTH KNOW I'VE GOT ONE FOOT ON THE SHORE.

Worldly attachments held me back from death as surely as they held the residents from enlightenment. The ashram line was that desires were the source of suffering, that earthly pleasures were meaningless, that only God was real.

You're nothing but a pack of cards.

Absorption in a book, the scent of rain on moss, hot mint tea drunk outside before dawn, water pistol duels with Rupali, the weight of history in the gray stones of Sinhagad, the luscious perfume of a fresh-plucked lychee, Walter's hands boosting me up a tree, a gecko's golden eyes, the haunting melody of the Muslim call to prayer, the blaze of stars in a sky undimmed by electric light—those things were real and meaningful and precious. How could I stop wanting more of them? Why should I?

How could I sacrifice the rest of this day? I was safe at home, and nothing terrible was likely to happen until tomorrow.

I got up, replaced the knife and the chair, and picked up *History of the Marathas*.

I could always kill myself later.

33

All the Fishes Come Home to Roost

Dad folded his arms behind his head, relishing the exercise of his debating skills. "Are we all taking it as a given that Baba is still going to break his silence some day even though he dropped the body without doing it in this incarnation?"

General agreement. The residents were having a sunset barbecue and bull session in the Compound's bad-luck backyard as the first bats of the evening swooped and chittered overhead. The shards of bottle glass atop the walls glowed like the skyline of a burning city.

The Goldberg turned over the sizzling chicken, and Carla dripped a spiced marinade over the pieces. The smoky scent of burning fat drifted over to me, making my eyes and mouth water.

Dad stretched back in his folding chair. "So the

only questions are a) is the breaking of the silence literal or metaphoric, b) is that when three-quarters of the world will be destroyed, c) is the end of the world literal or metaphoric, and d) what do we think will actually happen when the silence is broken?"

"I think they're both metaphoric." Carla set down the baster. "I don't think the world ends, like, it explodes. The end of the world means the end of our preconceived notions and mental garbage. It means we face up to who we are and what we've been doing. When Baba breaks his silence, all the fishes will come home to roost."

Everyone cracked up.

"What?" said Carla. "All the fishes come home to roost. It means the consequences of everything come home. The truth is known and spoken aloud. The—"

I put down *Biggles Takes It Rough*. "The saying is all the *chickens* come home to roost. Not fishes chicken. Fish don't roost."

"Oh, well," said Carla. "The point is . . ."

I returned to my book, but the adventures of the flying ace had lost their charm.

What would happen if I broke *my* silence? If I jumped up and denounced Baba, the ashram, Ahmednagar, Holy Wounds, and my parents for bringing me here?

Do any of you have any idea what goes on around here? I could ask. *Do you know what they do to children at Holy Wounds? Do you know how they beat them, how they force them to stand in the sun until they collapse from heat exhaustion, how they smash their heads against the wall?*

Do you know that kids throw rocks at me every time I leave the Compound? Do you know that Harry tied me up in front of a madman and left me there? Do you know that I took a knife and tried to cut my throat?

Do you care?

I could find out.

May I have your attention please, I could say. *Let me tell you—*

But I sat frozen, blood roaring in my ears, silent as Baba ever was.

Then I saw myself as if in an old photograph, from a distance of years I had not yet reached: a little girl curled up in a folding chair with her dress tucked carefully under her feet. Her hair was yanked into braids, and her face was wiped clean of feeling.

I didn't see the person looking at the photograph, but I knew her as one knows an old friend in another land, regardless of current appearance. Her hair was cut short or set free to tangle in the wind. She wore jeans or shorts because women could do that where she lived. Her expression was not empty but still, like a full glass in a quiet house.

Promise, said the girl. *Promise that you won't forget. Promise that you'll never say it was right. Promise that some day you'll say what really happened.*

The woman faded from my imagination. So I took the vow myself.

One day, I promised, I would break my silence.

The world wouldn't end. But all the fishes would come home to roost.

34

Home

One afternoon my front door wasn't locked. I pushed it open and peered inside. Dad was there, sitting on his bed. I hesitated in the doorway. Something was obviously up, and it was equally obviously nothing good.

"Come here, Mani," he said. "There's something I have to tell you."

I crept forward.

"I'm moving back to America—" he began.

I burst into tears. In the background, he was explaining that it had nothing to do with me and he still loved me. But all I knew was that he was abandoning me.

I cried nonstop for the next three days. Then I got an idea.

"Take me with you," I begged.

"We'll see," he said.

And then he left.

I moved through the next few weeks like a zombie. Mom was alternately weepy and relieved but always there to comfort me. The trouble was that her idea of comfort was telling me that Baba loved me and would always be there for me. But I didn't want Baba. I wanted Dad.

Then I got an idea. Talking to my parents had never changed anything. Keeping silent hadn't either. Nor had acting out or being good or praying. As far as I knew, only one thing I'd ever done had made enough of an impression on an adult that it had translated into action. The letter I'd written to Nancy, my Sukiyaki Sister, had made her Xerox it and use it as a class handout.

She had said I was talented. She had said I was a real writer. If one tossed-off letter had affected a hardened English teacher that much, maybe a letter could affect Dad.

I wrote to him every day for six months.

I begged him to let me come live with him. I listed one hundred and thirty seven reasons why Ahmednagar was driving me "inexorably insane." I offered to cook, clean, and help out in the shop. I swore that I wouldn't be a bother. I promised to do all my homework without complaint. I'd give him backrubs, sweep the floor, and water the plants. Had I mentioned that I'd cook and clean?

At about the one hundred and eightieth letter, I got the response I wanted. I could go home.

Mom cried, but Mom was always crying. She said she'd miss me and always love me, and that the mandali loved me and Baba loved me. She never asked me to stay, which I was grateful for, and she never asked if I'd want to live with her if she left too, which I was also grateful for.

Grateful, and guilty. I would rather have lived with Dad than Mom, but I would have left either parent in an instant to return to America with the other. The pinnacle of my guilt came when she said that she knew what a hard decision it had been for me. It hadn't been hard at all.

When I said goodbye to the mandali and residents, and they all told me how much they and Baba loved me, I wished I could honestly say that I'd miss them and so in some tiny way be sorry to go. But I wasn't sorry. Rupali's family had moved to Bombay at around the same time that Dad had moved to America, and so I'd already lost the person I would have missed the most.

Mom and I stood at the airport gates. She'd been crying for hours already, but I'd never started. I was abandoning her, and the best I could do was not mention that I couldn't wait to get on that plane. What sort of person could leave her mother forever and not care? I was the witch-child in the fairy tale, the girl who couldn't love or grieve; I was Princess Heart-of-Stone.

The final boarding announcement crackled over the loudspeakers. Mom and I hugged each other, and then I picked up my bags and walked away. I heard her shouting after me, her voice thick with tears: "Jai Baba! I love you! Jai Baba!" But I never turned around.

Dad picked me up at the Santa Barbara airport. I had meant to throw myself into his arms and pour out my happiness and gratitude. I would tell him everything I'd been keeping secret and how glad I was that it was over.

"Jai Baba, Mani," said Carla, stepping out from behind him.

I stood clutching my bags, puzzled and inhibited. How was I supposed to have my intimate talk with my father in the presence of his business partner?

Why had she come to the airport? Surely they would have known that I'd want some quality time with my father, whom I hadn't seen in half a year.

It was night and the air was cool. Dad loaded my bags into the trunk of the car, then got in the driver's seat.

Carla took the front seat.

As I slid into the back, the realization of how clueless I'd been crashed over me. Memories of all the conversations in which I'd assured people that the only reason Dad and Mom were splitting up was because he couldn't stand Ahmednagar any more and she would never leave leaped back to me in crushing word-for-word detail. One pilgrim had even asked me if there was another woman, and I'd assured her that there wasn't.

I was an idiot.

Everyone had known but me.

And nobody had told me. I glared at the back of Dad's head. Why hadn't he? Why hadn't Mom? Had it—horrors!—been so obvious that it never occurred to them that I needed to have it spelled out?

Dad pulled up at a McDonald's, and Carla went out to get us sodas.

He cleared his throat. "Uh, you know that Carla and I are pretty much boyfriend and girlfriend now."

"I kind of figured that out," I said.

We sat in silence until she returned, and drove in silence to the apartment.

Carla must be living with him. Which meant that I'd be living with her. Which meant that I had a stepmother.

I tried to remember all my interactions with her in Ahmednagar. Pro: She had gotten me hooked on fantasy and her friends had burned down a Bank of America. Con: She was almost as devoted to Baba as Mom was, and she thought that if you were unhappy, it was because you'd chosen to be.

The verdict: Who knew? I just didn't know her well enough to come to an informed conclusion.

I sucked down my Coke. It wasn't as sweet as I'd remembered.

Baba was waiting when we arrived at the apartment. Baba paintings decked the walls, Baba photos perched on tables, Baba books filled the shelves, and Baba magnets adorned the refrigerator.

I ostentatiously checked my watch. "Wow, it's nearly two in the morning. I better go to bed."

Dad and Carla seized upon the suggestion.

"Good night, Mani," said Dad.

"'Night, Mani," said Carla.

Dad and Carla, as I had guessed, were sharing a bedroom.

The door to my room had a lock on the inside. Not the deadbolts I was used to, but a wedge on a brass knob. I twisted it. It clicked. Locked.

There was no mosquito netting on my bed; there were no mosquitoes. I could hear the soft undistracting roar of the nearby freeway and some TV chatter from the apartment next door, rather than blaring Bollywood soundtracks, grunting old men, and crickets. The toilet was down the hall, not outside, and it came with a flush and soft paper and without giant rats. There was a shower with hot water.

There was a TV! There was a VCR, and a shop where I could rent movies. There were movie *theaters*, with movies in English, and bookshops, and a real library. There was Coke and hamburgers and cold milk and cookies and Hershey bars and blueberry pie and potato chips and steak and hash browns and macaroni and cheese.

I could get a cat. I could get two cats.

I lay back on the quilt, ankles crossed and shoes on. No one could come in through that locked door to punish me for putting my shoes on the bed. And when I did take off my shoes, I wouldn't have to tap them out for scorpions before I put them on again.

So I had a stepmother. I'd have to wait and see what she was like. She couldn't be *too* wicked, or she wouldn't have let me come at all.

The uncertainty and imperfection, the failure of my homecoming to be the joyous reunion I'd dreamed of, was also what made it feel real. I was only moderately worried that at any minute, I might wake up in Ahmednagar.

But my escape was, if not too good to be true, too good for me to deserve. I had fled the country without a second thought for the other kids at Holy Wounds. In my entire stay in Ahmednagar I had never, not once, done anything to stand up for them. Why should I be here when Shamim was still there? I wasn't better than him or any of them. I was just lucky enough to have American citizenship and a runaway Dad.

If Dad hadn't eloped with Carla, I'd never have gotten away. I hadn't forced my escape, I'd just taken advantage of an opportunity.

Some warrior.

I got up and paced around the room, then flopped back down on the bed. The mattress gave and bounced, and the quilt was soft and slightly cool. It was real.

Some warrior, I repeated like a mantra. *Some warrior.*

But not all warriors fought to the death. Some waited, and waited, and outlived the war.

Tarabai had lived to be eighty-six. I'd looked it up.

I had been so fixated on the flashy heroism of Shivaji and Rani Lakshmibai that I hadn't considered the quiet courage of the fighters for Indian Independence, people like Jawaharlal Nehru. He had been imprisoned by the British in the Ahmednagar Fort for seven years. He could have gotten shot in a hopeless escape attempt, hung himself in his guarded rooms, or let his jailers convince him that he was wrong to fight, wrong to want an India run by Indians, wrong to demand it *now*. But he waited instead, and wrote books and letters and fiery protest essays until he was released, and India gained its independence, and he became its first Prime Minister.

Perhaps my battle too had not been of the body but of the mind. If so, I'd won. After five years of Ahmednagar, I still didn't believe that Baba was God or that life wasn't real or that Holy Wounds was anything but a horror. I'd kept myself sane, and I'd written myself free.

A letter a day for six months equaled . . . I had never been good at mental arithmetic, even when it was taught in English. But Dad had left a blank notebook and a pen on the table, so I wrote it out. One hundred eighty letters, a jailbreak tunnel dug one spoonful of dirt at a time.

Even Shivaji hadn't created his victories from scratch. If that cliff face at Sinhagad hadn't been left unguarded, no amount of lizards would have gotten his men inside.

As if I were under a slow hot shower, warmth flowed from my head and down my body. Every inch of skin tingled as it passed by, and when the wave had finished its progress, I was left with an unaccustomed sensation, pleasant but unsettling. *Happiness,* I thought, but surely I had felt that before. Then I knew. It was freedom.

Perhaps will is like bone, and it can mend after it's been broken.

Perhaps it takes as much courage to live as it does to die.

I had another chance, so this time I'd do better. Who needed reincarnation? I had another life now, and I hadn't even needed to die first. But what was I going to do with it?

I had been so focused on getting out that I hadn't given any thought to what I would do when I *was* out. The moment had seemed too remote and unlikely to imagine, even when I knew it was coming. But here I was. Out.

Back in Hawthorne, before we left for Ahmednagar, my parakeet Chatter had escaped from his cage and taken off out the window. But because he wasn't used to freedom, or didn't like it as much as he'd thought he would, or wasn't quick enough on his wings, he flew to the roof and perched there until Dad climbed up and grabbed him.

I wasn't going to stop at the roof. And nobody was going to catch me again.

What was I going to do?

I chewed the pen I was holding, but nothing came to mind. Then I put pen and notebook back on the desk, got in bed, and turned out the lights.

I'd think of something.

INTERLUDE IV: 2004

Thanks for the Happy Childhood

When I was thirty, I wrote this book.

Less than a year after I put down my notebook that first night back in America, I picked it up again and never looked back. I wrote plays, teleplays, screenplays, articles, reviews, and several hundred thirty-second sound bites for a fitness show called *Body by Jake*. ("Did you know that carrots have forty-seven separate nutrients? They make good soup too.") But I did not respond positively when people asked me when I was going to write a true story about my actual childhood.

"It would kill me to spend that much time thinking about it."

"Nobody in my family knows that I don't believe in Baba. My mother would drop dead. Right after she finishes suing me. So never."

"Anyway, no one would believe it."

"Maybe after my parents and all the mandali die."

"Maybe after my mother dies."

"Maybe after I finish my novel/my screenplay/cleaning my apartment."

The trouble was, I didn't know *how* to write it. I'd tried a few times, but all my attempts had gotten bogged down in fury, self-pity, or wild speculations about my parents' motivation. I was bored reading them, and I wrote them.

Then I read *Running with Scissors*, a memoir by Augusten Burroughs. When he was fourteen, his insane confessional poet mother gave him away to her even crazier psychiatrist, who kept an obsessive-compulsive patient in the attic, an electroshock machine under the stairs, and a pedophile in the shed. His book was shocking, horrifying, and appalling. It was also extremely funny.

I was impressed. Lots of people have unhappy childhoods, but this was the first time I'd come across anyone who'd had one as *weird* as mine. I looked up Augusten Burroughs' Web page and e-mailed him a fan letter. At least, I intended to e-mail him a fan letter. But before I could get any further than "Dear Augusten" (I figured that my knowledge via his memoir that he had once used Queen Helene Cholesterol as a sexual aide put us on a first-name basis), my fingers became possessed and began madly typing a brief account of my own childhood, headlined "And I thought growing up in a cult was weird." It concluded,

OBVIOUSLY, I ADORED YOUR BOOK. IT MADE ME THINK THAT PERHAPS I TOO COULD WRITE A MEMOIR WITHOUT GETTING SHOT BY MY OUTRAGED CHARACTERS.

He replied the next day to suggest that I write my book in the same style in which I'd written the e-mail. I realized then that when I had

told him my story, without worrying about what my parents would think or fishing for sympathy or trying to do anything at all but say what happened in an amusing manner to someone who I thought would appreciate it, I had taught myself how to write my memoir.

I knew that if I did write it, it would hurt a lot of people's feelings, especially Mom's. Though I'd often found her infuriating, I didn't relish the idea of jumping up and down on her heart. But I was a writer and I had a good story that I knew how to tell, like a baseball player who sees the pitch and knows he can hit a home run. The bat swings almost of its own accord.

I did not inform my parents that I was writing a memoir. Dad and Carla, who had gotten married when I was sixteen, were still Baba-lovers. I once visited their house in Santa Barbara with a friend, Tracey. Dad and Carla were on vacation and had offered to let us sleep over while they were gone.

Tracey gazed up at a huge oil painting of Baba. "That's the guru, huh?"

"Uh-huh."

She inspected a dresser decorated with six framed Baba photos. "They sure have a lot of pictures of the guy."

"Eighty-nine," I said. "I've counted."

"You know, Rachel," she said, eyeing the Baba magnets on the refrigerator, "at first I thought I was being judgmental because it's some fringe religion I never heard of. But if I walked into a house and it had this many pictures of Jesus in it, I'd freak out."

I came out as an atheist on Christmas Day. I didn't mean it as an ironic statement. I hadn't intended to confess that day, but when I walked into my Uncle Danny's house, Dad and Carla were already there, and Dad was saying, "But your belief that this is reality is merely part of the great illusion."

I sat down by the fireplace and listened to Dad lecture on about Baba and illusion, with more smoke coming out of my ears than from the chimney.

"And of course the theories of quantum physicists completely support what Baba was saying in the 1930s. Baba spoke of sanskaric threads, just like the strings in string theory—"

"There's something I ought to tell you." I blurted out. "I hope you won't disinherit me, but I'm an atheist."

"Yeah, so?" said Dad instantly. "I'm an agnostic."

You have eighty-nine pictures of Baba in a ten-room house! I wanted to howl. *What kind of agnostic has eighty-nine pictures of God in his house?*

But if I said so, I'd get sucked into an argument over the definition of agnosticism and whether or not Baba-loving is a religion, and then everyone could go on believing that I believed whatever they preferred to believe that I believed.

I chose my words carefully. "I mean that I don't believe in God, including Baba. I do not believe that Baba is God."

"So?" said Carla.

"I don't know." We weren't even in an argument, but I felt like I'd already lost it. "I guess I just thought I should say so, to be honest. I should have told you guys years ago, but I thought you'd freak out."

"We. Don't. Care," said Dad.

I hadn't wanted them to weep and scream or rant and rave, but their lack of interest was equally disconcerting. While I was searching for a statement that would keep the topic open without sounding combative, Danny preempted me. "So what did Baba say about free will?"

"Free will is very complex," began Dad.

I gave up.

That night I dreamed that I was at another family party. All my relatives were there, even the dead ones, but that did not strike me as unusual. I went to the kitchen and popped a frozen duck into the microwave as an hors d'oeuvre. The microwave had a fax attachment, so I included, under the duck, a letter to a friend telling her about my memoir, complete with scandalous quotes. But when I removed the duck, now nicely browned and ready to eat, I found that it was not quite dead.

The duck lurched out on its reanimated feet and began staggering around the kitchen, causing a huge commotion. I pursued it with a cleaver to put it out of its misery. But when I slashed it in half, it became two flapping wretched zombie ducks. Then a familiar shriek arose.

During the ruckus caused by the resurrection of the roast duck, Mom had found my letter (damp with duck juice) and was reading it, over the sink in case it dripped.

"You're writing a memoir and you didn't tell me!" she screamed. "It's all lies! You've totally misrepresented me! None of this ever happened!"

As the ducks lurched horribly about the kitchen, and all my relatives, even the dead ones, crowded around to see what I'd done, and Mom shrieked and wept and threatened to sue . . . I woke up.

I didn't need Freud to analyze that dream. As William Faulkner said, "The past isn't dead; it's not even past." I decided that I had to confess before my memoir burst upon the Baba scene like a whole flock of zombie ducks. So I drove up to Dad and Carla's eighty-nine-Pictures-of-Baba abode.

"I got an agent for my book," I said. My heart banged against my chest as if I was a teenager who'd totaled the family car, not an adult announcing a career milestone. "I think he's about to sell it. But it's not the novel. It's a memoir about growing up in Ahmednagar."

"Wow!" said Dad. "That's great!"

"That's terrific!" said Carla.

"I bet it's hilarious," said Dad.

"When can we read it?" asked Carla. "I love a book that makes me laugh."

"Uh . . ." I said, recalling the entire chapter devoted to my suicide attempt. "Some parts of it are actually kind of depressing. . . . So, you guys aren't mad?"

"Of course not," said Carla. "Why should we be?"

"Well, it says what I really think about Ahmednagar."

"We all know what you really think about Ahmednagar," said Dad.

"Well, in that case, can I ask you about some things I always wondered about?"

"Shoot," said Dad.

I started with a softball. "When I came back from India, I was completely shocked that you guys were a couple. I figured I must have been the only person who didn't know, so—"

"Nobody knew," said Carla.

"What? Really?"

"Nope," said Dad. "We didn't think it was anyone else's business. So we didn't tell anyone."

"Oh." I pondered that. "But why didn't you tell me? I thought the only reason you didn't was that you assumed I'd figured it out already, and I thought I was stupid because I hadn't."

"Oh, no," said Dad. "I'm sorry about that. I had no idea you'd think that. Really, no one knew."

I gaped at Dad. It was the first time that I could remember him apologizing to me for anything. Usually I was the one apologizing

to him, for bills I'd forgotten to pay and errands I'd forgotten to run and the brilliant career I'd forgotten to have. But why should I always be scrambling after his approval when he'd forgotten to give me a happy childhood? Why shouldn't I ask him a few uncomfortable questions?

I pressed my advantage. "Okay. Next question: Did you always mean to take me back to America but you just never told me, or did my letters talk you into it?"

"I remember all those letters you sent," said Dad. He seemed relieved at the cheerier topic. "You promised to cook and clean and pick up after yourself."

"I specifically remember you insisting that you'd always clean your room," added Carla.

"And you never did any of it!" said Dad. "It was the world's biggest case of over-promise and under-deliver."

"But did my letters change your mind?" I asked.

Dad leaned back in his chair and considered the ceiling. Then he tilted it back and looked straight into my eyes. "Rachel, the truth is that I had no idea what I was doing when I left. I had no plans other than to start a business with Carla."

"Oh, no," said Carla. "You did have a plan. I know because once before we left, you said it might be nice to live on the East Coast and that Mani would like it there. So he always did mean to take you."

"That's right," said Dad. "I guess I always did."

One sentence worth of day-dreaming does not constitute a plan, I thought. But I let it lie. All the times I'd asked my parents the question I most wanted an answer to—why did you move to the ashram? Did you think about me at all?—the replies were always variations on what Dad had just said: "I don't know." "I don't remember." "I was young and naïve." "I guess I figured it would work out."

"Why did you move to India?" I asked.

Dad shrugged. "It seemed like a good idea at the time."

I then e-mailed Mom to inform her that I had sold a memoir and I didn't believe in Baba. She took my atheism with surprising grace, but began firing off letters demanding a copy of the manuscript. Figuring that the actual book couldn't be as bad as what she was imagining, I sent her the first seven chapters. Unfortunately, it turned out that it was even worse than she'd imagined. She began writing lengthy line-by-line critiques, starting with the first chapter:

Sweetheart, all the baskets of fruit and water and assorted snacks that I lugged around in those bulging cotton bags were not for me—they were for you! My suitcase was filled not just with clothes for me, but stuff for you. Yes you did have a backpack worth of books, but all the intention in the travel was to make it more pleasant for you and safe for you to eat and drink as need be. Neither your father nor myself were going on the vacation for ourselves but because we wanted to take you someplace fun!

Moreover, she informed me that she had never thought a fire truck was Baba breaking his silence but had only played along with Dad's belief because he was having a bad trip and freaking out, that she had never poked me in the ribs, that I had been overjoyed at the prospect of moving to Ahmednagar, that the Baba quote in Dr. Bergmann's office had not been on a bulletin board, that she and Dad had never seriously considered naming me Arwen Evenstar, that she had never in her life used the word "mandible," that Firoze had never given her a chapati with mango jam, that Baba was not a guru but an Indian Spiritual Master, that I'd misunder-

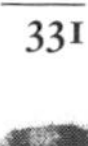

stood all of Baba's doctrines, and that I'd had many normal happy times at the ashram that I ought to put in the book.

The trouble is that one extreme experience is more memorable than many normal ones. If your childhood was unremarkable except for the time when your father raped you, when you grow up and go to a therapist, you won't mention the many normal happy times, but will zoom right in on that one rape. I could see why Mom thought I ought to have written more about baking cookies and less about decapitations. But the decapitations had made more of an impression on me.

It wasn't that I didn't sympathize. I just didn't sympathize enough to grind the sharp edges from my memories. Also, I found it acutely annoying that she sometimes signed her e-mails "with love from the horrible, stupid, despicable 'Da-nonna.'"

Greg Feeley, a writer friend of mine, suggested that I tell my mother to write her own book and call it *The Serpent's Tooth: Surviving Your Ungrateful Child's Memoir*.

The next time I visited Dad and Carla, they took me to an Argentine restaurant. Dad ordered a caipirinha, a cocktail made with lime and sugarcane brandy. I felt a pang of nostalgia for sugarcane, peeled and chewed raw for its juice. You can't get it in America, any more than you can get sweet limes or chikus or jamun berries.

"I'll have a caipirinha too," I said.

Halfway through our drinks, I began to suspect that they were stronger than they tasted. Dad stirred the melting ice cubes in his glass. "Did I ever tell you how your Mom and I got together?"

"No." He had, many times, but I always entertained the forlorn hope that he might some day slip off the story's well-worn tracks and say something revealing.

"When I was a boy, the only thing I ever wanted was to be a shortstop for the Yankees. But I was too short. I wasn't good enough to be the next Pee Wee Reese, and I don't think girls could even see me. Except for Amy Klein. Did I ever tell you about Amy Klein?"

"No." I tried not to sound too excited, lest I scare him, but he'd finally gone off the tracks. I'd never heard of Amy Klein.

Dad took a drink. "When I was a senior in high school, Amy Klein asked me out. She was really cute, and she was shorter than me, so we started dating, and . . . er . . . " Dad knocked back his caipirinha. "Fooling around. Excuse me!" He held up his glass to the waiter. "Another one."

"Same here," I said. Neither of us were big drinkers, but if he was going to tell me about his sex life, I wanted the details fuzzed over with sugarcane brandy.

Carla sat placidly sipping her glass of Chardonnay. None of this was news to her.

"When we'd been dating for about six months, she thought she was pregnant. In those days, if you got a girl pregnant, you had to marry her. I realized that I was going to have to marry into Amy Klein's boring, close-minded, bourgeois family. It was my worst nightmare, but I didn't see any way out of it. Well, it turned out that she wasn't pregnant, and then we broke up and went off to different colleges. I met your mother at USC. She was really cute, and she was shorter than me, so . . ."

"That's so shallow," I protested. "There must have been more you liked about her than that."

Our drinks arrived. Dad and I each took a gulp.

"She wasn't like Amy," said Dad. "She wasn't bourgeois. Do you know the play *David and Lisa*?"

"I saw the movie," I said. "They're in a mental hospital, right, and David's afraid to be touched, and Lisa's all sensitive and fragile and only speaks in rhymes?"

"Uh-huh. Well, your mother was Lisa. Without the rhymes. The

only thing she'd ever wanted to be was a ballet dancer. But she didn't have this thing called turnout, where your feet point in opposite directions. Apparently that's essential, and she didn't have it, so she quit. After that she got into tennis."

"Tennis?" I had no idea Mom had ever played sports.

"Sure," said Dad. "You got the amateur sports fanatic gene from both sides. No wonder you're into karate. Well, your mother was always obsessed with something. When she was into tennis, all she ever thought about or talked about was tennis. Then she got into Baba, and all she ever thought about or talked about was Baba. You're a bit obsessive too; you get it from her."

"Not like Mom," I protested.

"You *are* single-minded," remarked Carla.

"The difference is that you think about other things too," said Dad. "Your mother only ever focused on one thing at a time, and once she zoomed in on that, she literally never looked at anything else. Anyway, Da-nonna and I started going out, and then one day she showed up on my doorstep with a suitcase. Her parents had found out that we were . . . er . . . having sex, and they'd thrown her out. So I had to let her come live with me. Another caipirinha, please."

"Two more," I said.

"Your father is a very honorable man," interjected Carla.

"Her horrible father came and confronted me where I was working," Dad continued. "He said, 'I'm going to have you arrested for moral turpitude.' I said, 'I don't think there is such a crime.'"

Dad laughed. I couldn't tell if his eyes were out of focus or if mine were. "So we moved in together, and then we got into Baba—you know that story—and visited India before you were born. But what you might not remember is that after that, your mother went to India by herself. She was supposed to stay for two weeks, and she didn't come back for six months. You were three years old, and my mother was dying of cancer, and I had no idea if Da-nonna was ever going to come back. So when she started talking about Ahmednagar again, I figured she'd either go with us or without us."

Dad's eyes focused on me, and they were as sharp and clear as if he hadn't been drinking at all. "That's what you've always wanted to know, isn't it? Why I went. It was go with her or get left behind with a little child. Also your mother was . . . depressed. I thought she might commit suicide if I tried to stop her. I had no idea what was wrong with her or what to do about it, but I figured at the ashram, there'd be people who could take care of her."

The base of Carla's wine glass clinked against the wrought iron table. "So you went to save your family."

"Wait a minute," I said. "Carla, didn't you know all this already?"

She shook her head.

Dad spoke with over-articulated dignity. "I have never told anyone any of this stuff in my entire life."

I stirred my caipirinha and watched the ripples spread and widen. I wondered why Dad had been so intent on keeping his not-so-dark secret. Maybe he'd retrospectively awarded himself the most altruistic motives possible. But everyone in his story had acted in character: Dad trying to do the right thing via the path of least resistance, and Mom marching to Baba come hell or high water, equally convinced that she was right. What role had I played? Had I too been in character?

I said, "When Mom went to India for six months, do you remember what I thought about that? I know I was a little kid, but I must have said something."

Dad rubbed his index finger along his evening stubble. "My recollection is that you kept your counsel to yourself."

"When I was three?"

"You haven't changed since you were a baby," said Dad. "Even

before you could talk, I remember you sitting in your high chair, watching people and laughing to yourself. And you're still exactly the same."

The next morning, still woozy from all those caipirinhas, I received this message from Mom.

In my mind, whether or not you consciously accept Baba as the Avatar or even believe in God, does not deny your close connection to God but rather merely points to the fact that perhaps at this time in your life or for this life, your work is to believe otherwise, and He will use that for His purpose.

With all this said, I do want to share with you, Rachel, something that you have been given and that is yours. Perhaps you have forgotten the incredibly beautiful and revealing dreams that you had of Baba when you were little and living in India. They have always meant a great deal to me. It may seem strange to you but in some ways, they were a great solace to me when you chose to leave here and live with your dad. I felt so cut off from you and your life, I didn't know how to bridge that gulf, and I guess they somehow helped to give me the strength to accept what had happened and know well that you are Baba's no matter what happens.

Dreams that one has of Baba or God in any of His Advents have great significance. They are not the same as ordinary dreams. A dream in which God in Human Form appears to you means that He has indeed come to you.

I hope that you are glad to know of these dreams of yours. Even if they mean nothing to you today, it may well be that sometime in your life their meaning will become remarkably clear to you.

DREAM:

You are in the Samadhi, and you are playing alone there with a felt art board that I had made for you before we came to India. You are happily playing in silence, when you suddenly look up. Baba is standing barefoot on the marble. You rush to Him and kiss him, and He embraces you.

You think or say to yourself, "What am I doing playing with the toys of the world when God is standing before me?"

Though I didn't recall that dream, its content didn't seem implausible. But I was certain that, though I might have expressed the sentiment, I would never have used the phrase "the toys of the world."

Of course, Mom thought she would never have used the word "mandible."

I copied the e-mail into my manuscript. Since it seemed unlikely that Mom would write her own book and I had no intention of altering my memories to make them match with hers, it seemed only fair to give her this small chance to misrepresent me.

Months later, I went back to Santa Barbara for another visit. On the way to the restaurant—the same one that had been the site of that caipirinha-fueled evening—Dad said, apropos of nothing, "Do you remember that window seat you used to sit and write in when you were in high school?"

"Sure. Why?"

Dad gazed out at the freeway, satisfied and secretive. "Just keep remembering it."

"But—"

"We had a great time in Santa Fe," said Carla perkily. "We saw a convoy of baby quail on our first day there."

"Were they carrying teeny little rifles?" I asked, and forgot all about the window seat.

It was a pleasant dinner. I didn't have to censor my conversation to preserve secrets that I'd never wanted to keep. I wasn't frustrated with Dad over stories he refused to tell me and motivations he wouldn't reveal. And though Mom and I were not exactly connecting, I had managed to convince her to stop e-mailing me to complain that I said I'd worn a red dress when it had actually been blue.

If we'd never quite worked as a family, at least we'd all separately managed to get what we'd wanted. Dad shifted the responsibility for Mom on to the ashram and escaped from her and it without even a guilty conscience. Mom stayed at the ashram, secure in her belief that I was Baba's no matter what. I moved to a city where everybody's an immigrant and nobody's a foreigner, and used my miserable childhood as a stepladder to reach my goals.

"I almost forgot," said Dad. "Here's a present for you." He handed me a gift-wrapped object. I fingered it: clearly a picture in a frame.

His wicked grin made me suspicious. "God, what is it, a picture of Baba?"

"That's right," said Carla, with a matching wicked grin.

I unwrapped the package. It was a blow-up of a *New Yorker* cartoon.

A girl with a ponytail and glasses, who bore a remarkable resemblance to me as a teenager, sat in a window seat with a notebook in her lap. The caption read, "Dear Mom and Dad: Thanks for the happy childhood. You've destroyed any chance I had of becoming a writer."

I laughed.